U.S. Citizenship For Dummies®

Immigration Attorneys or Services to Avoid

Not all immigration attorneys or legal services are reputable. If any of the following apply to your attorney or service, consider it a sign that you should investigate further:

- Anyone who can't or won't give you an honest estimate, in advance, of what his services cost
- Anyone who asks for money to influence or bribe an immigration official
- Anyone who promises something that sounds too good to be true, or promises a quick, easy solution to your immigration problems
- Anyone who absolutely, positively guarantees to get you a visa after you pay him a designated fee
- Any attorney who does not have a license to practice law in the United States or, for other legal services, other evidence of reputation (for example, referral through known resources like the United Way, letters of accreditation for agencies with accredited representatives, and so on)

Important Immigration Resources

You're not taking the immigration journey alone. Many resources are available to help you — from the BCIS itself, to other government agencies, to low- and no-cost immigration services that can help you with your case or help you find reliable help:

- **The Bureau of Citizenship and Immigration Services (BCIS):** The BCIS Web site (`www.immigration.gov`) can tell you nearly everything there is to know about U.S. immigration and naturalization. If this site doesn't have the answer to your immigration questions, chances are you'll find a link to another source that does.

  You can also order immigration forms online at `www.immigration.gov` or by calling 800-870-3676 (toll-free in the U.S.). For other immigration questions and concerns, call the BCIS National Customer Service Call Center toll-free in the U.S. at 800-375-5283 (or 800-767-1833 for the hearing impaired).
- **Selective Service:** Register for the Selective Service online at `www.sss.gov` or pick up Selective Service mail-back forms at any U.S. post office or overseas at any U.S. embassy or consulate.
- **Immigration Lawyer Referral Service:** Find a qualified, reputable immigration attorney by calling the Immigration Lawyer Referral Service toll-free in the U.S. at 800-954-0254. This free service is part of the American Immigration Lawyers Association (AILA).
- **Executive Office for Immigration Review (EOIR):** The EOIR provides listings of competent, free immigration help throughout the country via their pro bono program. Find a listing for services in your geographical area by visiting the EOIR Web site at `www.usdoj.gov/eoir/probono/probonoassist.htm`.

Item 5463-8.
For more information about Wiley Publishing, call 1-800-762-2974.

U.S. Citizenship For Dummies®

Taking a Regulation BCIS Photo

With your naturalization application, you need to include two unretouched color (not black-and-white), high-quality photographs on glossy or matte finish. Here are some tips on what qualifies as a regulation photograph:

- The photograph should be at least 1 9/16 inches (40 mm) tall by 1 3/8 inches (35 mm) wide.
- The photo needs to show a three-fourths profile view of the right side of your face and your right ear.
- Your facial features must be visible.
- The image of your face in the photo should be 1 3/16 inches (30 mm) from the hair to the neck just below the chin and 1 inch (26 mm) from the right ear to the left cheek.
- The image of your face may not exceed 1 1/4 inches by 1 1/16 inches (32 mm by 28 mm).
- Unless your religion requires you to wear a headdress, your head should be bare in the photograph.
- Photos should be unmounted and printed on thin paper.
- Have your photo taken against a white or off-white background.
- Photos of very-light-skinned people should be slightly underexposed; photos of very-dark-skinned people should be slightly overexposed.
- Take your photos within 30 days of the date you will send them to the BCIS.
- Make sure your photo is taken with the acceptable instant color film, which has a gray-toned backing (the unacceptable non-peel-apart films have a black backing). Polaroid hybrid film is acceptable, although SX-70 type film or any other instant-processing type film is not accepted.

Assembling Naturalization Applications

The BCIS is picky about how they want your naturalization application assembled. These tips will help you keep everything in line.

- If you are submitting several documents, clip all the required fees to the top of your application packet.
- If you're being represented, your attorney or accredited representative should include a Form G-28 Notice of Appearance for you.
- Below your payment (or below the G-28 if you have a representative), include the actual application (the N-400), with photos in a separate envelope attached by a paper clip.
- Below the application, include any other documents relevant to your case (this could include affidavits, a form N-648 if you are requesting a waiver, and so on — see Chapter 4 for more information).
- Whenever you send something to the BCIS, make sure you use a method that ensures proof of delivery — certified mail (with return receipt), express mail, or some other similar method.
- After filing your application and paying your fees, you'll receive a receipt number. Don't lose your receipt numbers, because you'll need them to reference your case whenever you contact the BCIS to find out about the case's status.

Paying Immigration Fees

Keep these tips in mind when sending payments to the BCIS to ensure your payments receive proper credit.

- If a filing fee is required with your immigration form or application, attach it to the top of the application package and mail it all together.
- Never send cash for immigration fees — BCIS accepts money orders, cashier's checks, or personal checks for payment of fees.
- Always write your full name, your A-Number, and the form number in the memo area of your check.
- Make sure your check is signed and dated correctly.
- Submit a separate check (or cashier's check or money order) for each application you're sending.
- If part of your application requires fingerprinting, you must also include a check for the fingerprinting fee.

U.S. Citizenship FOR DUMMIES®

by Steven D. Heller and Cheri Sicard

Wiley Publishing, Inc.

U.S. Citizenship For Dummies®

Published by
Wiley Publishing, Inc.
909 Third Avenue
New York, NY 10022
www.wiley.com

Published by Wiley Publishing, Inc., Indianapolis, Indiana

Published simultaneously in Canada

For general information on our other products and services or to obtain technical support, please contact our Customer Care Department within the U.S. at 800-762-2974, outside the U.S. at 317-572-3993, or fax 317-572-4002.

Wiley also publishes its books in a variety of electronic formats. Some content that appears in print may not be available in electronic books.

Library of Congress Cataloging-in-Publication Data: Is available from the publisher.

Library of Congress Control Number: 2003101934

ISBN: 0-7645-5463-8

1B/QX/QX/QT/IN

Manufactured in the United States of America

10 9 8 7 6 5 4

About the Authors

Steven D. Heller is a New York attorney. He has practiced immigration law for over ten years, including stints as a supervisor with the INS and as a supervising attorney with the New York Association for New Americans (an immigrant-assistance nonprofit agency), as well as in private practice. He also writes and lectures on immigration matters, especially asylum.

Cheri Sicard is the author of *The Great American Handbook: What You Can Do for Your Country — Today and Every Day* (published by Berkley Books). She is also the editor of the popular Web sites FabulousFoods.com and FabulousTravel.com. Her freelance travel and food articles have appeared in countless magazines and newspapers. Cheri lives in Los Angeles, California.

Dedication

Dedicated to the memory of my grandfather, Albert Heller, who went through all of this long before I knew him, so I wouldn't have to, and to the memory of my mother, Alice, who traced her roots to the Revolution from which this country (whose citizenship we cherish) was born.

—Steven D. Heller

Dedicated to Chuck Burnes, for his unending support of all my endeavors, and for enthusiastically reading nearly everything I write — regardless of the topic.

—Cheri Sicard

Authors' Acknowledgments

Steven D. Heller: I would like to thank my wife, Sharon, my daughter, Lila, and my son, Leo (known as "the boy in the womb" while we were writing), for putting up with my late nights on this project. I would also like to thank my father, Robert, and brother, Marc, and the rest of my family, friends, and colleagues who supported me on this — and Lindsay Curcio and Janet Rosen, in particular, for getting me involved in the first place. I would especially like to thank my coauthor, Cheri Sicard, whose tireless research and writing really made this possible, and our legal technical editor, Susan Burgess (and, by extension, Stephen Brent, who referred her), whose tenacious editing kept us focused.

Cheri Sicard: I would like to thank my friends and family for putting up with me while I spent so much time in "immigration land" while working on this book, especially Mitch Mandell — I couldn't do any of this without you. I would also like to thank my agent, Sheree Bykofsky, who made this project possible. Janet Rosen and Megan Buckley, you guys are the best! My coauthor, Steven Heller, made a difficult project a joy to work on — thank you. Also, the fabulous editors that kept Steven and me on track, focused, and accurate: Elizabeth Kuball, Kathleen Dobie, Tracy Boggier, Susan Burgess, and Dale Kubicki — thank you all!

Publisher's Acknowledgments

We're proud of this book; please send us your comments through our Dummies online registration form located at www.dummies.com/register/.

Some of the people who helped bring this book to market include the following:

Acquisitions, Editorial, and Media Development

Project Editor: Elizabeth Kuball

Acquisitions Editor: Tracy Boggier

Technical Editors: Susan Burgess and Dale Kubicki

Editorial Manager: Michelle Hacker

Editorial Assistant: Elizabeth Rea

Cover Photos: © Joe Sohm, Chromosohm/Stock Connection/PictureQuest

Cartoons: Rich Tennant, www.the5thwave.com

Production

Project Coordinator: Maridee Ennis

Layout and Graphics: Seth Conley, Carrie Foster, Kristin McMullan, Tiffany Muth, Jacque Schneider

Proofreaders: John Tyler Connoley, John Greenough, Susan Moritz, Carl William Pierce, Kathy Simpson, TECHBOOKS Production Services

Indexer: TECHBOOKS Production Services

Publishing and Editorial for Consumer Dummies

Diane Graves Steele, Vice President and Publisher, Consumer Dummies

Joyce Pepple, Acquisitions Director, Consumer Dummies

Kristin A. Cocks, Product Development Director, Consumer Dummies

Michael Spring, Vice President and Publisher, Travel

Brice Gosnell, Publishing Director, Travel

Suzanne Jannetta, Editorial Director, Travel

Publishing for Technology Dummies

Andy Cummings, Vice President and Publisher, Dummies Technology/General User

Composition Services

Gerry Fahey, Vice President of Production Services

Debbie Stailey, Director of Composition Services

Contents at a Glance

Table of Contents

Introduction

So you want to live in America? You're in good company. In 2000, over 849,807 people became permanent legal residents of the United States. Sixty-nine percent of these new immigrants came to reunite with family members who had already made the move to the unparalleled freedom and opportunity the United States offers her people. Thirteen percent specifically came here to offer their skills to help keep the U.S. workforce strong. Still others came to escape persecution and tyranny in their homelands.

Many permanent residents choose to take living in the United States a step farther by becoming naturalized United States citizens. By becoming a naturalized citizen, these immigrants will experience nearly all the benefits granted to citizens born in the U.S. (the only exception is that they can't become President or Vice President of the United States).

During the fiscal year 2000, the Immigration and Naturalization Service (INS) processed about 1.3 million naturalization applications that resulted in about 900,000 new American citizens. For some, the process of immigrating to the U.S. and becoming a citizen was simple and straightforward. For others, the journey through the immigration and naturalization process became an endless parade of obstacles, delays, forms, and paperwork.

This book will help you get through this often confusing process, from determining how best to qualify to live permanently in the United States to gaining a green card to become a naturalized citizen of the U.S. Along the way, we point out the important requirements you need to meet and give tips and insights into dealing with the Bureau of Citizenship and Immigration Services (BCIS), as well as other government agencies you'll come into contact with while attempting to immigrate to the U.S. or become a citizen.

We wish we could tell you the immigration process is always simple, but each case is different and there are many special circumstances and exceptions to the rules that can come into play. In the aftermath of the tragic events of September 11, 2001, the complications have only increased. The U.S. immigration system has been under unprecedented public scrutiny. In most immigration cases, the services of a competent immigration attorney are highly recommended. Sometimes an attorney's help is absolutely necessary in order to protect your immigration chances and help you through the process. Often, you can get free or low-cost help from nonprofit immigration services, designed to help immigrants legally live in the United States.

About This Book

In this book, we let you know things you can do to make the immigration and naturalization process easier and less stressful, as well as where to find additional help in case you need it. You'll discover how to be proactive and stay a step ahead of the BCIS by anticipating what forms and paperwork you'll need in advance. We also alert you to important points that can help you protect your immigration case throughout the proceedings.

If you plan on becoming a citizen, we also get you ready to pass the English and civics portions of the naturalization interview. This part, more than any other, seems to fill potential citizens with fear. But you really shouldn't worry. The BCIS is not expecting you to be an expert. In this book, we show you how to find out what you need to know. In fact, you'll probably find practicing for the tests enjoyable, if not fun.

Why does a book on citizenship spend a fair amount of space on how to immigrate to the United States? Because you must first be a lawful permanent resident for a designated amount of time before you even qualify to try to become a naturalized citizen. So lawful immigration truly is the first step to naturalization.

Still, you will note this book is not called *U.S. Immigration For Dummies.* We'll help you identify potential ways to immigrate, but this room isn't long enough to walk you through actual petitioning and visa processing. We also avoid detailed discussion of nonimmigrant visas.

In all cases, we've kept the chapters *modular,* meaning you'll find all the information you'll need on a given subject, or we'll refer you to other chapters in the book for further detail, and you don't have to read the book from start to finish to understand the topic at hand.

Foolish Assumptions

Because you bought this book, we assume you are interested in living permanently in the U.S. or are a friend or relative of someone else who does. You (or your friend or relative) probably want to take the immigration process all the way to the end — naturalization — but regardless of your immigration goals, this book can help.

We don't assume that you have a legal background, or any familiarity with U.S. immigration. As such, we have made every attempt to explain the complicated legal process of immigration and naturalization in simple, easy-to-understand language. Nonetheless, we still strongly urge you to seek the advice of a competent attorney or immigration service to help you pursue your goals. Don't worry, we also tell you how to find reliable help.

How This Book Is Organized

U.S. Citizenship For Dummies is divided into seven parts, each of which you'll use at various times in your immigration and naturalization process.

Part I: Pursuing Immigration and Citizenship

The first chapter in this part will help you determine what you really want by introducing you to the benefits of becoming a citizen as well as the serious obligations that come with it. You'll discover how you can best qualify to immigrate to the United States and what requirements you need to meet to qualify to become a citizen. Chapter 2 guides you through the various visas and how to qualify and apply for them. In Chapter 3, you meet the major players in the immigration game, including the Bureau of Citizenship and Immigration Services (BCIS), the Directorate of Border and Transportation Security (BTS), the Department of Labor (DOL), the Department of State (DOS), and even the Federal Bureau of Investigation (FBI). You'll also find out about immigration forms and documents and additional paperwork you may need to provide, as well as know what you need to do to get ready for interviews with the BCIS.

Part II: Staying Up to Date and Out of Trouble

Being an illegal alien is no fun. Chapter 8 shows you how to effectively deal with the BCIS, what to do if your immigration or naturalization applications are rejected, and how to avoid the worst case scenario — removal. Chapter 6 brings you up date with recent changes in immigration law that can affect your chances for permanent residence or citizenship; it also tells you how to monitor changes that may occur as time goes by. You'll also figure out how to recognize when you need to seek professional help and where to find it.

Part III: Understanding U.S. Government

Part III begins to get you ready to pass your interview for naturalization. In order to become a naturalized citizen, you'll need to show a basic understanding of how the United States government is structured and how it works to protect the rights and liberties of U.S. citizens. Part III familiarizes you with government in the U.S. at the federal, state, and local levels. Think of this part as a user's guide to citizenship.

Part IV: Exploring U.S. History and Culture

In this part, your preparation for the naturalization interview continues with lessons about United States history from before the nation was formed to the present. We also cover the country's most important documents: the Constitution and the Declaration of Independence. In addition, you'll find out about important U.S. symbols like the flag, our national anthem, patriotic and other important holidays and celebrations, as well as America's most significant national heroes. Here, you'll not only find important exam material, you'll also gain insight into the fabric of life in the United States, and how it got to be that way.

Part V: Practicing for the Citizenship Test

In Part V, you see how to use your everyday life to practice for the naturalization English and civics exam as well as find fun quizzes and reviews to make sure you know everything you'll need to pass the test with ease. We even give you 100 sample questions, just like the ones you may be asked during your BCIS interview.

Part VI: The Part of Tens

The Part of Tens is a unique feature in every *For Dummies* book, and this one is no exception. In this part, you'll gather valuable tips that can help you pass your BCIS interview as well as discover ten things that hurt your chances of obtaining lawful permanent residence or naturalization in the United States. You'll also get up close and personal with our last ten presidents and identify their major accomplishments.

Part VII: Appendixes

No, you don't need to memorize the Constitution or the Declaration of Independence in order to pass the civics test. But if you really want to understand the essence of the United States, you may want to take the time to read these important documents. The beliefs and principles behind our country, as well as the events that helped form our nation, are in there. Also in this part, the document checklist will let you know, at a glance, which forms and documents to include with your naturalization application.

Icons Used in This Book

Icons are the pictures you'll see in the margins throughout this book. Although they're mighty fun to look at, they're there to serve a purpose: flagging your attention to key pieces of information. Here's what the various icons mean:

This icons calls your attention to information we cover elsewhere but that's so important we think it's worth repeating (and worth remembering).

The Tip icon points out practical advice that will make your naturalization and immigration process easier.

This icon highlights key points that can save you trouble, money, or in the worst-case scenario, forced removal from the country.

The Technical Stuff icon points out more information than you technically need, but provides interesting facts that explain the hows and whys of immigration.

Where to Go from Here

Depending on your goals and where you are in the immigration process, you can dive right into Chapter 1 and read the entire book, or skip to the chapters that best apply to your unique situation.

If you already hold an alien registration card and are now interested in gaining U.S. citizenship, you can easily skip over the chapters that deal with visas and gaining lawful permanent residence — although if you have friends or family members who also want to immigrate, you can certainly help them with this information.

If you're just beginning the process, you won't need to concern yourself with studying for the naturalization interview yet. But when that time comes, the information will be waiting for you in Parts III, IV, and V.

Part I
Pursuing Immigration and Citizenship

"I understand you're somewhat of an expert in the area of immigration law."

In this part . . .

The immigration process can be long and complex. Although we go into detail on important subjects later in this book, Part I gives you a broad overview of what to expect, from visiting the United States as a nonimmigrant, to gaining lawful permanent residence and the right to work here, to becoming a naturalized United States citizen. This part will give you clear information on how to best pursue your immigration goals, the government agencies you'll need to deal with along the way, and what steps you'll need to take to successfully complete the immigration and naturalization process.

Chapter 1

Getting In and Staying In the U.S.A.

In This Chapter

- Planning your way to immigration and citizenship
- Understanding the immigration process
- Preparing to prove your case

The decision to become a United States citizen is one of the most important choices you can ever make. Before you can become a U.S. citizen, however, you first must be a lawful permanent resident of the U.S. For this reason, before you begin the process, you need to know what you want to achieve — legal immigration or naturalization — and whether you can expect to qualify for it.

This chapter gives you an overview of your immigration options, helps you understand the benefits and disadvantages of becoming a U.S. citizen, and shows you what to expect during the process. Although we go into more detail later in the book, this chapter helps you determine what your immigration and citizenship goals are and shows you how best to pursue them.

Determining Whether You Really Want to Become a U.S. Citizen

Becoming a U.S. citizen carries important duties and responsibilities as well as rights, rewards, and privileges. Before you make the decision to pursue U.S. citizenship, you need to be aware of what you stand to lose and what you stand to gain and be sure you're ready to fulfill all the obligations of a good citizen.

Naturalization refers to the process by which immigrants become citizens. In most cases, if you were not born in the United States, you must be *naturalized* to become a U.S. citizen.

What you lose

When you become a U.S. citizen, you must give up all prior allegiances to other countries. Although nobody will care if you root for your birth country in a soccer match (actually, some soccer fans may care, but the U.S. government certainly won't), you won't be able to defend that country against the United States in times of conflict or war. You must also be willing to serve your new country, the United States of America, when required. What this means is that if the U.S. is at war or in the midst of some other type of crisis, you need to be willing to take up arms for the U.S. or otherwise aid the military effort in whatever capacity is needed.

Giving up your allegiances to other countries doesn't necessarily mean you have to give up your citizenship in other countries. You may be able to maintain your original citizenship(s) *and* hold U.S. citizenship (having citizenship in more than one country is known as *dual citizenship*). The United States allows dual citizenship (though it is disfavored). Some countries do not allow dual citizenship. If you are a citizen of such a country, you will likely give up your citizenship upon naturalizing to U.S. citizenship. This information may affect your decision to apply for U.S. citizenship. To find out if your citizenship can be affected, check with the embassy of each country where you have citizenship.

What you gain

The United States Constitution, the country's most important document and essentially the rulebook for how the U.S. government runs, guarantees all people living in the United States, whether U.S. citizens or not, certain rights. Freedom of religion and speech, the right to peaceable assembly, and the right to a fair trial if you're ever accused of a crime are all important freedoms guaranteed to everyone in the United States.

U.S. citizens, both born and naturalized, however, are eligible for many additional benefits based on their status as U.S. citizens. These include the following:

- The right to vote and, therefore, to have a voice in government
- The right to hold elected office (except for the offices of President and Vice President, which are reserved for natural-born citizens)
- Certain government jobs
- Public education
- Scholarships
- Grants
- The ability to petition for immediate relatives to join you in the U.S. without being subjects to visa limits
- Protection from forced removal from the country
- Certain types of public assistance

Your rights and responsibilities as a U.S. citizen

When you become a naturalized U.S. citizen, you must take the *Oath of Allegiance.* The Oath of Allegiance is your promise to the government and the people of the United States that you will

- Support and defend the Constitution and the laws of the United States against all enemies.
- Support, defend, and obey the laws of the United States.
- Swear allegiance to the United States.
- Serve the United States, if required, in times of war or national emergency. You may be called to serve in the military or help U.S. military efforts in some capacity.
- Give up any prior allegiances to other countries.

In addition to the responsibilities outlined in the Oath of Allegiance, U.S. citizens have other important duties:

- **Serving on a jury:** One of the most important rights in the U.S. is the right to a trial by a jury in most cases. Serving on a jury when asked is an important obligation of U.S. citizens in order to protect the U.S. system of justice, in which the power still rests with the people.

  Although there is a small chance you may never be called to report for jury duty, know that if you do receive a notice to report, you're legally compelled to do so. Failure to report for jury duty can result in a fine, jail time, or both.

- **Voting:** The United States has a government of the people, by the people, and for the people. The ultimate political authority is not in the hands of the government or of any single government official — instead, the ultimate political authority is in the hands of the people. Citizens of the United States have the right to change or abolish the government or to amend the Constitution. U.S. citizens exercise their power by voting for elected representatives.
- **Being tolerant of others:** The U.S. is a *melting pot,* a combination of many different cultures and ethnic races. People living here need to be tolerant of all races, religions, and cultures.

Although you aren't legally compelled to perform some of these duties — for instance, no one will take you to jail if you don't exercise your right to vote — you will deprive yourself of the important benefits of living in the United States if you don't participate.

Mapping Your Way to America: Typical Ways People Immigrate to the U.S.

Before you can even think about becoming a naturalized citizen of the U.S., you must be a lawful permanent resident of this country. A *lawful permanent resident* is a foreign national who has been granted the privilege of permanently living and working in the United States. Most adult applicants (those 18 or older) must have been lawful permanent residents of the United States for the five years prior to applying for citizenship. If you're married to and living with your U.S. citizen spouse, and your permanent residence is based on that marriage, the residence requirement drops to three years, as long as your spouse has been a citizen for the three years prior to your application. (We go over the eligibility requirements for naturalization in further detail in Chapter 3.)

Due to an immigration law passed in 1996, people who have stayed in the United States illegally for over 180 days and who leave the U.S. can be barred from reentering the country for at least three years. If the period of unlawful presence was less than a year, then the bar applies for three years (unless you leave voluntarily after removal proceedings start). If the period of unlawful presence was for a year or more, the bar is for ten years. The Bureau of Citizenship and Immigration Services (BCIS) won't count time you spent here illegally before April 1, 1997, nor will it penalize you for illegal time spent here while you were under the age of 18. The bottom line: Don't overstay your welcome. If you're in the United States on a temporary visa and you stay after your visa expires, you're putting your future chances for lawful permanent residence at risk. Being in the country illegally is grounds for removal and for denial of future immigration benefits. If you are currently in the country illegally, you should seek competent legal advice before leaving the U.S. to try to secure a visa.

What are children (besides people who ask you for money every time you turn around)?

The definition of a child has specific meaning in immigration law. When you read government documents that say, for instance, that you're able to sponsor "children," that means you can sponsor an unmarried son or daughter, under the age of 21 who was born in wedlock or is your legally recognized stepchild or adopted child. If, on the other hand, an immigration document refers to a "son or daughter," this refers to a child aged 21 or older.

To check whether your immigration status is currently legal, rely on your I-94 (Arrival-Departure Record). You receive this document from the Bureau of Customs and Border Protection (find out more about the BCBP in Chapter 2) upon entering the country, or from the BCIS if you extended your immigration status while already in the U.S. Many people believe the visa is what determines the amount of time you can stay in the U.S., but this isn't the case.

The BCBP is supposed to give a person the amount of time for which a visa petition is approved, rather than the amount of time the visa is valid — which is sometimes less than the amount of time granted in the petition. Likewise, the BCBP can approve entry for a lesser amount of time than the visa would indicate. ***Remember:*** If you stay in the U.S. for more time than your I-94 allows, you are out of status, even if your visa indicates a longer period.

TIP

Your visa can say it expires tomorrow, but the airport inspector can stamp your I-94 for six months. On the other hand, your visa can say it's valid through 2010, but the inspector can stamp you for only one month. The stamp is always your guide.

How can you achieve legal permanent residence? Although there are other ways, which we go into in Chapter 3, most people immigrate for one of two reasons:

- To reunite with family members already living in the U.S.
- To pursue a permanent employment opportunity in the U.S.

Reuniting with your family

In order to use family connections to immigrate to the United States, you must have a *close* relative already living here who is willing to sponsor you. So how close is close? If your relative is at least 21 years old and a U.S. citizen, born or naturalized, he or she may sponsor you if you are his or her:

- Husband or wife
- Unmarried child under age 21
- Unmarried son or daughter over age 21
- Married son or daughter
- Brother or sister
- Parent

Citizens may *not* sponsor their grandparents, grandchildren, aunts, uncles, cousins, or anyone else.

Legal permanent residents, or green-card holders — those legally living and working in the United States who have not become naturalized citizens — may only sponsor their:

- Husband or wife
- Unmarried son or daughter

Legal permanent residents (green-card holders) may *not* sponsor brothers or sisters, parents, grandparents, grandchildren, aunts, uncles, cousins, or anyone other than their spouse and children.

But wait, it's not so easy. More than a willingness to sponsor you, your relative must meet certain criteria in order to be eligible to become a sponsor:

- Your relative must be able to provide documentation of his or her immigration status — as a lawful permanent resident or as a United States citizen (born or naturalized).
- Your relative must be able to prove that he or she can financially support you (and any other family members he or she is financially responsible for) at 125 percent above the government-mandated poverty level. In other words, in order for a sponsor to bring a relative to live permanently in the United States, the sponsor must be both willing and able to accept legal responsibility for financially supporting that family member. You can find more information about how to meet this qualification in Chapter 3.

Pursuing employment opportunities

If you want to immigrate to the United States based on the fact that you have a full-time, permanent employment opportunity waiting for you here, both you and your prospective employer must meet a list of specific qualifications. Although one of the goals of the BCIS is to provide the U.S. with a strong and stable workforce, the BCIS also wants to be sure that immigrants aren't taking jobs that would otherwise go to unemployed U.S. citizens.

Before you even get started, keep in mind that your prospective employer has to first certify the position with the Department of Labor. This *Labor Certification* is required to show there are no qualified, available U.S. workers to fill the job.

The BCIS grants permanent residence based on employment skills in one of five categories:

- **Priority Workers (category EB-1)** have extraordinary ability in the arts, education, business, science, or athletics, or are considered to be outstanding professors or researchers. Notice the superlatives: *extraordinary, outstanding.* This category is one of the most difficult ones to qualify for, unless you're a Nobel Prize winner or hold other such prestigious and public accolades in your given field. You may qualify, however, by presenting extensive documentation proving your professional or academic achievements in one of the listed fields as well as evidence of your financial success in your field and your ability to substantially benefit the United States. Another way to qualify for the Priority Workers category is if you happen to be a manager or executive of a company that has transferred you to one of its branches in the United States.
- **Professionals with Advanced Degrees or Persons with Exceptional Ability (category EB-2)** are members of the professions holding advanced degrees, or their United States equivalent or persons with exceptional ability in business, sciences, or the arts who will benefit the interests or welfare of the United States. In order to qualify for this category, be prepared to show how your becoming a legal permanent resident will be good

for the economy or culture of the United States or how you can help meet the academic needs of the country. You may also qualify for this category if you're a qualified physician and you agree to practice medicine in an area of the United States that is medically underserved.

- **Skilled or Professional Workers or Other Workers (category EB-3)** have less stringent requirements for qualification than people who qualify under the EB-1 and EB-2 classifications, but this category sometimes has a much longer backlog of people waiting for visas, especially in the Other Workers category. You can qualify for a classification EB-3 employment visa in three ways:
  - As a Skilled Worker: If you can fill an open position that requires at least two years of experience or training, you can qualify as a Skilled Worker. The Department of Labor determines which jobs are considered skilled, as opposed to unskilled labor.
  - As a Professional: Professionals must hold a U.S. baccalaureate degree or the foreign equivalent degree normally required for the profession. Education and experience may not be substituted for the actual degree.
  - As an Other Worker: Those who fall into the category of Other Workers have the skills to fill jobs that require less than two years of higher education, training, or experience. This category receives the most petitions, so if you fall in this group, you may have to wait many years before being granted a visa.
- **Special Immigrants (or category EB-4)** primarily are members of religious denominations that have nonprofit religious organizations in the United States. You must be able to prove that you have been a member of this organization and have worked for the organization for at least two years before you applied for admission, and you must be coming to the United States to work as a minister or priest or other religious vocation that helps the organization. You may also qualify if your work helps the organization in a more professional capacity; however, this means that a U.S. baccalaureate degree, or the foreign equivalent, is required to perform the job.
- **Immigrant Investors (or category EB-5)** must agree to make a "qualified investment" in a new commercial enterprise. All Immigrant Investors must demonstrate that their investment will benefit the United States economy, as well as create a specified number of full-time jobs for qualified U.S. citizens.

  This category is often known as the "million-dollar visa" because the minimum investment (which is subject to change) is, you guessed it, a million dollars. You can invest less and still qualify, if you invest in a *targeted employment area* (a rural area or area of high unemployment).

  A special pilot program allows an investor within an approved regional center to receive an EB-5 visa when he or she shows that his or her investment will create jobs indirectly through revenues generated from increased exports, improved regional productivity, job creation, or increased domestic capital investment resulting from the new commercial enterprise. Currently, of the 10,000 EB-5 visas available annually, 5,000 are set aside for this program.

Winning the visa lottery

Even if you qualify for one of the visa categories listed in the preceding section, entering the Diversity Visa (DV) Lottery Program makes sense, because it can speed up your process of receiving a visa, especially if you find yourself in one of the lower preference categories.

Entering the visa lottery is easy. You just have to fill out a single form. (For more details on the lottery, turn to Chapter 3.)

Surprise!: You may already be a U.S. citizen

If you were actually born in the United States — including, in most cases, Puerto Rico, Guam, and the U.S. Virgin Islands — you're considered a U.S. citizen at birth. Your birth certificate serves as proof of your citizenship. The one exception to this rule is if one or more of your parents was a foreign diplomat at the time of your birth (you would be considered a permanent resident in that case).

Are there ways to be born abroad and still be a U.S. citizen? Yes, under certain specific conditions. If you were born abroad but both your parents were U.S. citizens, and at least one of those two parents lived in the United States at some point prior to your birth, then you are considered a U.S. citizen in most cases.

If you were born abroad but only one of your parents was a U.S. citizen, and the other parent was an alien, you will be considered a citizen in most cases if, before you were born, your citizen parent lived in the U.S. for at least five years. In order to qualify, at least two of those five years had to have taken place after your citizen parent's 14th birthday.

Notice how we keep saying "in most cases"? The previous explanation is current law, and it's a generalization. Whether you acquired U.S. citizenship at birth depends on the law that was in effect at the time of your birth. This is one of the toughest areas of immigration law, filled with loopholes and exceptions, so getting expert help in these cases is always a good idea. Be sure to seek and get competent legal help *before* you need it. (You can get more information on finding legal help in Chapter 7.)

If you receive a visa through the Diversity Visa Lottery Program, you'll be authorized to live and work permanently in the United States, as well as bring your husband or wife and any children under the age of 21 along with you.

Each year 55,000 immigrant visas become available to people who come from countries with low rates of immigration to the United States. The Department of State randomly selects about 100,000 applicants from among the qualified entries. Why do they pick 100,000 when only 55,000 visas are available? Because they know that not all the applicants will be able to successfully complete the visa process. When 55,000 applicants have qualified and completed the immigration process, no further Diversity Lottery visas are issued for that year.

Documenting Your Immigration Status

Your entry document (such as an I-94 card for nonimmigrants) or a green card (if you're a permanent resident), serves as the important documentation you need to prove that you're in the United States legally and that you're entitled to all the rights and privileges that come with that status. As long as you hold a valid BCIS entry document or green card, are maintaining lawful status, and have not committed a removable offense, you don't have to worry about being forced to leave the country. For naturalized citizens, a Certificate of Naturalization or a U.S. passport serves as the same proof of immigration status.

Depending on where you are in the immigration process, you'll need various forms and documentation.

Just Visiting

A *nonimmigrant,* or temporary, visa allows you to legally stay in the United States for a given length of time, after which you must leave the country. In order to qualify for a temporary visa, you'll usually need to prove that you have a residence outside the U.S., as well as binding ties to your home country, such as a family or a job. The U.S. government wants to be sure you'll return home at the end of your visit. In most cases, you'll also need to show that you have enough money to support yourself while in the United States.

The type of temporary visa you get will depend on the reasons why you want to visit the United States. You can gain temporary access to the United States in many ways, including the following:

- As a visitor or tourist
- For business
- To seek medical treatment
- As a temporary worker or to receive work training
- As a student, either for academic or vocational training
- By participating in an educational or cultural exchange program
- As a fiancé(e) of an American citizen
- As a NAFTA professional

Qualified citizens of Canada and Mexico may obtain temporary TN (Trade NAFTA) status. This status is available to certain professionals under the North American Free Trade Agreement (NAFTA). These citizens are *visa exempt,* meaning they don't have to obtain visas at a U.S. consulate in order to enter the U.S. in this status. Through the agreement, a citizen of a NAFTA country may work in a professional occupation in another NAFTA country, providing he or she can meet the following conditions:

- The profession is on the NAFTA list.
- The person has the necessary skills and qualifications to fill the position.
- The position requires someone in a professional capacity.
- The person will be working for a U.S. employer.

Under this particular status, you will be allowed to bring your spouse and unmarried children under 21 with you, although they will not be allowed to work in the U.S. unless they qualify for work authorization on their own.

Travelers from certain eligible countries also may be able to visit the U.S. (for business or pleasure only) without a visa through the Visa Waiver Program. Check with the Department of State (`www.travel.state.gov/vwp.html`) to see if your home country qualifies.

Here to stay

To become a lawful permanent resident, an alien must first be admitted as an immigrant. Most people get their immigrant visas because a qualified relative or employer has sponsored them as follows:

1. The employer or relative filed a petition with the BCIS.
2. The BCIS approved the petition and then forwarded it to the National Visa Center for further processing.
3. The State Department issued a visa after an immigrant visa number became available.

If you're already living in the United States, you may be eligible to adjust your immigration status from temporary to lawful permanent resident without leaving the country. And here's some good news: As an applicant, you may apply for a work permit while your case is pending. (You can find out more about this in Chapter 3.)

If you plan to leave the U.S. while applying for adjustment to permanent resident status, you must receive advance permission, called *advance parole,* to return to the United States. If you do not apply for advance parole *before* leaving the U.S., the BCIS will assume you have abandoned your application and you may not be permitted to reenter the United States.

In most cases, as an alien applying for permanent residence, you will need to provide

- A valid passport
- Three photographs
- Birth and police certificates
- Marriage, divorce, or death certificates of your current and/or prior spouse(s)
- Proof of financial support
- Proof of medical examination

You can get more-specific details about what to provide at the National Visa Center (NVC); requirements vary slightly from consulate to consulate. An automated recorded message system can answer many simple questions, 24 hours a day, 7 days a week (call 603-334-0700). Operators are available to respond to more-complex questions from 8:00 a.m. to 6:45 p.m. (eastern time) Monday through Friday. (***Note:*** You can only obtain information on the status of your case, and you can only get access to an operator, by entering your NVC case number or BCIS receipt number on a Touch-Tone telephone.) You can visit the NVC Web site at `www.travel.state.gov/nvc.html` for more information.

Written inquiries, changes of address and requests to upgrade petitions due to naturalization of the petitioner should be sent to The National Visa Center, 32 Rochester Ave., Portsmouth, NH 03801-2909.

The NVC is not open to the public. Unfortunately, some people have traveled long distances to inquire about their case in person, only to discover that NVC staff is unable to meet with them.

Seek competent legal help if you have been in the United States illegally. If you leave the U.S. to obtain an immigrant visa abroad and the unlawful presence accrued after March 31, 1997, you will be barred from reentering the U.S. for three years (if the continuous unlawful presence was from 181 days to one year) or ten years (if the continuous unlawful presence was for more than one year).

Joining the club

Naturalization, the process by which lawful permanent residents become U.S. citizens, is the next step in the immigration process. Many lawful permanent residents stop before achieving citizenship, but if you bought this book, chances are you're interested in going all the way.

As a naturalized citizen, a person has the exact same rights, responsibilities, and benefits of natural-born U.S. citizens, with two exceptions: Only natural-born citizens may become President or Vice President of the United States.

Serving your way to citizenship

In times of peace, legal permanent residents on active duty in the military can become naturalized after living here three years, rather than the usual five. In times of war or other declared hostilities, members of the U.S. armed forces may naturalize without even being lawful permanent residents. Such periods are designated by law or by Executive Order of the president and have included World War I, World War II, the Korean War, the Vietnam police action, and the Gulf War. Most recently, the War on Terror, was added, allowing all active-duty military personnel serving on or after September 11, 2001, until a date to be determined, to be naturalized without regard to prior permanent resident status.

In most cases, naturalization applicants must prove they can meet these requirements:

- **A designated period of continuous residence in the United States (usually three or five years immediately prior to applying) as a lawfully admitted permanent resident.**
- **Physical presence in the U.S. for at least half the designated time.**
- **Residence in a particular BCIS district prior to filing, usually for at least three months.** Districts are geographical areas, serviced by local BCIS offices. You can get up-to-date information about districts at www.immigration.gov/graphics/fieldoffices/index.htm.
- **The ability to read, write, and speak basic English.**
- **A basic knowledge and understanding of U.S. history and government.**
- **Good moral character.** Applicants for naturalization must be "of good moral character," meaning that the BCIS will make a determination based on current laws. Conviction for certain crimes will cause you to lose your eligibility for citizenship. If you have ever been convicted of murder or convicted of an aggravated felony (committed on or after November 29, 1990), you may never become a citizen of the U.S. Other lesser crimes may delay your immigration or citizenship goals, because they prevent you from appl ing until a specified amount of time has passed since you committed the crime. In determining good moral character, however, the BCIS can consider conduct that would have been a crime even if you were never arrested, charged, or convicted. (You can find more on good moral character in Chapter 3.)
- **Attachment to the principles of the U.S. Constitution and a favorable disposition toward the United States.** This means that you must be willing to take the Oath of Allegiance to the United States of America, giving up any prior allegiances to other countries.

Don't worry if this sounds like a lot. The purpose of this book is to help get you ready to successfully complete your immigration goals all the way to becoming a U.S. citizen. We go into greater detail on all these requirements later in the book.

Making Sense of the Immigration Process

If you bought this book, you're obviously interested in being more than just a temporary visitor to the United States. You want to be a U.S. citizen. But first you must become a lawful permanent resident (with one exception — see the "Serving your way to citizenship" sidebar, earlier in this chapter).

Doing the paperwork

The type of application you file will depend on your path to immigration — in most cases, through family or through employment. (You can find more details on specific forms and paperwork in Chapter 4.)

After the BCIS approves your sponsor's immigrant visa petition, the Department of State must determine if an immigrant visa number is immediately available to you or if you will be on a waiting list. When an immigrant visa becomes available to you, you can process your immigrant visa through a U.S. consulate.

If you're already in the United States, you may only apply to change your status to that of a lawful permanent resident *after* a visa number becomes available for you.

Proving your identity

In order to gain your Permanent Resident Card, if you're adjusting your status while in the U.S., or to become a naturalized citizen, you're going to have to prove your identity. Be prepared to be fingerprinted and provide the BCIS with at least two photographs, in addition to documents and paperwork that must be included with your application (you can find more information on this in Chapter 4).

Even if you have a Permanent Resident Card, you'll have to be fingerprinted and photographed when applying to become a naturalized citizen. After you've filed an application with the BCIS, you will receive a fingerprinting appointment letter, usually advising you to go to a local application support center or police station. The BCIS will do a criminal background check, cross-referencing your fingerprints with the Federal Bureau of Investigation (FBI). In some cases, the quality of the fingerprints is not sufficient for the FBI to read. If this happens, the BCIS will notify you of another fingerprinting appointment. Don't worry — you'll only have to pay a fingerprinting fee ($50 as of this writing) once.

If the FBI rejects your fingerprints twice, you'll most likely be asked to provide police clearances for every place you've lived since you were 16 years old. Contact the local police departments in those cities or towns to obtain the clearances. If you're processing through an overseas consulate, as opposed to adjusting your status while in the U.S., you'll need to provide police clearances for every place you have lived (for your country of nationality if you lived there six months or more; for all other countries, if you lived there for at least one year).

In some cases, especially if you live far away from the nearest fingerprinting station, a mobile fingerprinting van will travel to perform the process.

It's not easy being green

A Permanent Resident Card is evidence of your status as a lawful permanent resident. Although in popular lingo it's called a green card, the Permanent Resident Card is officially known as BCIS Form I-551. At one time in its history, the Permanent Resident Card was known as the Alien Registration Receipt Card. The cards used to actually be green, too. Even though today's cards are no longer green, the name has worked its way into the *slang,* or popular language, and people still refer to Alien Registration Receipt Cards or Permanent Resident Cards as green cards.

Being Interviewed by the BCIS

Presuming you plan on following the immigration path all the way to the final step of naturalization, you can plan on interviewing with the BCIS at least twice: once to qualify for your permanent resident status or green card, and again when you become a naturalized U.S. citizen (unless your visa processing took place at an overseas consulate, in which case you'll only interview with BCIS once — for naturalization.

The interviews fill many potential immigrants and citizens with terror. "How will I ever remember everything?" they worry. Relax. Passing the BCIS interview is far easier than you think. In fact, you probably already have most, if not all, of the skills and information you need. And if you don't, this book has you covered.

Interviewing for a green card

You need to live in the U.S. as a lawful permanent resident for at least three to five years before you can qualify for naturalization. Look at obtaining your green card as taking the first step toward citizenship.

Wives or husbands of U.S. citizens who die while honorably serving in the U.S. military (not necessarily during a time of hostilities) do not need to meet the residence or physical presence requirements; they just need to be a legal permanent resident at the time they file for naturalization.

So, let's assume you're a qualified applicant for permanent residence and you have a qualified sponsor — usually your employer or a spouse or other family member. You can prove these facts and have sent the BCIS all the necessary applications and documents we cover in Chapter 4. You've prepared your case and have kept careful records of all the paperwork you've ever sent to the BCIS. Because immigration laws can be complicated, you've probably consulted an attorney or received other professional help in preparing your case up to this point. It's been a long road, but you've done the work and now you're ready to take the final step toward lawful permanent residence — interviewing with the BCIS (if you're adjusting your status while in the United States) or interviewing with a consular officer (if you're applying at an overseas consulate).

In many employment-based cases, the BCIS does not require an interview. If you receive an interview notice, however, don't be nervous about your interview. Be prepared! Here's what to expect: At the beginning of the interview, the BCIS officer will place you under oath. This means that you swear to tell the truth at all times during the interview. The officer will then review your file and ask you questions about the answers you gave on your application. Be prepared to answer questions about whether you have a criminal record or have ever been involved in deportation proceedings or any of the other permanent or temporary bars to immigration outlined in Chapter 8.

The BCIS officer will also review your medical examinations. He or she will ask if there is anything you want to correct about the background and biographical information you provided the BCIS. If anything has changed or you feel your documents contain inaccurate information, now is the time to speak up.

If your case is based on employment, the officer may also review your Department of Labor paperwork. He or she could ask questions about your job to determine if you really worked in the occupation you claim when you lived in your native country. The officer may also want to know whether you have the necessary skills to perform the job in the United States.

Be prepared to answer questions designed to determine if you've been working illegally while waiting for your green-card application to be approved. ***Remember:*** Some applicants aren't allowed to work in the U.S. while waiting to get their green cards — and working illegally provides grounds for the BCIS to deny your application. As long as you're truthful and have followed the rules, you should have nothing to worry about.

If your case is based upon your marriage to a U.S. citizen, the interviewing officer will ask questions about your marriage and life together. The BCIS wants to feel confident that yours is a true marriage and not a union of convenience designed to get you into the country. The BCIS will require your spouse to come to the interview, and they can choose to interview you separately or as a couple.

In some cases, the officer will need additional information and paperwork in order to make his or her decision. If this happens in your case, the BCIS officer will reschedule you to return with the requested items another day.

If all goes well and the officer doesn't need any more documentation, he or she will issue you an approval and you'll be asked to return to the BCIS to get your passport stamped — as a lawful permanent resident. If you've been married to your U.S.-citizen spouse for less than two years, your passport will be stamped as a *conditional permanent resident* — conditioned on your still being married after two years. At that time, you may have the condition removed to become a full lawful permanent resident, which may require another interview with the BCIS. In either case, you won't actually receive the green card itself for several months, although your new immigration status takes effect with the stamping of your passport.

All applicants for adjustment of status are entitled to work authorization. If you're in the U.S. waiting to go to an overseas consulate to process, you have to maintain a status that permits employment (see Chapter 3 for more information) and only work pursuant to your status.

Obtaining U.S. citizenship

Let's assume you've been a lawful permanent resident of the United States for at least five years or, if your permanent resident status is based on marriage, you've been married to and living with your U.S. citizen spouse for at least three years. If you're a man between the ages of 18 and 26, you've registered for the draft with Selective Service. You've properly completed and filed your Application for Naturalization Form (Form N-400), and supplied the BCIS with all the necessary documents and paperwork (you can find more on this in Chapter 4). Now comes the final step in the process of becoming a citizen: the BCIS interview.

Although it only takes about 40 minutes, the interview fills many prospective citizens with fear and dread. After all, you not only have to be prepared to answer questions about yourself, you also have to prove that you know how to read, write, and speak English and that you have a basic understanding of U.S. history, government, and civics.

We know it sounds intimidating, but if you do your homework, you'll have nothing to worry about. BCIS examiners don't expect you to know *everything* about the United States. Nor do you have to be an English professor to pass the language test. If you can read and understand this book, you can pass the English text. If you're having trouble, don't worry. We give you some fun and easy ways to improve your skills in Chapter 17.

BCIS officers are required to give "due consideration" to your education, background, age, length of residence in the United States, opportunities available, and efforts made to acquire the requisite knowledge, along with any other elements or factors relevant to appraising your knowledge and understanding. As far as U.S. history and civics are concerned, the

BCIS wants to know you understand the principles that the U.S. stands for. Finding out about history helps you understand how the United States became the great nation it is today. Parts III, IV, and V of this book help you prepare for the history and civics test, but we predict you already know more than you think you do.

After your interview, you'll get a BCIS Form N-652, which simply tells you whether your application was granted, denied, or continued. Here's an explanation of what each of these three possibilities means:

- **Granted:** Congratulations! If your application was granted, you'll soon receive a notice of when and where to go for your swearing-in ceremony, where you'll take the Oath of Allegiance. You don't become a U.S. citizen until you attend this ceremony and take the Oath of Allegiance.
- **Denied:** If the BCIS denies your application for naturalization, you'll receive a written notice telling you why. If you feel you were wrongly denied, you can ask for a hearing with another BCIS officer to appeal your case. On the back of your denial letter, you'll find BCIS Form N-336 "Request for Hearing on a Decision in Naturalization Proceedings." You'll also conveniently find full instructions on how to file and what fees you'll need to pay. If your application is again denied at your second hearing, don't give up — you still have one more chance: You can file to have your application reviewed in U.S. district court.

Keep in mind that you only have 30 days after receiving your denial letter to file for an appeal hearing. After 30 days, the case is considered closed, and you'll have start the entire process over again if you want to reapply.

- **Continued:** Cases are most often *continued,* or put on hold, because the applicant didn't provide all the documents the BCIS needed or because the applicant failed the English or civics test. If the BCIS requires more information, they will give you a Form N-14, which explains exactly what information or documents they're looking for. The form will also tell when and how you should provide these papers.

You're close to gaining citizenship, and details count. Follow the instructions on Form N-14 carefully. Not paying attention to details can result in your application being denied. If you don't understand the instructions, ask for help and make sure you deliver what's asked for on time. (See Chapter 7 for information about finding competent and ethical help.)

If you failed the English test and/or the civics test, the BCIS will give you a time to come back and try again in another interview. Study hard, because if you fail the tests a second time, your application will be denied. Don't worry — you'll have plenty of time to prepare for your second test (usually between 60 and 90 days).

Recognizing Permanent and Temporary Bars to Naturalization

Are there any situations in which you can be automatically disqualified from ever becoming a U.S. citizen? You bet. Having committed certain crimes may cause you to lose your chance at citizenship — these are known as *permanent bars to naturalization.* A murder conviction on your record is a permanent bar to naturalization. If you were convicted of an aggravated felony that was committed on or after November 29, 1990, you've also lost your chance of becoming a U.S. citizen.

Disability and age exceptions to the English and civics requirements

In order to accommodate those with disabilities, certain applicants — those with a physical or developmental disability or mental impairment — may not be required to take the English and/or civics test. If you think you, or an immigrant you are assisting, may qualify for these exceptions, be prepared to file BCIS Form N-648 "Medical Certification for Disability Exceptions" along with the naturalization application. Don't send in the application until a licensed medical or osteopathic doctor or licensed clinical psychologist with knowledge of the case has completed and signed Form N-648. If you qualify for the English language proficiency portion of the test, be prepared to bring a qualified interpreter with you to your interview.

When it comes to gaining U.S. citizenship, age has its privileges in the form of easier English and/or civics test requirements:

- **If you are over 50 years old** and have lived in the U.S. as a lawful permanent resident for periods totaling at least 20 years, you won't have to take the English test. You will, however, be required to take the civics test in the language of your choice.
- **If you are over 55 years old** and have lived in the U.S. as a lawful permanent resident for periods totaling at least 15 years, you won't have to take the English test. You will be required to take the civics test in the language of your choice.
- **If you are over 65 years old** and have lived in the U.S. as a lawful permanent resident for periods totaling at least 20 years, you won't have to take the English test. You'll also be given a simpler version of the civics test in the language of your choice.

You must meet the age and permanent residency requirements at the time you file your Application for Naturalization in order to qualify for an age exception. Your time as a permanent resident need not be continuous, but it must total a period of at least 15 or 20 years. (We cover this topic in more detail in Chapter 4.)

Other crimes are *temporary bars to naturalization,* meaning you must wait a designated time after committing the crime before you can become eligible to apply for citizenship. In Chapter 8, you can find out more about other ways you can be disqualified for citizenship.

Failure to pay child support, or support other legal dependents, can present a bar to naturalization. Make sure your legal financial obligations to any dependents are current and up to date before applying for citizenship.

Attending Your Swearing-In Ceremony

Assuming you pass your interview, you'll receive a notice of when to attend your swearing-in ceremony, where you'll take the Oath of Allegiance. (In some cases, the interviewing officer will give you the oath on the spot, and you'll become a naturalized citizen then and there, but most often you'll return another day for a ceremony.)

The Oath of Allegiance plays an important part in becoming a U.S. citizen, and it carries serious implications. The oath serves as your solemn promise to the government of the United States that you:

- **Formally renounce or give up all ties with your former country's government.** You may still have feelings of respect and admiration for your former homeland. You may even have family and friends still living there. However, in order to take the oath, your government loyalty must be to the United States and only to the United States.

- **Declare total allegiance to the United States of America, vowing to support and defend the Constitution.**
- **Pledge your willingness to serve the United States.** When required by law, you must be willing to fight in the armed forces or help the U.S. military through civilian service.

Taking the Oath of Allegiance is also known as *Attachment to the Constitution.* In this case, the word *attachment* means loyalty or allegiance.

Receiving your Certificate of Naturalization

After you've taken the Oath of Allegiance, you'll be presented with your Certificate of Naturalization. Congratulations! You are now officially a citizen of the United States of America, and you can use your certificate to prove it. This legal document is quite ornate in appearance, resembling a diploma — one personalized with your photograph.

Applying for a passport as soon as you receive your Certificate of Naturalization is a good idea. A passport can also serve as proof of your citizenship, and it's much easier to carry than the certificate itself. If you ever lose your certificate, getting a replacement can sometimes take up to a year. If the certificate serves as your only proof of citizenship, a year can feel like a mighty long time — especially if you want to travel. You can usually pick up a passport application at your swearing-in ceremony. If not, your local post office has passport applications, or you can download one at www.travel.state.gov/download_applications.html.

TECHNICAL STUFF

Modifying the oath

We take freedom of religion seriously in the United States, which is why the BCIS allows the oath to be *modified,* or changed, in some cases, by leaving out these phrases:

- **". . . that I will bear arms on behalf of the United States when required by law":** In order for these words to be left out of the oath, you must provide evidence that your objection to fighting for the United States is based on your religious beliefs and training.
- **". . . that I will perform noncombatant service in the armed forces of the United States when required by law":** If you can provide enough evidence that your religious training and beliefs completely prohibit you from serving in the armed forces in any capacity, the BCIS will also leave out this portion of the oath.
- **". . . so help me God":** If your religious beliefs keep you from using the phrase *so help me God,* the BCIS will omit the words.
- **". . . on oath":** If you are unable to truthfully swear using the words *on oath,* the BCIS will substitute the phrase with *solemnly affirm.*

If you think you qualify to take a modified oath, you'll need to write the BCIS a letter explaining why and send it along with your Application for Naturalization. Be aware that the BCIS will probably ask you to provide a letter from your religious institution explaining its beliefs and declaring you are a member in good standing.

If you have a physical or mental disability that prevents you from communicating your understanding of the oath's meaning, the BCIS will probably excuse you from this requirement.

Chapter 2

Meeting the Major Players in the Immigration Game

In This Chapter

- Identifying the goals of the U.S. immigration system
- Introducing the Big Three: The DHS, the Department of State, and the Department of Labor
- Recognizing other agencies that affect immigration

Before you start your journey on the path to immigration, knowing whom you're dealing with is helpful. This chapter introduces you to the government agencies you'll encounter and work with during the immigration and naturalization processes. Knowing the goals and missions of these government agencies can help you identify the ways they can impact you, as someone seeking lawful permanent residence or citizenship, and how to most effectively deal with them.

Understanding the Goals of the U.S. Immigration System

The Bureau of Citizenship and Immigration Services (BCIS) administers immigration benefits, including legal permanent residence and naturalization for qualified applicants. The BCIS replaced the immigration benefits part of the Immigration and Naturalization Services (INS) when the INS was eliminated. (See the "Surprising INS statistics" sidebar later in this chapter for more information about the former duties of the INS.)

The U.S. immigration system works to achieve three main goals:

- **Bringing and keeping families together:** U.S. immigration laws are designed to encourage families to stay together when possible. ***Remember:*** Immigrating through a family connection is the most common way people come to the United States.
- **Supplying a qualified workforce to keep the U.S. prospering:** Another of the BCIS's duties is to help supplement the U.S. workforce by ensuring there are enough foreign workers to fill positions not filled by U.S. workers.
- **Providing safe refuge and asylum:** The BCIS also exists to help those who are seeking a safe refuge in the U.S. from political, religious, or social persecution in their home countries.

Identifying the Major Players and Their Roles in the Immigration System

A popular American expression with its origins in baseball, the country's national pastime, says, "You can't know the players without a score card." And so it is with immigration. During the immigration and naturalization process, you'll work with several government agencies. This section is your "score card" of the major players in the immigration game.

The Department of Homeland Security

Effective January 24, 2003, the new Homeland Security Act represents the most significant and extensive transformation of the U.S. government in over 50 years. In the aftermath of the terrorist attacks against the United States on September 11, 2001, President George W. Bush decided 22 domestic agencies could better serve and protect the country if they were coordinated into one department. The new department reorganizes a patchwork of government agencies under the authority of the Department of Homeland Security (DHS).

The DHS encompasses a wide range of duties and responsibilities. Although you may only interact with one or two parts of the DHS, all the department's activities are ultimately aimed at accomplishing three primary missions:

- Preventing terrorist attacks within the United States
- Reducing the country's vulnerability to terrorism
- Minimizing the damage from potential attacks and natural disasters

One of the potential major advantages of the DHS is that it gives state and local officials one main contact instead of many when it comes to homeland-security needs. In theory, this will streamline the process of efficiently obtaining necessary supplies and equipment and training emergency personnel like police and firefighters, as well as medical personnel, to manage security emergencies. The DHS also manages federal grant programs, protects the U.S. borders, and more.

As of March 1, 2003, the DHS started administering the nation's immigration laws. Prior to this, the INS oversaw these matters. But the INS was overworked, understaffed, and plagued by problems. Many experts attributed part of the INS's difficulties to the fact that the former INS did double duty as both an immigration-benefits administration agency and immigration enforcement agency. The DHS addresses the dual-function issue by dividing the former INS into two separate government entities: the Bureau for Citizenship and Immigration Services (BCIS) and the Directorate of Border and Transportation Security (BTS).

The Bureau for Citizenship and Immigration Services

Through the Bureau for Citizenship and Immigration Services (BCIS), the DHS will take over half of the INS's former duties, including:

- *Adjudicating* (hearing and deciding on) immigrant and nonimmigrant petitions
- Adjusting the immigration status of immigrants already in the United States
- Issuing work authorization and other permits
- Naturalizing qualified applicants for U.S. citizenship
- Processing asylum and refugee cases

Surprising INS statistics

Of course, you always hear horror stories about things the former INS did wrong — terrorist suspects and the like slipping past borders. INS mistakes were a big part of the motivation behind creating the Department of Homeland Security, although to be fair, a restructuring of the immigration system had already begun before September 11, 2001. To understand how such "mistakes" could have happened, you need to understand the sheer volume of work the INS dealt with. For instance, according to INS statistics, the Immigration and Naturalization Service:

- Held more than 43 million files, including approximately 20 million active files.
- Received 7.4 million naturalization applications from 1998 through 2001, more than had been received in the previous 42 years combined.
- Received 7.9 million applications for immigration benefits, including naturalization, in 2001, nearly 31 percent more than received in 2000.
- Removed 176,549 criminal and other illegal aliens in 2001. The number of criminal aliens removed (71,346) alone exceeded the total number of all illegal aliens removed in 1995 (50,924).
- Apprehended 1,235,000 illegal aliens along the Southwest border in 2001.
- Oversaw more than 300 land, air, and sea ports of entry. In 2001, the INS conducted more than 510 million inspections of individuals arriving in the United States at these ports.
- Collected approximately $1.7 billion in fees for services in 2001, more than double the amount collected in 1993.

And a collective employment staff of about 36,000 people accomplished all this.

The Directorate of Border and Transportation Security

The former Immigration and Naturalization Service also handled many law-enforcement duties. Under the new DHS, the duty of maintaining the security of the nation's borders and transportation systems falls under the jurisdiction of the Directorate of Border and Transportation Security (BTS). The BTS assumes immigration-related duties that used to be delegated to other government branches, namely:

- The border inspection functions of the United States Customs Service (part of the U.S. Treasury Department)
- The border inspection and enforcement functions of the INS (formerly part of the Department of Justice)

Under the authority of the BTS are two subagencies: the Bureau of Immigration and Customs Enforcement (BICE), which enforces immigration laws, including removal, and the Bureau of Customs and Border Protection (BCBP), which protects and monitors the nation's borders.

The BTS will work to make sure that the U.S. continues to welcome nonimmigrants and immigrants who seek opportunity in the country while excluding terrorists and their supporters. Under the heading of immigration enforcement, the BTS can

- Prevent aliens from entering the country unlawfully
- Detect and remove those who are living in the U.S. unlawfully
- Prevent terrorists and other criminal aliens from entering or residing in the U.S.
- Conduct border and port-of-entry inspections
- Detain and remove criminal aliens from the country

- Apprehend and prosecute illegal aliens and workers, including performing worksite enforcement of immigration laws
- Enforce laws regarding immigration document fraud
- Decide matters of removal from the United States
- Answer questions about and help find solutions to immigration concerns brought by the public, special-interest groups, and other government agencies, as well as the U.S. Congress

The Department of State

As the leading U.S. foreign-affairs agency, the Department of State (DOS) maintains diplomatic relations with about 180 countries as well as with many international organizations. With the primary mission of maintaining and improving relationships with these countries, the Department of State runs nearly 260 diplomatic and consular posts around the world, including embassies, consulates, and missions to international organizations.

To be sure, the State Department (just another way of referring to the Department of State) has many important duties, including providing support for U.S. citizens at home and abroad; helping developing countries grow strong, stable economies and governments; bringing nations together to address global concerns; and combating threats like terrorism, international crime, and narcotics trafficking. But the DOS also provides many services to U.S. citizens traveling and living abroad, including:

- Issuing passports (over 7 million passports were issued in 2000 alone)
- Providing information about safely traveling and living abroad
- Warning travelers of particularly dangerous areas
- Helping U.S. citizens traveling overseas to obtain emergency funds
- Checking on the whereabouts or welfare of U.S. citizens traveling or living abroad
- Helping families in the event a U.S. citizen loved one dies while traveling overseas
- Aiding U.S. travelers who become sick while traveling overseas
- Providing assistance to U.S. travelers who get arrested overseas
- Assisting in international adoptions and custody disputes
- Protecting and assisting U.S. citizens living or traveling abroad during international crises
- Distributing federal benefits payments
- Assisting with absentee voting and Selective Service registration

In addition to providing services to U.S. citizens, the Department of State issues visas for foreigners who want to enter the U.S. In fact, they issued more than 9 million visas in 2000. When it comes time for you to get a visa, whether it is a temporary visa or a permanent visa, you'll deal with the Department of State.

The BCIS must first approve your immigrant visa before forwarding it to the National Visa Center (NVC), a processing facility of the U.S. State Department, for further processing. The NVC will issue more paperwork for you to complete and, when you've completed that paperwork satisfactorily, the NVC will assign you an immigrant visa number. The State Department issues a monthly guide called the *Visa Bulletin,* explaining the status of various classes of immigrant visas. The *Visa Bulletin* charts visa availability for both family- and employer-sponsored immigrants based on *priority date* (the date the sponsoring petition was filed). Some categories, such as the fourth preference for siblings of U.S. citizens, are usually several years behind, while other categories may be current. (You can find out more about preference categories in Chapter 3.)

To access the *Visa Bulletin* go to the State Department Web site (`www.dos.gov`) or fax 202-647-3000 and request Document 1038. You can obtain past issues of the *Visa Bulletin* at `http://dosfan.lib.uic.edu/ERC/visa_bulletin`.

The State Department also has a huge impact on refugees and those seeking asylum — the millions of people each year who are displaced by war, famine, and civil and political unrest or those who are escaping persecution and the risk of death and torture in their home countries.

The difference between those seeking asylum and refugee admission is important. A *refugee* is someone who is living outside the U.S. *and* outside his or her home country who petitions the U.S. government for lawful permanent residence in order to escape intolerable conditions in his or her home country. An *asylum-seeker* is someone already in the U.S. or someone seeking admission at a U.S. entry point when he or she applies to the U.S. government for permission to stay.

Each year, the DOS prepares a Report to Congress on proposed refugee admissions. Congress then advises the president on the proposed *ceilings* (limits) on refugee admissions for that *fiscal* (financial) year. Asylum-seekers are not subject to the refugee admissions set by Congress — at least not until they become *asylees* (those granted asylum) and seek permanent residence.

For the 2003 fiscal year (October 1, 2002, through September 30, 2003), the total ceiling is set at 70,000 admissions, divided among six geographic regions and a catchall unallocated category called "reserve admissions." Here's how those 70,000 admissions are divided:

- **Africa:** 20,000
- **East Asia:** 4,000
- **Eastern Europe:** 2,500
- **The former Soviet Union:** 14,000
- **Latin America and the Caribbean:** 2,500
- **The Near East and South Asia:** 7,000
- **Reserve admissions:** 20,000

The Department of Labor

The U.S. Department of Labor (DOL) is responsible for protecting the nation's workforce by making sure workers enjoy safe conditions and fair employment practices. If you're applying for immigration through employment, your potential employer and your employer's attorneys will need to interact with the DOL.

Before a U.S. employer can hire a foreign worker, the employer will usually have to first obtain a DOL-issued *labor certification.* The certification is the DOL's way of officially letting the BCIS know that there are no qualified U.S. workers available and willing to work at the prevailing wage in the occupation for which the employer wants to hire you. After a labor certification is obtained, the potential employer must petition the BCIS. If everything passes

BCIS approval, the case then goes to the NVC to await a visa number, or if you are in the U.S., you may be eligible to apply for adjustment of status. Even if the DOL issues a certification, you aren't guaranteed a visa. Whether you get a visa is ultimately up to the BCIS or State Department and also depends on visa availability. Nonetheless, applicants for a labor certification must prove they're able to pass other necessary immigration qualifications, like those outlined in Chapter 3.

The Federal Bureau of Investigation

The Federal Bureau of Investigation (FBI) is the national law-enforcement agency in the U.S. The FBI's headquarters in Washington, D.C., provides direction and support to 56 field offices, about 400 satellite offices, 4 specialized field installations, and more than 40 liaison posts. Each foreign liaison office is headed by a legal officer who works with both U.S. and local authorities abroad on criminal matters that fall under FBI jurisdiction, including cases of immigration and visa fraud.

Even if you're an immigrant already living in the U.S., you'll have some dealings with the FBI, because applicants for *all* immigration benefits are required by law to have their fingerprints taken by the BCIS or a designated state or local law-enforcement agency. The fingerprints are then checked against the FBI's international database. Before allowing you to live here, the U.S. government wants to make sure you're not currently wanted for any crimes and that your record is free from crimes that present bars to immigration and naturalization (you can find more about this in Chapter 3). If your record has nothing to show, you may never realize you had a brush with the FBI, but rest assured that your BCIS-obtained fingerprints did.

Helping refugees: The United Nations

The Office of the United Nations High Commissioner for Refugees was established to lead and coordinate international action to protect refugees and resolve refugee problems worldwide. Striving to safeguard the rights and well being of refugees, the agency has helped an estimated 50 million people restart their lives in the last 50 years.

Today, a staff of around 5,000 people in more than 120 countries continues to help an estimated 19.8 million people find safe refuge in other countries.

Chapter 3

Finding Out about Immigrant and Nonimmigrant Visas

In This Chapter

- Visiting the United States on a temporary basis
- Safeguarding your future immigration plans
- Obtaining a green card
- Making sense of the preference categories

Whether you're just visiting the United States on a nonimmigrant basis or hoping to live here permanently, you'll need to know about visas and how to get them in order to remain in the country legally.

All visa applicants should be aware that having a valid visa does *not* guarantee you entry into the United States. Upon arrival in the U.S., you'll receive a form I-94 "Arrival-Departure Record" from the Bureau of Customs and Border Protection (BCBP). (You can find out more about this in Chapter 1.) This document states the amount of time you're allowed to remain in the U.S. legally.

Just Visiting: Nonimmigrant Visas

Nonimmigrants enter the U.S. for a temporary period of time, and their activities in the U.S. are restricted to the reasons their visas are granted. In other words, if you enter the U.S. on a tourist visa, you may not legally work while you're in the U.S., because that would necessitate an employment visa.

Business travelers who stay for pleasure after their business concludes — provided they leave the country within the time period authorized when they are admitted to the U.S. — do not need to go through the paperwork of changing their status from visitor for business to visitor for pleasure.

Determining whether you need a visa

You may not need a visa to enter the U.S. if you're entering under NAFTA or under the Visa Waiver Program (VWP). (We discuss NAFTA in Chapter 1.) The VWP allows foreign nationals from certain designated countries to enter the U.S. as nonimmigrants for business or pleasure under limited conditions, and for no more than 90 days, without first obtaining a nonimmigrant visa.

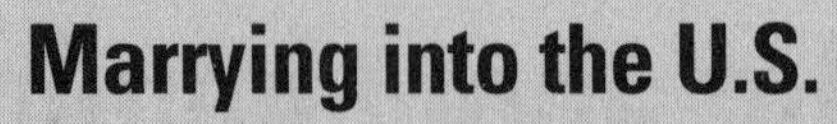

In order for a U.S. citizen to bring his or her foreign-born fiancé(e) to the United States, the citizen must file a Form I-129F with the Bureau of Citizenship and Immigration Services (BCIS). After the form is approved, BCIS forwards the petition to the relevant U.S. embassy or consulate abroad. The embassy or consulate will contact the fiancé(e) to schedule a visa interview. The U.S. citizen and his or her foreign-born fiancé(e) must marry within 90 days from the day the fiancé(e) enters the country.

You and your fiancé(e) may be romantics, but the BCIS is not. They don't automatically assume you will actually marry. After the wedding, the U.S. citizen must again contact the BCIS to change his or her spouse's immigration status from nonimmigrant to legal permanent resident.

The U.S. government believes that the countries accepted in the VWP are not likely to compromise U.S. law-enforcement or national-security interests — including the enforcement of immigration laws. Countries can be added or deleted from the program at any time, so be sure to consult the U.S. Department of State for the latest information (go to `www.travel.state.gov/vwp.html` for information). Countries on the Visa Waiver Program list as of this writing are Andorra, Austria, Australia, Belgium, Brunei, Denmark, Finland, France, Germany, Iceland, Ireland, Italy, Japan, Liechtenstein, Luxembourg, Monaco, the Netherlands, New Zealand, Norway, Portugal, San Marino, Singapore, Slovenia, Spain, Sweden, Switzerland, the United Kingdom, and Uruguay. Although not specifically listed as a Visa Waiver country, Canada's citizens and landed immigrants also can enter the U.S. for business or pleasure without visas.

In terms of visas, the United Kingdom means citizens with the unrestricted right to lawful permanent residence in England, Scotland, Wales, Northern Ireland, the Channel Islands, and the Isle of Man.

Discovering the common types of nonimmigrant visas

Most nonimmigrants in the U.S. fall under the categories of business or pleasure visitors:

- **Business visitors:** The B-1 nonimmigrant category includes those coming to the U.S. to conduct business with a company here. This type of visa does *not* allow the visitor to hold a job or work for pay in the United States.
- **Pleasure visitors:** The B-2 nonimmigrant category includes tourists or those visiting the U.S. for the pure enjoyment of the many attractions this country has to offer. It also includes those who come to this country for a number of other purposes, including seeking medical treatment. In our experience, most medical treatments are hardly pleasurable, but nonetheless, the government lumps them into the same category as pleasure visitors.

Students, temporary workers, crewmen, journalists, and all others planning to travel to the U.S. for a purpose other than business or pleasure must apply in a different visa category. The State Department issues a huge range of visas for all different types of circumstances. For additional detailed information about your unique nonimmigrant visa needs, consult the State Department Web site (`http://travel.state.gov/nonimmigrantvisas.html`).

Changing or adjusting your nonimmigrant status

Certain individuals who are already legally in the country may qualify to *change* or *adjust* their immigration statuses. They may be eligible to *change* from one category of nonimmigrant status to another or may even have the opportunity to *adjust* from nonimmigrant to lawful permanent resident status.

Petitioning in one nonimmigrant status for change to another nonimmigrant status is referred to as *changing status;* applying for permanent residence while in the U.S. as a nonimmigrant is referred to as *adjusting status.*

Unlawful presence in the U.S. had serious consequences, so be sure your immigration status always remains legal. For example, sometimes people in the first family preference category think that because they are married, they can stay in the U.S. until their petition is processed and a visa number becomes available, only to find out that they aren't eligible for adjustment of status because they've been out of status during that wait. Upon leaving the U.S. to visa-process after having been unlawfully present for more than 180 days or a year, they find they are barred from re-entering the U.S. for three or ten years (depending upon how long you were in the country). There are some exceptions and some waiver provisions, which is why we stress the importance of consulting a qualified immigration attorney or legal services if you have any unlawful presence time in the United States.

To check whether your immigration status is currently legal, rely on your I-94 "Arrival-Departure Record" — the document you received from the BCBP (find out more about them in Chapter 1) upon entering the country, or from the BCIS if you extended your immigration status while already in the U.S.

Switching nonimmigrant visa categories

If you want to change the purpose of your visit while you're in the U.S., then you, or in some cases your employer, must ask the BCIS to change your nonimmigrant status. Not all requests will be honored. For instance, if you're a tourist who wants to become a student in the U.S., you should state that you're looking into schools when you first enter the United States on a tourist visa. Otherwise, you'll need to first leave the country before being able to obtain a student visa.

If you were admitted to the U.S. in one the following visa categories, you may *not* apply to change your nonimmigrant status (you will first need to leave the country in order to change your immigration status):

- **VWP:** As part of the Visa Waiver Program
- **D:** As a crewman
- **C:** As an alien passing through the U.S., in transit from one country to another
- **K:** As a fiancé(e) or spouse of a U.S. citizen or dependent of a fiancé(e) or spouse
- **S:** As an informant (or accompanying family of an informant) on terrorism or organized crime

The only exception to the rule that limits nonimmigrant visa holders to the activity stated on their visas are business travelers who stay for pleasure after their business is over — providing they leave the country within the time period designated on their I-94 cards. Everyone else who wants to change the nature of their visit from the purpose stated on their visa must submit an application to change status to the BCIS. Failing to do so constitutes breaking U.S. immigration law, which in turn damages your chances at future temporary or permanent visas.

Adjusting status from nonimmigrant to immigrant

Providing that a visa number is available through the Department of State (unless you're in a category that is exempt from numerical limitations — you can find more on this later in this chapter), certain nonimmigrants may adjust their immigration status from nonimmigrant to immigrant. Immediate relatives of U.S. citizens usually are exempt from waiting for visa numbers and can adjust their status right away.

If you have to wait for an immigrant visa number and are outside the United States when it becomes available, you'll be notified to go to the local U.S. consulate to complete the processing.

If you are inside the U.S. and are waiting for an immigrant visa number so that you can adjust your status while in the U.S. or leave the country to visa-process at an overseas consulate, you must maintain valid nonimmigrant status while in the United States, or you risk encountering a three- or ten-year bar to naturalization.

Gaining Permanent Resident Status (or a Green Card)

As we discuss in Chapter 1, most people gain lawful permanent residence through a family connection or through employment. In the following sections, we explore these categories in more detail, as well as other ways people can legally live and work in the U.S. on a permanent basis.

Understanding the family preference categories

Family-based immigrant visa numbers are distributed according to preference categories. The higher you rank on the preference scale, the sooner you're likely to receive a number. The following are the four family-preference categories:

- **First preference:** Unmarried sons and daughters (age 21 or older) of U.S. citizens
- **Second preference:** Spouses of lawful permanent residents and their unmarried children of any age
- **Third preference:** Married sons and daughters of U.S. citizens
- **Fourth preference:** Brothers and sisters of U.S. citizens who are 21 or older

After the visa petition filed for them by their sponsoring relative is approved by the BCIS, the immediate relatives of U.S. citizens — parents, spouses, and unmarried children under the age of 21 — usually don't have to wait for an immigrant visa number to become available.

Marrying your way to permanent residence

Although it's usually relatively easy for the foreign-born spouses of U.S. citizens or lawful permanent residents to come to the U.S., the BCIS doesn't take kindly to folks who marry for the sole purpose of obtaining a green card. The countless TV sitcom and movie plots we've all seen on this subject are close to the truth. The BCIS will want to see evidence that yours is truly a marriage and not just a union on paper. You and your spouse should expect to answer questions about each other and about the marriage as well as provide physical evidence of the relationship. For this reason, in addition to important documents like your marriage certificate, be sure to save things like travel documents, vacation and family photos, billing statements, and other tangible evidence of your life together.

Marrying a U.S. citizen

If your spouse is a U.S. citizen, either born or naturalized, you are considered an immediate relative and are likewise usually eligible for an immigrant visa immediately, providing your Petition for Alien Relative (the form your sponsoring relative filed on your behalf) has been approved by the BCIS..

If you've been married less than two years when you gain lawful permanent resident status, that status is given on a conditional basis — conditional on your still being married after a full two years. At that time, you and your spouse will need to apply together to remove the condition.

You must apply to remove conditional status within 90 days *before* the two-year anniversary of the date your conditional permanent resident status was granted. If you fail to file during this time, you'll be considered out of status as of the two-year anniversary, and may be subject to removal from the country. Use BCIS Form I-751 to apply to remove the condition.

Marrying a green-card holder

If you marry a lawful permanent resident of the U.S., you aren't considered an immediate relative. Instead, you fall under the family second preference category. If your spouse's Petition for Alien Relative form is approved, the Department of State will notify you when a visa number becomes available.

If you were married before your husband or wife became a permanent resident, you cannot obtain permanent resident status along with your spouse without being subject to visa limits. If, for whatever reason, you did not physically accompany your spouse to the U.S. when he or she became a permanent resident, you may be eligible to receive *following-to-join benefits.* This means your husband or wife won't have to file a separate Petition for Alien Relative form and you won't have to wait any extra time for an immigrant visa to become available. You may be eligible for following-to-join benefits, provided your marriage still exists and your husband or wife received his or her lawful permanent residence status in one of the following ways:

- Through a diversity immigrant visa (wining the visa lottery)
- Through an employment-based immigrant visa
- Based on a relationship to a U.S. citizen brother or sister
- Based on a relationship to U.S. citizen parents after you were already married

Legally marrying abroad

Although no exact document exists in the U.S., all civil-law countries require proof of legal capacity to enter into a marriage contract. This means you must obtain certification by competent authority that no impediments to the marriage exist. Unless the foreign authorities will allow such a statement to be executed before one of their consular officials in the United States, the parties of a prospective marriage abroad must execute an affidavit at the U.S. embassy or consulate in the country where the marriage will occur. This affidavit of eligibility to marry states both parties are free to marry. Some countries require witnesses to these affidavits. Check the law where you plan to marry.

Making the best of a bad situation: The Violence Against Women Act

In order for an alien to qualify for family-based immigration, a U.S. citizen or lawful permanent resident must file a Petition for Alien Relative form with the BCIS on the alien's behalf. When, or even if, the petition is actually filed is strictly up to the relative petitioner.

Unfortunately, some people use their control of this process to abuse family members by threatening to report them to immigration authorities. As a result, most battered immigrants are afraid to report the abuse or their abusers.

Passed by Congress in 1994, the Violence Against Women Act (VAWA) allows the spouses and children of U.S. citizens or lawful permanent residents to self-petition for permanent legal immigration status. In order to protect the victims from their abusers, provisions of the VAWA allow certain battered immigrants (women or men) to file for immigration relief without their abusive relative's assistance or even knowledge. Children of these self-petitioners also receive *derivative benefits,* meaning they can gain lawful permanent residence along with their parents.

Remember: If you are a victim of domestic violence, help is available to you through the National Domestic Violence Hotline. Call 800-799-7233 or 800-787-3224 [TDD] for information about shelters, mental health care, legal advice, and other types of assistance, including information about self-petitioning for lawful permanent residence.

Using family connections

Family connections provide the most common path to immigration, and family reunification is a primary goal of the U.S. immigration system. Nonetheless, immigrating through a family connection can be a complex and challenging proposition. Sponsoring relatives have significant obligations to meet before they can bring family members here.

In order to immigrate through a family connection, your relative must file on your behalf with the BCIS an I-130 Petition that includes proof of your familial relationship.

Born or naturalized citizens may sponsor their spouses, children, brothers and sisters, and parents. Lawful permanent residents may only sponsor their husbands or wives and children.

Assuming the BCIS approves the I-130 Petition your relative filed for you, the State Department must determine if a visa number is immediately available. If you're an immediate relative of a U.S. citizen, a visa will be available at once. If you fall within a family preference category, you will be placed on a waiting list (you can find more information on preference categories later in this chapter).

You can check the status of a visa number in the Department of State's *Visa Bulletin.*

In order for your relative to be eligible to sponsor you to immigrate to the United States, he or she must meet the following criteria:

- He or she must be a citizen or a lawful permanent resident of the U.S. and be able to provide documentation proving his or her citizenship or immigration status.
- He or she must be at least 18 years old, in most cases, and at least 21 years old for U.S. citizen sons or daughters sponsoring a parent.

- He or she must prove and document his or her relationship to you, the relative being sponsored.
- Your relative must also document and prove that he or she can support you and any other financially dependent relatives at 125 percent above the mandated poverty line.

Your relative must prove he or she can support you by completing an Affidavit of Support (Form I-864) for you to file with the BCIS (if you're adjusting your status) or with a U.S. consulate (if your visa is processing — there is a filing fee in this case). To complete an Affidavit of Support, your relative must live in the U.S. as their primary residence. The Affidavit of Support states that the sponsoring relative accepts legal responsibility for financially supporting you. Your relative must be able and willing to accept this legally enforceable responsibility until you go through the entire immigration and naturalization process and become a United States citizen or until you can be credited with 40 quarters of work (which usually takes about 10 years).

Your relative must also complete an affidavit of support if he or she has filed an employment-based immigration petition (Form I-140) as the employer on your behalf or if he or she has a significant ownership interest (5 percent or more) in a business that filed an employment-based immigrant petition for you.

In determining his or her income amount, your relative can include in the count:

- Money held in savings accounts, stocks, bonds, and property
- Your income and, in some cases, your assets
- The income and, in some cases, the assets of members of your relative's household related by birth, marriage, or adoption or of those listed on your relative's most recent federal income tax return (whether or not they reside with your relative)

Not surprisingly, meeting the financial support qualifications presents an insurmountable obstacle to many otherwise willing and qualified potential sponsors. In some cases, if the relative visa petitioner's household income doesn't quite reach the minimum 125 percent above the government-mandated poverty level, a joint sponsor may also be allowed to sign an additional affidavit of support. A *joint sponsor* is someone, other than the family member who is sponsoring you for immigration, who is willing to share legal responsibility, along with your family member, for supporting you if for any reason you are unable to support yourself after immigrating to the U.S.

A joint sponsor must meet the same sponsorship qualifications as the sponsoring relative with one important exception: The joint sponsor does *not* need to be a relative of any kind (he or she can be, but that isn't required in order for the person to qualify).

The joint sponsor (or the joint sponsor and his or her household) must meet the 125 percent income requirement on his or her own. You cannot combine your income with that of a joint sponsor to meet the income requirement the way you can with your primary sponsor.

So how much is 125 percent above the mandated poverty level? The U.S. Department of Health and Human Services sets the annual poverty guidelines. The guidelines are available from the U.S. Department of Health and Human Services (HHS), 200 Independence Ave. SW, Washington, DC 20201. You can call toll-free 877-696-6775 to order a copy, or go online to `http://aspe.os.dhhs.gov/poverty/poverty.shtml`.

The guidelines are also on the BCIS's Web site (`www.immigration.gov`) as part of Form I-864, but often those guidelines are not updated as quickly as they are at the HHS, so checking with HHS first is always a good idea.

Identifying exceptions to the sponsorship requirements

As with all things related to U.S. immigration, there are exceptions to most rules, including the family member sponsorship requirements.

If you are the immigrant, and you can prove you already legally worked in the U.S. a total of at least 40 qualifying quarters as defined in Title II of the Social Security Act, an affidavit of support is not required. Keep in mind when calculating qualifying work quarters that you may not count any qualifying quarters worked during any period after December 31, 1996, when you received a federal means-tested public benefit. These benefits include *most* public assistance benefits like food stamps, Supplemental Security Income (SSI), Temporary Assistance for Needy Families (TANF), Medicaid (although not emergency Medicaid), and the State Children's Health Insurance Program (CHIP).

If the immigrant is the child of a citizen and if the immigrant, if admitted for permanent residence on or after February 27, 2001, would automatically acquire citizenship under the Immigration and Nationality Act, as amended by the Child Citizenship Act of 2000, he or she is exempt from sponsorship requirements. Approved in October 2000 by President Clinton, the Child Citizenship Act of 2000 states that a child born outside the U.S. automatically becomes a citizen of the U.S. when *all* the following conditions apply:

- At least one parent of the child is a citizen of the U.S., either born or naturalized.
- The child is under 18 years old.
- The child is living in the U.S. in the legal and physical custody of the citizen parent after being admitted as a lawful permanent resident.

It's important to realize that, in order to qualify under the Child Citizenship Act, an applicant must have met all three of the preceding requirements as of or after February 27, 2001. If an applicant meets all the requirements except that his or her 18th birthday fell *before* February 27, 2001, the applicant legally remains an alien until he or she can go through the normal naturalization process as outlined in this book.

Working for a Green Card

A second goal of the U.S. immigration system is to allow U.S. employers to hire citizens of other countries when no qualified U.S. citizens or legal residents can fill the positions. Each year, a minimum of 140,000 employment-based immigrant visas become available in five preference categories.

In most cases, you will need a solid offer of employment from a qualified employer who is willing and able to sponsor you for immigration. In addition to filing forms and guaranteeing employment, in many cases the employer should also be prepared to show evidence that no qualified U.S. citizens or lawful permanent residents are available to fill the position.

After determining if you qualify for an employment-based visa, you and your employer will usually be required to obtain a labor certification from the U.S. Department of Labor (Form ETA 750), as well as file an Immigrant Petition for Foreign Worker (Form I- 140) with the BCIS. As always, you'll probably have to file other forms and paperwork — you can find more on this in Chapter 4.

Making sense of employment preference categories

Just like family-based visas, U.S. immigration laws allow people to gain lawful permanent residence legally through several preference categories.

First preference: Priority workers

Priority workers receive 28.6 percent of the yearly worldwide allotment of employment visas, plus any left over from the fourth and fifth preference categories. Within this preference category, you'll find three subgroups. Although qualifying for a first preference visa is quite difficult, none of these categories requires labor certification, which saves processing time.

REMEMBER

People with extraordinary ability

In order to qualify in this category, be prepared to prove your extraordinary ability or past employment record to qualify.

If you can offer extensive documentation showing sustained national or international acclaim and recognition as a person of extraordinary ability in the sciences, arts, education, business, or athletics, you won't be required to have a specific job offer or a sponsoring employer to immigrate to the United States — provided you're coming here to continue work in your established field. An employer can petition for you, however.

Keep in mind the first priority classification is reserved for those with *truly extraordinary* achievement (for instance, Nobel Prize winners). If you haven't yet won such a prestigious award, other documentation that can help you prove your case as a person of extraordinary ability includes

- Receipt of nationally or internationally recognized prizes or awards for excellence in your field
- Membership in associations that demand outstanding achievement of their members
- Published material about yourself in professional or major trade publications or other major media attention
- Evidence that you have judged the work of others, individually or as a member of a professional panel
- Evidence of contributions of major significance to your field
- Evidence of authorship of scholarly articles in professional or major trade publications or other major media
- Evidence that your work has been displayed at artistic, business, educational, scientific, or athletic exhibitions or showcases
- Evidence that you perform a leading or critical role in distinguished professional organizations
- Evidence that you command a high salary in relation to others in your field
- Evidence of your commercial successes in your field
- Other comparable evidence

Outstanding professors or researchers

No labor certification is required if you can prove to the satisfaction of the BCIS that you are an internationally recognized outstanding professor or researcher with at least three years experience in teaching or research. You must be entering the U.S. in a tenure or tenure-track teaching capacity or in a comparable research position at a university or other institution of higher learning. If your prospective employer is a private company rather than an educational institution, the department, division, or institute of the private employer must employ at least three persons full time in research activities and have achieved documented accomplishments in an academic field in order to sponsor you for immigration.

You cannot self-petition in this category (an employer must petition on your behalf). In order to qualify as an outstanding professor or researcher, you'll also need to be able to document at least two of the following:

- Receipt of major prizes or awards for outstanding achievement
- Membership in associations requiring their members to demonstrate outstanding achievements
- Articles in professional publications written by others about your work in the academic field
- Participation, on a panel or individually, as a judge of the work of others in the same or allied academic fields
- Your original scientific or scholarly research contributions to your field
- Authorship of books or articles in scholarly journals with international circulation

Certain foreign executives or managers employed by U.S. companies or their affiliates, subsidiaries, or branches

If you're a foreign executive or manager, and you were employed at least one of the three preceding years by the overseas affiliate, parent, subsidiary, or branch of a U.S. company, your U.S. employer can petition for you without having to file a labor certification application. Of course, you must be immigrating in order to continue work for that same company in a managerial or executive position.

Second preference: Professionals

Professionals holding advanced degrees, or persons of exceptional ability in the arts, sciences, or business receive 28.6 percent of the yearly visa allotment, plus any leftover first preference employment visas. In most second preference category cases, you must have a firm offer of employment and your U.S. employer must file a BCIS petition on your behalf. In most cases, an employer must also obtain labor certification from the Department of Labor (DOL) before filing the petition.

The labor certification is the DOL's way of officially letting the BCIS or State Department know that there are no qualified U.S. workers who are willing and able to take the position. Working in conjunction with State Workforce Agencies (SWAs), the Department of Labor, through its Employment and Training Administration (ETA) reviews the proposed employment for compliance with U.S. wage and occupational practices and may guide the actual hiring process. The government wants to be sure that employing an immigrant under the terms described in the application will not adversely affect wages and working conditions of similarly situated U.S. workers.

For more information about labor certifications or for an online application, visit the DOL Web site at `www.ows.doleta.gov/foreign`.

Even if the DOL issues a labor certification, this does not guarantee you a visa. Whether you get a visa is ultimately up to the BCIS or State Department and also depends on visa availability.

TECHNICAL STUFF

Immigration through the national interest waiver

If you're a qualified physician who is willing to work in an underserved area of the United States or at a Department of Veterans Affairs (VA) facility, you may be able to skip the labor certification process. In some instances, you'll be allowed to self-petition for second preference classification, although a qualified employer may also file a national interest waiver on your behalf. In order to fulfill the obligations of obtaining this waiver, you'll be required to complete an *aggregate* (accumulated) five years of qualifying full-time clinical practice during the six-year period that begins when you receive the necessary employment authorization documents. You can find information on how to apply by visiting the BCIS Web site (`www.immigration.gov`). If you need more detailed information or have questions not answered on the Web site, consulting qualified legal counsel is a good idea — they can best help you prepare the documentation needed for your unique case and circumstances.

Another, very restrictive and therefore rarely used, national interest waiver is available on a case-by-case determination of whether foregoing labor certification is in the national interest. This type of waiver is available to nonphysicians also. Unlike the physician national interest waiver, however, approval of this type of national interest waiver waives only the requirement of labor certification, which means it also waives the requirement for a job offer. Therefore, in addition to proving all the elements needed for the national interest waiver, you (or the petitioning employer) also must prove that you hold an advanced degree or are an alien of exceptional ability, as described earlier in this chapter.

Because of labor certification backlogs, the standard procedure can take years. Measures to expedite the process, and a new process to be implemented after this book is published, promise to improve the situation in the future. This is a complicated area of immigration law that requires familiarity with how different positions are defined, their standard requirements and wages, and how to approach both DOL and BCIS processing.. Your sponsoring employer should work with a qualified immigration attorney or legal organization (see Chapter 7 for more information about finding reliable help).

Members of the professions holding advanced degrees (professors and researchers) must be internationally recognized in their particular area, and meet other requirements, including having earned a master's degree or a bachelor's degree with at least five years of post-baccalaureate, progressive experience in the specialty (such as advancing levels of responsibility and knowledge).

Regulations vaguely define exceptional ability as "having a degree of expertise significantly above that ordinarily encountered in the sciences, arts, or business." In order to document your qualifications as an alien of exceptional ability, be prepared to show at least three of the following:

- An official academic record showing you have a degree, diploma, certificate or similar award from a college, university, school, or other institution of learning relating to your area of exceptional ability
- Letters documenting at least ten years of full-time experience in your chosen occupation
- A license to practice the profession or certification for a particular profession or occupation
- Evidence you have commanded a salary that demonstrates exceptional ability
- Membership in professional associations
- Recognition by peers, government entities, or professional or business organizations for your achievements and significant contributions to your field

Your employer may not need a labor certification before petitioning under the second preference category if one of the following is true:

- Exemption from labor certification would be in the U.S. national interest.
- You qualify for one of the shortage occupations in the Labor Market Information Pilot Program, which defines up to ten occupational classifications in which there are labor shortages. For aliens within a listed shortage occupation, a labor certification will be deemed to have been issued for purposes of an employment-based immigrant petition.
- You are employed in an occupation designated as Schedule A. In these cases, the Department of Labor delegates authority to approve labor certifications to the BCIS. Schedule A, Group I includes physical therapists and professional nurses. Schedule A, Group II includes aliens of exceptional ability in the sciences and arts (except the performing arts).

Third preference: Skilled or professional workers

This category receives 28.6 percent of the yearly worldwide employment visa pool, plus any unused first and second preference category visas. Unless the job qualifies for a Schedule A designation, or as one of the shortage occupations in the Labor Market Information Pilot, all third preference petitions must be accompanied by a labor certification.

The Labor Market Information Pilot Program defines up to ten occupational classifications in which the U.S. has labor shortages. For aliens within a listed shortage occupation, a labor certification will be deemed to have been issued for purposes of an employment-based immigrant petition.

The Department of Labor delegates authority to the BCIS to approve labor certifications to occupations in the Schedule A Group — Group I includes physical therapists and professional nurses; Group II includes aliens of exceptional ability in the sciences and arts (except the performing arts).

Within the third employment-based preference group are three subcategories:

- **Skilled workers** are persons capable of performing a job requiring at least two years' training or experience. For an extensive listing of skilled-worker positions, see the State Department Web site at `http://travel.state.gov/ONET.html`. You then can find descriptions of the positions at `http://online.onetcenter.org`.
- **Professionals** must hold a U.S. baccalaureate degree or a foreign equivalent degree. Unfortunately, a combination of some education and experience cannot be substituted for the actual degree in order to qualify.
- **Other workers** are those persons capable of filling positions requiring less than two years of training or experience.

Note that the third preference category usually generally becomes oversubscribed or backlogged before the higher categories. Also, the "other worker" subcategory of third preference generally becomes oversubscribed or backlogged before the skilled or professional worker categories.

You can track visa availability trends by referring to past issues of the DOS *Visa Bulletin*. Find an online archive at `http://dosfan.lib.uic.edu/ERC/visa_bulletin`.

Fourth preference: Special immigrants

Special immigrants receive 7.1 percent of the yearly worldwide limit. Thirteen subgroups qualify as special immigrants, the most notable of which is the religious worker special immigrant. Other special immigrants include certain juveniles and battered spouses, certain overseas employees or retirees of the U.S. government, certain members of the U.S. armed forces, certain current and former employees of the Panama Canal Company, retired employees of international organizations, and certain dependents of international organization employees.

The religious worker category receives 5,000 of the allotted special immigrant visas. Religious workers are those who will work for a religious denomination that has a bona fide nonprofit religious organization in the U.S. and who are coming to work as ministers of religion, to work in a professional capacity in a religious vocation, or to work in a religious occupation. The worker must have been a member of this religious denomination and must have worked for the denomination for at least two years before applying for admission to, or adjustment of status in, the United States.

Fifth preference: Immigrant investors

Employment creation investors receive 7.1 percent of the yearly employment visa total. To qualify in this category, be prepared to invest about $1,000,000 (or the U.S. dollars equivalent in your currency), depending on the employment rate in the geographical area where you will set up business. Your U.S. enterprise will also need to create at least ten new full-time jobs for U.S. citizens, permanent resident aliens, or other lawful immigrants, not including you and your family.

If you plan on establishing a business in an area of high unemployment, you may only have to invest $500,000 to qualify for the fifth preference.

Discovering Other Ways to Qualify for Permanent Residence

What if you don't qualify for family- or employment-based immigration? Are there other ways you can gain lawful permanent residence in the U.S.? Thankfully, yes, but only under some specific conditions and restrictions.

Immigrating through asylum

If you are a potential immigrant already in the U.S. (legally or illegally) or you're applying for admission at its borders, you may petition the government for asylum by demonstrating you have a "well-founded fear of persecution" in your home country, based on race, religion, nationality, membership in a social group, or political opinion. Proving you belong in one of these protected categories can be complicated, because the legal definitions of *well-founded fear* and *persecution* are vague at best. We strongly recommend you seek the advice of a qualified immigration attorney. (You can find out more about hiring qualified and ethical help in Chapter 7.)

In most cases, if you're seeking to enter the U.S. and you indicate a desire to seek asylum, the Directorate of Border and Transportation Security (BTS) places you in expedited removal, where an asylum officer from the BCIS determines if you have a credible fear. If the asylum officer determines that you do have a credible fear, you're allowed to apply before an immigration judge (who is part of the Department of Justice).

Although the BCIS won't grant work authorization for the first 150 days after the filing of an asylum claim (unless of course, asylum is granted in the meantime), work authorization is automatic for cases on the docket longer than 180 days — as long as you're not the one who caused the delay.

Be sure to file your asylum application within one year after entering the United States. Failing to file the application on time can result in rejection of the claim, and removal from the U.S. After one year, applications will only be considered in certain cases of changed or extraordinary circumstances. You may still be eligible for withholding of removal, but it is only a temporary form of relief, from which you cannot gain permanent residence.

If you have held asylum status for at least one year, you may be eligible to adjust your status to lawful permanent resident by filing an application to adjust status (currently Form I-485). You will be required to provide evidence that you were physically present in the U.S. as an asylee for at least a total of one year prior to filing the adjustment of status application. For this reason, keeping important paperwork throughout the immigration process is essential. Examples of documents that can help prove physical presence include:

- A copy of your INS or BCBP Arrival-Departure Record (Form I-94), obtained when you first entered the country
- A clear copy of the letter granting your asylum status
- Any documentation of the conditions being removed (if you were originally granted conditional asylum)
- Copies of documents covering large periods of time, such as apartment leases, school enrollment records, or letters of employment

If you arrived in the country before March 1, 2003, the former Immigration and Naturalization Service (INS) processed your Arrival-Departure Record. If you arrive any time after March 1, 2003, the Bureau of Customs and Border Protection (BCBP) , part of the Department of Homeland Security, will administer your Arrival-Departure Record.

Looking for safe refuge

Refugees are those living outside the U.S. and outside their home countries who petition the government for lawful permanent residence in order to escape intolerable conditions in their home countries.

Benefits the U.S. government provides for qualified refugees include

- A no-interest travel loan to the U.S.
- Eight months of Refugee Cash Assistance (RCA) and Refugee Medical Assistance (RMA)
- Food stamps to help pay for groceries
- Housing assistance, furnishings, food, and clothing
- A Social Security card
- School registration for children
- Referrals for medical appointments and other support services
- Employment services
- Case management through community-based nonprofit organizations
- Adjustment of status from refugee to legal permanent resident for refugees who have been physically present in the U.S. as refugees for a total of at least one year prior to filing for adjustment (see "Immigrating through asylum" earlier in this chapter for more information about documenting your presence in the U.S.).

Making the most of your birthplace

If you're trying to come to the U.S., where you come from may help your chances of obtaining permanent resident status if you qualify under special laws. These cases are often complicated, so seek the advice of a competent immigration attorney if you think you may qualify.

The Cuban Adjustment Act of 1966 (CAA) provides for a special procedure under which Cuban citizens and their accompanying spouses and children may obtain a haven in the United States as lawful permanent residents. This act gives the Attorney General discretion to grant permanent residence to Cuban nationals, admissible as immigrants, seeking adjustment of status if they have been present in the United States for at least one year after inspection and admission or parole. Because many of the rules on immigration do not apply to adjustments under the CAA, you don't have to be the beneficiary of a family-based or employment-based immigrant visa petition. The CAA may also apply to your spouse and children, regardless of their citizenship or place of birth, provided the relationship existed at the time you obtained lawful permanent residence and they are now living with you in the U.S.

In ordinary circumstances, the arrival of a potential immigrant to the U.S. at a place other than an open port of entry is a ground of inadmissibility. However, a Cuban national or citizen who arrives at a place other than an open port of entry may still be eligible for adjustment of status, providing the former INS or the Bureau of Customs and Border Protection (BCBP) has paroled them into the United States.

The Nicaraguan Adjustment and Central American Relief Act of 1997 (NACARA), provides various forms of immigration benefits, including relief from deportation to certain Nicaraguans, Cubans, Salvadorans, Guatemalans, and nationals of former Soviet bloc countries and their dependents. The Victims of Trafficking and Violence Protection Act of 2000, designed to help and protect victims of crime, added two more categories of individuals eligible to apply for relief from removal under NACARA.

The Haitian Refugee Immigration Fairness Act of 1998 (HRIFA) established procedures for certain Haitian nationals, who have been living in the United States, to become lawful permanent residents without having to first apply for an immigrant visa at a U.S. consulate abroad. The law also waives many of the usual requirements for immigration. Principal applicants wanting to apply for lawful permanent residence under HRIFA initially had until March 31, 2000, to file for the adjustment of status. After March 31, 2000, in most cases, only *dependents* of aliens who met HRIFA's requirements are able to apply for lawful permanent residence under HRIFA.

In your immigration proceedings, you may come across the word *parole*. In immigration-speak, parole is a way to gain legal entry into the country, although it is not an official admission under one of the visa categories. Parole serves a specific purpose — for example, humanitarian parole or parole for the purpose of proceeding with adjustment.

Investing in the U.S.

You don't necessarily need talent, family connections, a job, or sympathy to get a green card. Money talks. The Immigration Act of 1990 created the immigrant investor program as the fifth preference within the employment-based category (EB-5). For a minimum investment of $1,000,000 — or as little as $500,000 in a *targeted area* (a rural area or area of high unemployment) — alien entrepreneurs who employ at least ten U.S. workers may be eligible to immigrate based on their investment in the U.S.

Each year, about 10,000 EB-5 visas are allotted to qualified investors and their spouses and children. At least 3,000 of the visa numbers are reserved for investments in targeted areas.

Immigrant investors are admitted for two years in conditional permanent resident status. During that time they must invest the required capital and create the required employment. The condition may be removed if the investment was sustained throughout the period of the investor's residence in the United States.

If you're a prospective immigrant investor, you must petition for yourself on BCIS Form I-526 "Immigrant Petition by Alien Entrepreneur," which you file with the required fee and supporting documentation with the BCIS's Texas or California Service Center, depending on which office has jurisdiction over the area where the commercial enterprise will principally be doing business. The required documentation must show that you have invested, or are investing, the required lawfully gained capital in a qualifying commercial enterprise within the U.S., and that you will create full-time (at least 35 hours per week) jobs for at least ten U.S. workers (U.S. citizens, lawful permanent residents, asylees, or refugees). At the end of the two-year period, you must file INS Form I-829 "Petition by Entrepreneur to Remove the Conditions" and demonstrate that the investment has been completed and sustained for the conditions to be removed.

The investment must be in a for-profit commercial enterprise. The business may be a:

- Sole proprietorship
- Limited or general partnership
- Holding company
- Joint venture
- Corporation
- Business trust
- Other public or privately owned entity

In addition, a new commercial enterprise may be established through

- The creation of an original business
- The purchase of an existing business and restructuring and reorganizing it into a new commercial enterprise
- The expansion of an existing business through a 40 percent net increase in its net worth or in the number of employees

The Immigrant Investor Pilot Program was created in 1993 to broaden investment opportunities. Under this program, you may invest the required capital in BCIS-designated regional centers, allowing you to claim indirect job creation through revenues generated from increased exports, improved regional productivity, job creation, or increased domestic capital investment. Currently, 5,000 EB-5 visas are set aside for the pilot program. The Pilot Program currently runs through October 2003. Check the BCIS Web site (`www.immigration.gov`) for further information.

Winning the green-card lottery

Entering the Diversity Visa Lottery Program can speed up your chances of receiving a visa, especially if you find yourself in one of the lower preference categories. Even if you're currently on a waiting list, you have nothing to lose by entering the visa lottery — it's easy, and it costs nothing but your time and the price of a few BCIS-style photographs. (Find out more about taking a good photo BCIS-style in Chapter 4.)

Understanding the priority date

In the case of a relative immigrant visa petition, the *priority date* is the date on which the petition was actually filed. In the case of an employer-sponsored petition, the priority date is the date the labor certification was filed with the Department of Labor or, if no labor certification is required, the date the petition was filed.

You can track changes in priority date availability with the *Visa Bulletin* (www.travel.state.gov/visa_bulletin.html).

If you receive a visa through the Diversity Visa Lottery Program, you will be authorized to live and work permanently in the United States, as well as bring your husband or wife and any children under the age of 21 along with you.

Each year 55,000 immigrant visas become available to people who come from countries with low rates of immigration to the United States. The qualifying countries can change from year to year, so check with the Department of State (www.travel.state.gov) to get the latest list of qualifying countries and detailed instructions for applying.

The Department of State randomly selects about 100,000 applicants from among the qualified entries. They pick 100,000 applicants when only 55,000 visas are available because they know that not all the applicants will qualify to successfully complete the visa process. After 55,000 applicants have qualified and completed the immigration process, no further diversification lottery visas are issued for that year. The following year, the process starts all over again — so if you didn't win this year, try again next year, and if necessary, the year after that, and so on.

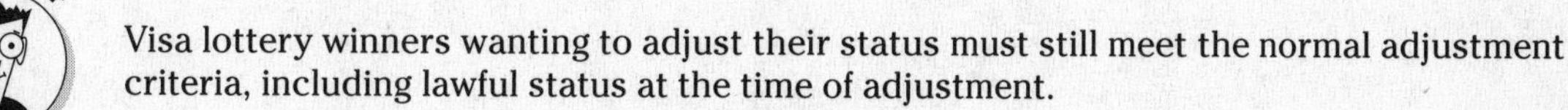

Visa lottery winners wanting to adjust their status must still meet the normal adjustment criteria, including lawful status at the time of adjustment.

Many unscrupulous companies prey on the insecurities of aliens. They charge big bucks for the service of helping them fill out their visa lottery applications. Don't pay it! Filling out the visa diversification lottery application is one of the easiest things you'll do during the entire immigration process. If you have doubts about your ability to fill it out properly, you and an English-speaking friend or family member should be able to figure it out in less than 20 minutes.

Even though filling out the form is easy, be sure to read and follow the instructions carefully. If you don't do everything as required in the instructions, your application will not be considered.

Waiting for a Visa

Several factors influence how long the process of getting an immigrant visa can take.

The U.S. government does not impose a limit on the number of immediate-relative visas that can be issued in any given year. Therefore, BCIS workload permitting, processing often begins upon receipt.

On the other hand, preference categories for both family and employment visas are numerically limited. A visa must become available before the Department of State can start to process the case or before you can apply to adjust status in the United States.

The reason for lengthy waits — priority dates that are months or several years away — is that each year many more people apply for immigrant visas than can be allowed to enter the country under the yearly preference limits set by law.

Chapter 4

Filling Out the Forms

In This Chapter

- Making sense of the forms
- Getting the right forms
- Filling out the paperwork

In the immigration process, you'll encounter a form for just about every situation and purpose that can occur. In fact, forms, paperwork, and immigration documentation can be so complex that getting qualified help from an attorney or immigration service is usually a good idea. (You can find out how to get reliable help in Chapter 7.)

To give you an idea of the types of forms you may encounter, check out the document checklist in Appendix C of this book. This checklist, prepared by the INS, can show, at a glance, the immigration forms you'll need to include with your naturalization application.

Keep in mind that as we write this, the U.S. immigration system is undergoing a major restructuring. The forms will more or less stay the same, but the names may change slightly. Odds are that an INS Form N-400 will simply turn into a BCIS Form N-400, and so on with other forms.

Obtaining the Forms You Need

The easiest place to get immigration and naturalization forms is the Internet. Why is the Internet such a great resource? For several reasons, including the following:

- **When you get your forms from the Internet, you always get the latest version of the forms available.** Forms change from time to time, but you can rest assured that what you get from the Internet is always up to date.

  Many nongovernment Web sites (those other than `www.immigration.gov`, `www.dhs.gov`, or any other Web site that does not carry a `.gov` suffix) offer downloadable immigration forms for a fee. Be aware that these sites are *not* affiliated with the Department of Homeland Security, the BCIS, the INS, or any other U.S. government entity. In many cases, these sites may have older versions of the forms — and using out-of-date forms can result in your case being rejected. You're much better off getting your forms from the official government Web sites. It won't cost you anything and you'll always get the latest versions of the forms available.

- **Downloading and printing the forms you need is free.**
- **Although you can't actually file your forms online, you can fill out many of the forms on your computer instead of writing them by hand or using a typewriter.**
- **You can download forms 24 hours a day.** If you have a computer and an Internet connection at home, you can even download forms in your pajamas, if you want, and your immigration officer will be none the wiser.

The amazing magic changing government agencies

In order to make the transition from the INS to the BCIS as smooth as possible, the BCIS is attempting to keep as many things consistent and practical as possible. Therefore, keep in mind the following:

- Official forms and documents issued by the former INS are still valid and will continue to be accepted by the BCIS and other agencies as evidence of status in the United States.
- BCIS local offices will remain in existing INS locations, including Application Support Centers and Service Centers. There will be no immediate change in office locations.
- You should continue to mail forms to the address indicated in forms and notices.
- The National Customer Service Call Center will continue to be available at 800-375-5283, or for the hearing impaired at 800-767-1833.
- You will still be able to download forms and check the status of your case online (for cases pending adjudication at Service Centers). The new Internet address for BCIS is `www.immigration.gov`.

If you don't have a computer at home, see if you can borrow a friend's computer, use a computer at work (make sure your company allows this), or use one at your nearest public library or at an Internet cafe.

If you still don't want to (or can't) use a computer, you can also order forms by phone by calling 800-870-3676 (toll-free in the U.S.). If you have a lot a free time (and don't mind waiting in line), you can go to the nearest BCIS office and request forms in person.

If you're outside of the United States, you can pick up immigration forms at the U.S. embassy serving your area.

Sometimes the instructions for completing and filing forms change before the powers that be actually get around to changing the forms. The Internet always contains the most up-to-date versions of forms, but even the Net versions may not always be completely accurate. However, accurate information about changes is contained on the Internet page where you select a form for downloading. Be sure to always read carefully the instructions before downloading forms — this will let you know about any special things you need to do or provide, along with the correct fees you'll need to pay (not all forms need fees, but many do). The instructions should also tell you if you need to send originals or if copies will suffice.

Failure to follow the instructions on immigration forms can result in your application being delayed or even denied. If you're not sure about something, ask for help (you can find more about this in Chapter 7).

When you have a choice in the matter, send copies and keep track of original documents in your own files (keeping copies of your original documents doesn't hurt — just store them someplace other than where you store the originals). Even when you're required to send original documents, make sure to always keep at least one copy of everything in your files, so you can prove your case if the BCIS ever loses your paperwork.

You'll be required to include additional documentation with many immigration applications. If you don't have a required document and cannot obtain a certified copy of the original, you can try submitting a certification from the recording authority that explains why you cannot provide the documentation. In cases such as this, the BCIS will consider other evidence such as notarized affidavits. A good country-by-country resource as to what alternative documents are acceptable can be found in the State Department's Foreign Affairs Manual (FAM), which you can access from `http://foia.state.gov/famdir/Fam/fam.asp`.

Downloading forms

The BCIS provides most public-use forms free of charge through its Web site in Adobe Portable Document Format (PDF). In order to view, print, or fill out your forms, you should use the latest version of Acrobat Reader. If you don't have Acrobat Reader, you can download it for free at www.adobe.com. Although the free version of Acrobat will allow you to fill out the form, it will not allow you to save the form to your computer, so be sure to print it out before quitting the program. If you happen to own Adobe Acrobat Approval or the full Adobe Acrobat software, you'll be able save forms to your personal computer.

Unfortunately, although you can download and fill out forms from the Internet, you can't file them online (at least not yet). After you download and fill out your form or application, you must print it out and mail it in to the appropriate BCIS office.

Recognizing Frequently Used Forms

Although including an explanation of every individual immigration-related form would put the sheer size of this book in the same category as a Manhattan phonebook, we did think going into detail about the most common forms — the ones nearly everyone will encounter when going through the immigration and naturalization process — was a good idea.

Keep in mind that in the course of your individual immigration and naturalization experience, you're likely to encounter many more official immigration forms than these most common examples. The U.S. immigration system has an official form for everything — from notifying the government of a change in your address, to requests for proof of military service, to applying for *posthumous* (after-death) citizenship.

As we write, the U.S. immigration system is in the midst of changing from being administered by the Immigration and Naturalization Service (INS), part of the Department of Justice, to the Bureau of Citizenship and Immigration Services (BCIS) and the Directorate of Border and Transportation Security (BTS), both under the jurisdiction of the Department of Homeland Security (DHS). The form numbers in the following sections are the INS form numbers, because at this time there are no BCIS forms. The BCIS may change the form numbers at some time, but the form's function should not change, so you'll still be able to apply this information. Also, the fee information is current as of this writing, but details like this change all the time. To be sure of the current status, check with the BCIS before filing.

New online filing

In an effort to deliver immigration services in an easier, more efficient and more customer-friendly manner, the BCIS made immigration history on May 29, 2003, when it began allowing applicants to file two of the most commonly used immigration forms electronically.

You can now file form I-90 "Application to Replace Permanent Resident Card" and Form I-765 "Application for Employment Authorization" electronically over the Internet. Part of a ten-year effort to transform the immigration system, e-filing allows applicants to conveniently check the status of their applications online at www.bcis.gov. Although these two forms are the first to allow electronic filing, the BCIS plans to make other forms available for electronic filing in the near future. Check the Web site for the latest additions.

The BCIS will electronically store your photograph, signature, and fingerprints so they can later be used to verify your identity. You don't have to submit photographs or fingerprints when e-filing. The BCIS will set up a convenient time for you to visit an Application Support Center (ASC) in order to take care of these details after they receive your electronic application. In order to schedule your appointment, call the National Customer Service Center at 800-375-5283.

Applying for citizenship: Form N-400

Assuming you meet all the qualifications for becoming a United States citizen, you'll most likely apply for naturalization using Form N-400 Application for Naturalization. You'll need to include a $260 fee with this application (as of February 27, 2003). You'll probably also need to include a separate fee — currently $50 — for fingerprinting.

You'll probably be asked about the answers you give on your Application for Naturalization at your citizenship interview, so remember what you say, be clear about what you mean, and be truthful. (You can find more information about the actual interview in Chapter 5.)

Here are some tips for completing the Application for Naturalization (Form N-400):

- **If you're actively serving in the military at the same time you're applying for naturalization, the BCIS recommends you go to your service's personnel office for information about, and help in, preparing your application.** Of course, if you feel more comfortable securing your own representation, you can do that too.
- **Do not apply too early, because doing so can cause your application to be returned to you or denied.** If you're qualifying based on five years as a permanent resident or three years as a permanent resident married to a U.S. citizen, you may file for naturalization up to 90 days before you have met the continuous residence requirement.
- **Include two photographs in the approved format.** You can find details about what the BCIS looks for in a photograph in Chapter 1.
- **Include a photocopy of your green card (front and back).**
- **Assemble the necessary documents you need to include.** Exactly which documents you need depends on your individual immigration situation. See the document checklist in Appendix C of this book for more information.
- **Include any explanations you may need to give to the BCIS, such as absences from the U.S. greater than six months, prior criminal convictions on your record, failure to register for the draft, and so on.** You must file these explanations in the form of affidavits. The government may or may not accept your explanation, but you still need to include it. If you feel you need to explain something about your application, you should always seek out the services of a qualified immigration attorney (see Chapter 7).

Researching your history: Form G-639

How can you make sure the information in your immigration files is accurate? By filing a Freedom of Information/Privacy Act Request (Form G-639) to access your files. This is where many attorneys start with a new client, especially clients who do not have personal records of prior dealings with the INS. By getting copies of previous filings, you can confirm what forms were filed, what information was on the forms, and what the INS did with them.

The fee charged for a Freedom of Information/Privacy Act Request may vary. See the instructions on the form itself for further details. You don't need to send any money with your request.

The Freedom of Information Act (FOIA), enacted in 1966, gives the American people the right to access records in the possession of agencies and departments of the Executive Branch of the United States government. The Privacy Act of 1974 regulates federal government agency record keeping and disclosure practices, allowing most individuals to access federal agency records about themselves. It also restricts the disclosure of personally identifiable information by federal agents and prohibits the government from using information gathered for one purpose from being used for another purpose. The Privacy Act states that personal information in federal agency files be accurate, complete, relevant, and timely, and gives the subject of a record the right to challenge the accuracy of the information in his or her own files.

Say cheese!: Taking a good photo, BCIS-style

If you neglect to send the BCIS proper photographs with your naturalization application, or with other applications such as an adjustment of status application, they will simply return the application, delaying the entire process. In most cases, you won't have to worry, because the photographer will have experience taking photographs for this purpose. But it doesn't hurt to know what the BCIS wants.

So what does a good photo mean in BCIS terms? They don't care how glamorous you look or if you were having a good hair day. The BCIS wants to be able to clearly identify that the person in the photograph is you. Likewise, they do have some specific photo requirements and restrictions:

- With your application, include two unretouched color (not black-and-white), high-quality photographs with glossy or matte finish.
- The overall photograph size should be at least $1\frac{9}{16}$ inches (40 mm) tall by $1\frac{3}{8}$ inches (35 mm) wide.
- The image of your face in the photo should be $1\frac{3}{16}$ inches (30 mm) from the hair to the neck just below the chin and 1 inch (26 mm) from the right ear to the left cheek. The image may not exceed $1\frac{1}{4}$ inches by $1\frac{1}{16}$ inches (32 mm x 28 mm).
- Photos should be unmounted and printed on thin paper.
- You should be photographed against a white or off-white background. Contrast between the image of your face and the background is essential. Photos of very light skinned people should be slightly underexposed, and photos of very dark skinned people should be slightly overexposed.
- Above all else, your facial features *must* be visible. The photo needs to show a three-fourths profile view of the right side of your face and your right ear.
- Unless your religion requires you to wear a headdress, your head should be bare in the photograph, but either way, your face *must* remain visible.
- The photos need to have been taken within 30 days of the date they are sent to the BCIS.
- Polaroid hybrid film is acceptable, however SX-70 film or any other instant-processing film is not accepted. Acceptable instant color film has a gray-toned backing, whereas the unacceptable nonpeel-apart films have a black backing.

Other common naturalization forms

Although the forms and documents you need will depend on your individual case, here are some common forms that many naturalization candidates will encounter.

- **Application to Preserve Residence for Naturalization Purposes (Form N-470)** allows certain lawful permanent residents who need to leave the United States for employment purposes to preserve continuity of status as an immigrant in order to pursue naturalization.
- **Application for Certificate of Citizenship (Form N-600)** is filed by those seeking naturalization based on parentage.
- **Application for Certificate of Citizenship in Behalf of an Adopted Child (Form N-643)** is filed to give adopted foreign children of United States citizens the benefits of becoming a U.S. citizen. The BCIS suggests you file this form as soon as your foreign adoption comes through.
- **Application for Transmission of Citizenship Through a Grandparent (Form N-600/Form N-643 Supplement A)** is a form filed along with Form N-600 or Form N-643, that allows a U.S. citizen parent who lacks sufficient U.S. physical presence to transmit citizenship to his/her child to rely on the physical presence of the child's grandparent(s). Keep in mind that the grandparent must be living in order to use his or her residence to qualify for U.S. citizenship.
- **Medical Certification for Disability Exceptions (Form N-648)** must be completed by a licensed medical doctor or a licensed clinical psychologist and filed along with an application for naturalization (Form N-400) for those who qualify for an exemption from taking the English or civics test portion of the naturalization interview (find out more about this in Chapter 5).

Who are approved representatives?

An immigration attorney will be the representative in most immigration cases, but there are other individuals who may be authorized to represent you before the BCIS. Law school graduates and current law students who are supervised by an attorney may represent you so long as you do not pay them. Some nonlawyers are also authorized through a process known as *accreditation,* under which the Board of Immigration Appeals grants permission to a representative of a recognized religious, charitable, or social-service organization.

Other common lawful permanent residence forms

Depending on individual circumstances, many people will encounter these forms during the naturalization process:

- **Petition for Alien Worker (Form I-140)** is filed by an employer to petition for an alien worker to become a permanent resident in the United States. The filing fee $135.
- **Petition for Alien Relative (Form I-130)** is filed by a citizen or a lawful permanent resident to establish a relationship to certain alien relatives who want to immigrate to the United States. You must file a separate form for each individual qualifying relative who wants to immigrate. The filing fee is $130.
- **Affidavit of Support (Form I-864)** is a promise made to the United States government that a sponsoring relative will be financially responsible for their alien relative. The sponsor is promising that the alien will not become a public charge. Sponsors must file separate forms for each relative they are sponsoring.
- **Application to Register Permanent Residence or to Adjust Status (Form I-485)** is submitted by applicants who want to obtain permanent resident status. You will usually file this form with supporting evidence that you qualify for upgrading your immigration status from temporary to permanent resident, and you may file this form at the same time as other applications or petitions. This form carries a fee of $255 for applicants over 14 years of age and $160 for applicants under 14. Applicants aged 14 or older must be fingerprinted at an additional cost of $50 per applicant.
- **Change of Address (Form AR-11)** is used to report the change of address of an alien in the United States to the BCIS. ***Remember:*** Failing to report an address change to the BCIS within ten days of moving is a removable offense. Always make sure the BCIS has your current address.
- **Application to Replace Permanent Resident Card (Form I-90)** is used to obtain replacement for a lost green card.

Documenting immigration help

If you're using an attorney or other approved representative, they must file another form with your application package — the G-28, Notice of Appearance. The representative may ask you to sign the G-28; your signature tells BCIS that you grant them permission to communicate directly with your attorney or representative. If multiple applications are submitted for other family members or for different petitioners, make sure that a separate G-28 is submitted for each party being represented.

If you're using an attorney, he or she will probably include a cover letter that outlines the immigration benefit you're seeking and the evidence included in the packet that demonstrates your qualifications. ***Remember:*** When using an attorney, you should read everything the attorney is planning to file with the BCIS (if you have questions, ask them before the forms are filed). Get a copy of the forms for your own files.

Preparing Your Application

The better prepared your immigration applications or petitions are, the less time it should take to process them. Here are some tips to help you stay organized and minimize the time it takes to process your applications:

- **Make your forms and applications easy to read.** Fill them out on a computer or type them if possible. Make sure the text is dark enough to easily read. If for some reason you cannot use a computer or typewriter, be sure to write clearly and legibly with a dark-colored ink pen. Never use pencil to fill out immigration forms.
- **Fill out the forms *completely*.** If you don't have an answer or the question doesn't apply, do not leave the question blank. Simply write "None" or "N/A" (for "not applicable") in the answer space.
- **Make sure required photos conform to BCIS requirements (and always put your name and A-Number [your Alien Registration Number] on the back of each photo).** Place the correct number of photos (read the instructions on the application carefully) in a separate envelope. Then use a paper clip to attach the envelope to its corresponding application. Never staple photos to applications. Stapled photos are unusable by the BCIS, and the application may be returned to you, with the entire process unnecessarily delayed.
- **If you are submitting other documents or paperwork with your immigration application, place all the additional documents in a single envelope and clearly write the contents on the outside of the envelope — listing the documents included.**
- **Avoid using tape on all four sides of an envelope.** Try to leave at least one side free of tape.

Make a copy of everything you submit. If the original application is ever lost (and it does happen), you can quickly submit a duplicate. Also, if you need to go over any errors or problems with the BCIS, you can look at the same forms they're looking at while you're on the phone. Of course, if the BCIS ever loses your application, it's a good time to get professional help from an attorney or a qualified immigration service.

TIP

Assembling immigration applications

In order to ensure the fastest processing of your application, here's the order the government likes to see applications assembled, from top to bottom:

- **Money:** The thing to put at the top is any fees you need to include with the application. Assemble *all* fee payments on the top of each and every case, whether or not the case is filed with one fee payment or multiple fee payments. In other words, if you're submitting several applications or documents, clip the fees for all of them to the top of your application packet.
- **Form G-28 "Notice of Appearance":** Next in the stack is a Form G-28 "Notice of Appearance" — but only if you're represented by an attorney or other approved representative (he or she will file this form for you). If you are not represented, you don't need to worry about this element.
- **The actual application:** Next comes the actual application or petition, with photos in a separate envelope attached by a paper clip (if your particular application needs photos).
- **Any additional evidence:** Now put in the envelope other paperwork and evidence (if applicable).
- **Supporting documentation:** If you need to include any other documents to help prove your case, add them at the bottom of the pile.

Wait a minute Mr. Postman! Whenever you send something to the BCIS, make sure you use a method that ensures proof of delivery — Certified Mail (with a return receipt), Express Mail, or something similar.

Paying the Price

A filing fee is required with many immigration forms. The fee must be included with and mailed in the same package as the application form. The BCIS can give you general information about the current amount of fees. You can also find fee information with the filing instructions for each form or application (if a fee is required).

TIP

After filing your application and paying your fees, you'll receive a receipt number. Don't lose your receipt numbers! You'll need them to use the BCIS case-status service online, or to reference your case whenever you contact the BCIS about your case.

TIP

Keep these tips in mind when sending in fee payments to the BCIS:

- **Do not send cash!** The BCIS accepts money orders, cashier's checks, corporate checks, or personal checks for payment of fees. They do *not* accept cash (besides, sending cash through the mail is never a good idea).
- **Be sure to sign your check and make sure it's correctly dated.**
- **Place the check on top of your application and secure it with a paper clip at the upper-left corner.**
- **If you're filing more than a single application, the BCIS wants you to submit a separate check (or cashier's check or money order) for each form.** This is designed to save you time in the long run. With separate checks, the BCIS doesn't need to return the entire package, should any one part of it be unacceptable.
- **If part of your application requires fingerprinting, don't forget to also include the fingerprinting fee with your petition or application.** Do not submit a completed fingerprint card with your request. Just include the payment for the service. The BCIS will contact you by mail, advising you of the time and place where your fingerprints will be taken.

Organizing your files

As you may be beginning to realize, you can accumulate a whole lot of paperwork during the course of immigration and naturalization. Maintaining accurate and organized files and always keeping copies of everything are important. If the BCIS ever loses anything important, you'll be able to replace it or prove your case. Keep extra copies of important documents (birth and marriage certificates, for example), in a separate location, so you'll have a backup.

A good way to keep organized files is to get a small file box or an alphabetical accordion file organizer. Organize the paper in a way that makes sense to you — so you will be able to quickly find the paperwork you need at a moment's notice. Get a separate file box for each member of the immigrating family.

Having well-organized paperwork in a single small location will allow you to bring your entire file with you, if you need to.

Chapter 5

Interviewing with the BCIS: It's Easier than You Think

In This Chapter

- Anticipating the interview
- Preparing for the English and civics tests
- Knowing what to do after the interview

There's no way around it: To become a naturalized citizen of the United States, you have to go through a minimum of two interviews with the BCIS — once to gain lawful permanent resident status (a green card) and a second time to become a naturalized citizen.

In this chapter, we let you know what to expect at your naturalization or citizenship interview. (See Chapter 1 to find out more about the permanent residence interview.)

Who Needs to Interview with the BCIS?

Everyone applying for naturalization has to interview with the Bureau of Citizenship and Immigration Services (BCIS), although not all people have to complete *all* parts of the interview. Everyone, except those with certain physical or mental disabilities, must take the Oath of Allegiance.

Age exemptions

Age has its privileges when it comes to interview exemptions. If you are over 50 years old and have lived in the United States at last 20 years, review Chapter 1 to see if you may be exempt from taking the English test. You may also be allowed to take the civics test in the language of your choice, or be given an easier version of the test.

Keep in mind that in order to meet the residency requirements for an age exemption, the time you spent living in the United States as a permanent resident need not have been continuous. Although you cannot count time spent out of the country, you can get credit for the total time you spent here. To see if you qualify:

1. **Add the total number of years you've been a United States lawful permanent resident.**

   Note: You may not count time spent living in the United States before you got your green card.

2. **Subtract from this any extended periods (more than six months) you spent outside the U.S.**

In order to qualify for BCIS interview exemptions, you must meet the requirements *as of the time you filed your application.* Even though you may be 50 years old by the time you actually interview with the BCIS, if you were 49 when you filed your application, you will still be expected to pass the English test.

Disability exemptions

People with disabilities — physical or developmental handicaps or mental impairment — may not have to take the English and civics tests.

You must file a Medical Certification for Disability Exceptions (Form N-648) with the BCIS if you think you qualify for a disability waiver. Unfortunately, the BCIS requires more than just your word. You'll need to get a licensed medical or osteopathic doctor or licensed clinical psychologist to complete and sign your form. In order to qualify for a disability exception, your condition must be expected to last at least one year and cannot have been caused by illegal drug use.

Even if you gain a disability waiver, you'll still be required to take the Oath of Allegiance — unless your condition is so severe that you are truly unable to do so. Plan to bring an interpreter with you to your interview if you do qualify for an English proficiency waiver (an exemption from having to speak, read, and write English).

Passing Your Naturalization Interview

No other part of the immigration process fills as many potential citizens with fear as the interview. They fret and worry about what kind of questions they'll be asked, how they'll be judged, and if they can possibly speak well enough and demonstrate enough knowledge of history, civics, and government to live up to the examiner's standards.

Relax. Passing the BCIS interview is far easier than you may think. In fact, if you make it through the maze of forms, documents, and paperwork necessary to be in the position to be interviewed for citizenship, you've made it through the hardest part.

The BCIS is not looking for brilliance or perfection. They just want to know that you have a basic understanding of how to read, write, and speak English, along with an understanding of U.S. history and how our government functions.

Arriving prepared

You already know you'll be asked about U.S. history and civics, and that you'll need to demonstrate a working knowledge of the English language. But in order to be completely relaxed and prepared for your interview, be aware that the officer may ask you to talk about any of the following:

- Your background (where you came from, your education, your occupation, and so on)
- Evidence and documents that support your case for naturalization (things like your employment records, marriage, and involvement in your community)
- Where you live and how long you've lived there
- Your feelings about the United States, its Constitution, and its government
- Your willingness to take the Oath of Allegiance (you can find more on the Oath of Allegiance later in this chapter)

Acing the interview

We know that no matter how much we tell you not to be nervous, you're going to be, so try to give yourself a break. By following these easy tips, you'll take off some of the pressure in advance.

- **Be on time!** Why rush yourself? Find out where to go ahead of time. Some BCIS offices have separate entrances for people with particular appointments. Even with an appointment notice, you may still have to wait as much as an hour at some offices just to get into the building — and then wait again after you get to the office waiting room. Expect lines and you won't be disappointed. Also, everyone entering a federal building must pass through security, which takes time (follow instructions and that should speed your passage). Talk to people familiar with the process in your area (friends in the community, lawyers, or other service providers); they can help you anticipate how far in advance you should plan to arrive so you'll have time to relax — the day is stressful enough already.
- **Dress as though you're going to a job interview.** You want to make a good impression on the BCIS officer, and although there are no hard and fast rules for the kind of clothing you should wear, looking nice, neat, and tidy doesn't hurt.
- **Bring copies of any paperwork you think you may need.** If you've taken our advice and kept accurate, organized files and copies of all your documents, you'll be able to easily bring your entire file with you, so you're always super-prepared.
- **In addition to BCIS documents, bring paperwork that will prove your job or standing in your community.** Bring things like payroll stubs, apartment leases, or membership cards in clubs or organizations — anything that helps establish your residence and participation in your community.
- **Tell the truth and don't be nervous — you'll do fine.**

Remember: The calmer and more relaxed you are, the easier the interview will go. Before you know it, the whole thing will be over and you'll be a giant step closer to becoming a United States citizen.

Be sure to bring to your interview your Alien Registration Card, your passport, and any reentry permits you obtained. Also, if your appointment letter specifically asks for any additional documentation, be sure to bring it.

Lying to the BCIS in writing or during the interview will immediately disqualify you. Even if the BCIS finds out you lied *after* you have been granted citizenship, your citizenship can be taken away. Being truthful with the BCIS is serious business, but as long as you've been truthful at every step of the process, you should have nothing to worry about. Note that when we talk about the kind of lying that results in disqualification, we're talking about untruths that you *knew* were untrue at the time that you told them. In other words, if you lied about your criminal record, you'll be disqualified; if you've committed an *inadvertent misstatement* — unknowingly providing incorrect information, such as being a digit off on your telephone number or having a new address — you should be fine. However, it's important to note that failing to notify the BCIS of a change of address within ten days of moving can be a removable offense. Always keep your whereabouts current with the BCIS.

Practicing for the Big Three: Reading, writing, and speaking English

Unless you qualify for an age or disability exemption, you must be able to read, write, and speak English to be eligible for naturalization. The BCIS officer doesn't expect you to have perfect grammar, diction, and accent. He or she just wants to know you can speak and understand *basic* English — enough to get around and function well within U.S. society.

How does the officer determine your English proficiency? He will probably ask you to read or write some simple sentences in English, as well as ask you a few questions about what the words mean:

- **Reading:** You may be asked to read out loud parts of Form N-400, the Application for Naturalization you sent the BCIS or INS when you first started the naturalization process. Or the officer may ask you to read some simple civics questions out loud and to answer them. Typical questions may be, "How many stars are on our flag?" or "What are the three branches of government?" Don't worry if you don't know the answers to these questions yet — we cover them in Parts III and IV of this book.
- **Writing:** The officer will probably ask you to write a couple simple sentences in English to test your writing skills. The sentences may be something like "I want to be a United States citizen," or, "Today I am going to the store."
- **Speaking:** The officer evaluates your ability to speak English by the answers you give throughout the interview, so you don't have to worry about studying for this separately.

Preparing for the English proficiency part of your BCIS interview is easy. After all, English surrounds you in the United States. Listen to conversations, have a conversation with someone yourself, read the newspaper or even signs and billboards, watch television, listen to the radio — opportunities to improve your English proficiency are everywhere! See Chapter 17 for lots of tips and strategies that will help you communicate in fluent English in no time.

Studying for the civics test

During your interview, you'll also be required to show you know about U.S. history and government. You don't need to be an expert and know every important historical event and date that ever happened in the United States. The BCIS just wants to make sure you understand and appreciate what it means to be an American. Find out the important principles that make up our government's foundation, and show a basic understanding of the history and events that made our Founding Fathers structure our government the way they did, and you're sure to pass.

It may seem like a lot to absorb, but if you stay aware, you can't help but pick up new knowledge every day — even by simply watching television! We'll cover what you need to know, in detail, in Parts IV, V, and VI of this book.

Communicating with the BCIS

Be sure to notify the BCIS each and every time you move. Your accurate address is the only way they have to stay in touch with you. If your interview appointment notification gets sent to the wrong address, you can miss your opportunity for naturalization, simply because you didn't know about it. Don't take chances with your immigration proceedings by being careless about communications.

What should you do if you have to miss your BCIS interview appointment? Unless you have absolutely no other choice, do everything in your power *not* to miss your scheduled interview. Yes, you can reschedule, but be aware that rescheduling is likely to add several months to the naturalization process. If you must miss your interview call the National Customer Service Center (NCSC) at 800-375-5283 to request rescheduling. The NCSC will record the information and pass it on to the local office, which will make the final decision whether to reschedule your appointment. To be on the safe side, also send a request by certified mail (with return receipt) to the BCIS office where your interview is scheduled and ask to have it rescheduled as soon as possible — the earlier the better!

If you miss your scheduled appointment without notifying the BCIS, they will close your case. If you let this happen, there may still be hope as long as not more than one year has passed since your case was closed. Contact the BCIS and ask for your interview to be rescheduled. If you knew about the interview and let more than one year go by since your case was closed, the game is over — your request and application will be denied, and the only way to get it started again is to file a new application.

Following Up: What Happens After the Interview

After your interview, you'll get a letter from the BCIS (currently Form N-652), which simply tells you whether your application was granted, denied, or continued. If your application was granted, congratulations! The letter will tell you where and when to go to attend your swearing-in ceremony.

If your application was *continued* (put on hold) or even denied, don't panic. The game is not over yet. If your case is continued, you probably just need to provide more documents or retake the English or civics portion of the test. If your application was denied, you still have an appeal process that may result in the denial being overturned. Chapter 1 gives more detail about both scenarios.

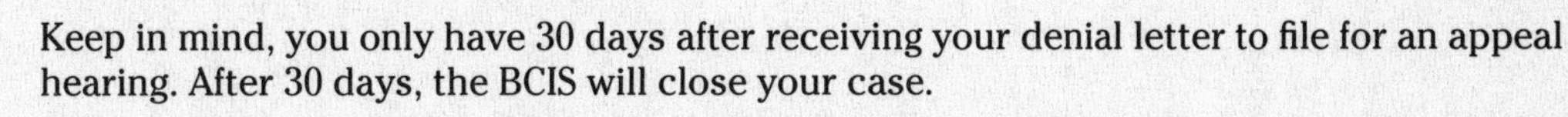

Keep in mind, you only have 30 days after receiving your denial letter to file for an appeal hearing. After 30 days, the BCIS will close your case.

Assuming your interview and tests went well, you'll probably be scheduled to come back for a swearing-in ceremony where you'll take the Oath of Allegiance. Taking the Oath, also known as Attachment to the Constitution, demonstrates your loyalty and allegiance to the United States of America. At some BCIS offices, you can choose to take the Oath the same day as your interview rather than come back for a group ceremony. If you choose this option, you will usually be asked to come back later that same day. The BCIS officer will then give you the Oath on the spot. Most new citizens, however, come back at a later date for a group ceremony at the BCIS office or in a court. In either case, you officially become a naturalized citizen as soon as you take the Oath of Allegiance to the United States.

After you become naturalized, be ready to surrender your green card. Don't worry, you won't need it anymore. After you take the oath, you have all the rights and benefits given to United States citizens who were born here. Well, almost — you won't be eligible to become President or Vice President, but other than that, the sky's the limit!

Apply for a passport as soon as you receive your Certificate for Naturalization. A passport also serves as proof of your citizenship and it's much easier to carry than the Certificate itself (not to mention the fact that getting a replacement certificate, if you ever lose your original, can take up to a year). Pick up a passport application at your swearing-in ceremony or at your local post office — or online at `www.travel.state.gov`.

Part II
Staying Up to Date and Out of Trouble

"The funny thing is, he keeps answering all the questions on the citizenship test correctly."

In this part . . .

Any time you deal with government agencies, things can get complicated. This part gives you tips and information that can help you navigate through the immigration system, avoiding problems and pitfalls whenever possible. You'll discover how to stay up to date with the latest changes in immigration law. Should difficulties ever arise, we give you resources to help you deal with them. We also show you how to find competent immigration help at a price you can afford, and how to avoid unscrupulous attorneys or immigration services who take your money but don't deliver on their promises.

Chapter 6

Keeping on Top of Changes in Immigration Law

In This Chapter

- Feeling the aftereffects of September 11, 2001
- Understanding legal changes in recent history
- Keeping up with new immigration law

Immigration laws change constantly. In the past 13 years, there have been two major revisions of the entire body of immigration law, as well as a variety of measures that have enhanced security and provided additional benefits to would-be immigrants. And it's not just the laws that change — just this year the entire United States immigration authority was restructured.

This chapter not only fills you in on the newest and most significant changes in immigration law, it also shows you how to stay up to date with any new changes that may take place long after this book is published.

Breaking Up Is Hard to Do: Understanding the Post-9/11 Changes to the Immigration System

The terrorist acts of September 11, 2001, which were perpetrated by non-U.S. citizens, prompted policymakers to examine how the U.S. polices its borders and administers immigration.

Balancing the prevailing notion that immigration is good for the U.S. (and part of our heritage) with border-security concerns, Washington decided against maintaining a unified immigration authority. Instead, lawmakers separated the primary functions of deciding eligibility for benefits and enforcing restrictions on immigration, taking them out of the Department of Justice, and placing them under the authority of a new government agency — the Department of Homeland Security (DHS). Two separate divisions now handle these functions:

- The Bureau of Citizenship and Immigration Services (BCIS) administers immigration benefits.
- The Directorate of Border and Transportation Security (BTS) acts as the law-enforcement arm of the U.S. immigration system.

Where did the other INS duties go?

Although the BCIS took over the immigration benefits portion of the INS, most of the INS's other functions are now performed by one of these two agencies (also part of the Department of Homeland Security):

- **The Bureau of Immigration and Customs Enforcement (BICE):** BICE has taken over the duties of the investigative and interior enforcement functions of the INS, the U.S. Customs Service, and the Federal Protective Services. The government believes that allowing BICE to take over the law-enforcement tasks of these agencies will help enhance security at home and abroad, in the air and on the sea.
- **The Bureau of Customs and Border Protection (BCBP):** Staffed by about 30,000 employees — many of them former agricultural quarantine inspectors, INS border agents, and customs inspectors — the BCBP seeks to coordinate border enforcement by focusing on the international movement of goods and people between the United States and other countries.

As of March 1, 2003, the INS technically ceased to exist and the BCIS took over the immigration benefits portion of the INS's former duties. Designed to enhance the service of the tens of thousands of people who interacted with the INS in the past, as well as new immigration cases, the bureau now serves the following functions:

- *Adjudication,* or judgment, over family- and employment-based immigration petitions
- Issuance of employment authorization and travel documents
- Asylum and refugee processing
- Naturalization and implementation of special status programs such as Temporary Protected Status

The BCIS is made up of some 15,000 employees and contractors headed by a director who reports to the Deputy Secretary for Homeland Security.

Overhauling Immigration Laws in 1990

The Immigration Act of November 29, 1990, (IMMACT90) significantly overhauled and changed the system. In some ways the laws broadened opportunities for people wanting to immigrate to the United States, but in other ways it made immigrating a lot tougher. Important points of the 1990 changes include the following:

- It increased the total number of immigrants allowed to legally live and work in the country.
- It revised the grounds for exclusion and deportation, especially on the grounds of politics or ideology. For instance, the act repealed the bar against the admission of communists as nonimmigrants.
- It gave the Attorney General the power to grant temporary protected status to undocumented alien nationals of designated countries subject to armed conflict or natural disasters.
- It revised certain existing nonimmigrant visa categories as well as established new ones.

- It established the Diversity Visa (DV) Lottery Program.
- It substantially altered existing permanent resident categories by establishing new employment categories and redefining who constitutes an "immediate relative" in case of family-based immigration.
- It broadened the authority to naturalize aliens to allow administration of the oath by the Attorney General, as well as by federal district and certain state courts.
- It changed some requirements for naturalization, including reducing residency requirements.
- It broadened the definition of *aggravated felony* and imposed new legal restrictions on aliens convicted of such crimes.
- It revised criminal and deportation provisions.
- It restructured the 32 grounds for exclusion into 9 categories, including revising and repealing some of the grounds (especially some health grounds).

After the 1990 restructuring, changes continued to be made in immigration law, but they were either smaller changes or laws that affected only certain small groups of immigrants. However, by the time 1996 rolled around, U.S. immigration law underwent another round of major changes.

Understanding the Significance of the 1996 Immigration Law Changes

The immigration law changes of 1996 (known as the Illegal Immigration Reform and Immigrant Responsibility Act, or IIRAIRA) made things considerably tougher for many immigrants. Spurred by terrorist activities abroad, a growing domestic crime problem, as well as financial worries, the laws got tougher on crime, reduced government benefits to immigrants (both legal and illegal immigrants), and sought to better protect the U.S. borders.

Getting tougher on crime

The 1996 immigration laws took the issue of crime very seriously, expanding criteria for removal, including allowing deportation of nonviolent offenders prior to completion of their sentence of imprisonment. In addition, those with criminal records had a harder time immigrating, because the law also

- Established a criminal alien identification system
- Provided access to certain confidential immigration and naturalization files through court order
- Granted the government authority to conduct alien smuggling investigations
- Expedited the process of removing criminal aliens from the United States
- Established deportation procedures for certain nonimmigrant criminal aliens

The Immigration and Nationality Act of 1952

The Immigration and Nationality Act (INA) — the basic body of immigration law in the United States — collected and restructured the many immigration-related laws of the time. Over the years, the Immigration and Nationality Act has been *amended,* or changed, many times. Amendments allow Congress to change or modify one or more parts of a law, without having to rewrite the entire statute. Sometimes the changes or amendments cover entire sections of the act; other times the changes are as subtle as a word or two that provides further clarification of an issue.

Technically, deportation proceedings don't exist anymore — thanks to IIRAIRA. In the past, there were two kinds of proceedings in immigration court:

- **Exclusion,** for folks stopped while trying to come into the country
- **Deportation,** for folks already here, whom INS wanted to ship out

Now there is just one form of proceeding: removal. However, you can get involved in removal proceedings in one of two ways:

- Through being denied admission to the U.S. (which is based on exclusion grounds)
- Through being required to leave the U.S. after being admitted (which is based on deportation grounds)

These two bases for removal are similar to the prior deportation procedures.

Proving you won't be a burden to the system

Meeting financial obligations and requirements also got tougher for immigrants in 1996. The Personal Responsibility and Work Opportunity Reconciliation Act severely limited access to public benefits for non-U.S. citizens — whether in a legal immigration status or not — in the following ways:

- **It barred non-U.S. citizens (with certain exceptions) from obtaining food stamps and Supplemental Security Income (SSI) and most other federal public-assistance programs as well as established screening procedures for current and future recipients of these programs.** Of course, the law also prohibits illegal aliens from receiving most federal, state, and local public benefits.
- **It provided states with flexibility in setting public benefit eligibility rules for legal immigrants, allowing them to bar legal immigrants from both major federal programs and state programs.**
- **It increased responsibilities for those sponsoring family members, including instituting a new, legally enforceable affidavit of support.** (You can find out more about the affidavit of support in Chapter 3).

- **It required immigration status to be verified in order for eligible aliens to receive most federal public benefits.**

All the preceding applies to both legal and illegal aliens as well as nonimmigrants.

Protecting America's borders

The Illegal Immigration Reform and Immigrant Responsibility Act of 1996 increased border personnel, equipment, and technology at ports of entry, increasing penalties for illegal entry, passport and visa fraud, and failure to depart. The law also sought to enforce laws and protect the U.S. by

- Increasing penalties for alien smuggling.
- Speeding deportation proceedings.
- Instituting temporary bars to admissibility for aliens seeking to reenter the country after having been unlawfully present in the United States.
- Prohibiting those individuals who renounced their U.S. citizenship in order to avoid U.S. tax obligations from reentering the country.

Recognizing Helpful Immigration Law Changes

Not all new immigration laws are designed to make things tougher for the people trying to immigrate. Through the years a variety of laws have been passed to help victims — victims of violence, victims of war, victims of oppressive regimes, and so on. Some of the most important new laws of this type include

- **The Violence Against Women Act (VAWA), 1994; expanded by the Victims of Trafficking and Violence Protection Act, 2000:** To help victims of domestic violence (both men women) escape the cycle of violence, these laws allow abused spouses and children of sponsor citizens or Legal Permanent Residents (LPRs) to self-petition for immigration benefits. It is important to note that even though this is known as the Violence Against *Women* Act, it is not for women only. Abused husbands can also seek relief through this avenue.
- **The Nicaraguan Adjustment and Central American Relief Act (NACARA), 1997; expanded by the LIFE Act, 2000:** Provides eligibility for adjustment to certain Nicaraguans, Cubans, Guatemalans, Salvadorans, and nationals of the former Soviet bloc.
- **The Haitian Refugee and Immigration Fairness Act (HRIFA), 1998; expanded by the LIFE Act, 2000:** Provides eligibility for adjustment to certain Haitians.
- **The Legal Immigration and Family Equity (LIFE), 2000:** Expands eligibility for certain benefits to all applications filed by April 30, 2001, provided the beneficiary was in the U.S. on December 21, 2000 (the date the LIFE Act was signed). Also created new nonimmigrant visas to allow spouses and dependants of lawful permanent residents and citizens to come to the U.S. when processing of their permanent resident petitions is delayed.

- **The Child Status Protection Act (CSPA), 2002:** Allows child/dependent-beneficiaries of citizens to maintain their eligibility even after they *age out* (turn 21) as long as the original petition was filed before the child turned 21. However, if the sponsor is an LPR, different rules apply, based on the priority date.

Staying Abreast of Changes in Immigration Law

With immigration laws changing so frequently, how can you keep up with what's going on? The BCIS Web site (www.immigration.gov) should keep you up to date with the latest changes in immigration law. Reading newspapers or listening to or watching comprehensive television or radio news should also keep you up to date with major changes (although some smaller ones may not get coverage). *The Immigration Law Daily* (www.ilw.com), an Internet-based immigration publication is also a good source of news.

Another great source for immigration laws changes is the nonprofit National Immigration Law Center. Specializing in immigration law and the employment and public benefits rights of immigrants, the Center protects and promotes the rights and opportunities of low-income immigrants and their family members. Find their Web site at www.nilc.org or locate their offices in:

- **Los Angeles:** 3435 Wilshire Blvd., Suite 2850; Los Angeles, CA 90010; phone: (213) 639-3900
- **Oakland:** 405 14th St., Suite 1400; Oakland, CA 94612; phone: (510) 663-8282
- **Washington, D.C.:** 1101 14th St. NW, Suite 410; Washington, DC 20005; phone: (202) 216-0261

TECHNICAL STUFF

Fighting the war on terror

United States immigration law was fighting the war on terrorism long before the events of September 11, 2001. The Antiterrorism and Effective Death Penalty Act of 1996 made it easier for the U.S. to identify someone as having a connection to terrorism and to quickly remove that person from the U.S. on that basis, with limited judicial review. The law also changed asylum procedures, making involvement in terrorism a bar to asylum.

The U.S.A. Patriot Act, enacted weeks after September 11, 2001, along with the Enhanced Border Security and Visa Reform Act, expand the definition of terrorism and terrorist activity to include fundraising, solicitation, and material support of terrorist organizations. In addition, the laws

- Expand detention powers, including indefinite detention of certified terrorist suspects or threats to national security
- Facilitate greater information sharing between immigration and law enforcement agencies
- Call for implementation of an entry/exit tracking system and use of machine-readable documents using tamper-resistant, biometric technology
- Update student and exchange visitor tracking mechanisms
- Restrict issuance of nonimmigrant visas to citizens of countries the Secretary of State designates as a "state sponsor of terrorism"

The controversy over tracking immigrants

Seizing the initiative to implement expansive tracking of nonimmigrants, the Department of Justice published regulations in 2002 calling for special registration of certain nonimmigrants. Using laws that have existed since World War II — but were rarely enforced — the regulation requires registration, fingerprinting, and photographing of nonimmigrants in three classifications:

- Nationals of countries designated by the Attorney General
- Perceived nationals of countries designated by the Attorney General
- Individuals who are perceived to meet criteria that warrant monitoring

By notices published in the Federal Register, the Attorney General has designated the relevant nationalities to include the following: Afghanistan, Algeria, Bahrain, Eritrea, Iran, Iraq, Lebanon, Libya, Morocco, North Korea, Oman, Pakistan, Saudi Arabia, Somalia, Sudan, Syria, Qatar, Tunisia, United Arab Emirates, and Yemen.

Immigration advocates have been fiercely opposed to the special registration requirements, and it remains to be seen whether the program will be expanded to all nationalities (as the Attorney General has suggested) or scrapped entirely.

Rumors of amnesty and other provisions often spread through immigrant communities. If you hear of something that you think may benefit you, the best thing to do is to check with a qualified immigration attorney or legal service provider. You can find out more about hiring a reputable attorney in Chapter 7.

Chapter 7

Getting Help When You Need It

In This Chapter

- Determining whether you need help
- Finding ethical, reliable people to assist you
- Seeking free and low-cost resources

The immigration process can be complex. Sometimes even seemingly simple cases can get bogged down in endless rounds of documentation and complicated forms and paperwork. Often, the best thing you can do is get professional help. But how do you find ethical, reliable help? Not all attorneys or immigration services are worth the money. Some may not be what they seem, or may make false promises. In this chapter, we show you how to find attorneys and organizations that can help you in your quest for citizenship, and we help you avoid those that can waste your time or money.

Recognizing When You Need Professional Help

In almost all cases, potential immigrants and/or citizens can benefit from consulting with a qualified immigration attorney or legal service provider, especially if your case involves any unusual circumstances such as criminal record, long-term absences from the U.S., or being out of legal immigration status.

An *immigration attorney* is licensed to practice law by at least one state or the District of Columbia and should have some level of expertise in immigration matters. Your attorney may or may not have studied the subject of immigration in law school, but he or she should have some foundation in the subject and continually work to keep up with changes in the law.

You can also find lots of nonattorney legal-service providers, which provide legal-service programs for immigrants. These programs are usually staffed primarily with nonattorneys — sometimes called *counselors.* Counselors do much the same work that attorneys do, and some have been doing it much longer than most attorneys you'll meet. Legal services provided by a reputable organization — whether an attorney or a counselor — should be satisfactory. You should feel confident that any work done by a counselor in a reputable organization is reviewed by an attorney. Generally, counselors are not authorized to represent you before the Bureau of Citizenship and Immigration Services (BCIS) or in court — unless they become accredited immigration representatives.

Not quite attorneys, *accredited immigration representatives* are like super-counselors, specially trained in immigration law. In order for a representative to be accredited, the U.S. government must officially recognize the organization that counselor works for. In order to qualify for recognition, the organization must agree to keep any fees for their services low. ***Remember:*** These organizations exist to help people who cannot otherwise afford the services of a qualified immigration attorney.

The designation of accredited representatives is given by the Executive Office for Immigration Review (EOIR), part of the Department of Justice. Technically, an agency must first apply to be recognized by the EOIR, and then apply to have its non-attorney staff accredited.

Of course, free or low-cost legal services don't necessarily have to be provided by a recognized agency or an agency with accredited representatives. For instance, an agency that relies solely on lawyers for representation does not need to be recognized or have accredited representatives.

An attorney or accredited representative can advise you on what to expect from the immigration process, as well as warn you of the risks. He or she can help you obtain legal status from the BCIS or represent you in immigration court.

Applying for the Diversity Visa Lottery is quite simple. Many services will be happy to take your money in exchange for writing out some basic information about yourself. Before you fork over any of your hard-earned cash, take a look at the rules yourself (they're posted at the State Department Web site, `www.travel.state.gov`). Be aware, however, that the rules may vary from year to year, and that incomplete or incorrect applications will be rejected without notice. You can find out more about the Diversity Visa Lottery in Chapter 1.

You'll find lots of Web sites that will offer you the privilege of downloading or filling out forms online for a fee. Don't pay it. Not only can you download forms for free at the BCIS Web site (`www.immigration.gov`), but also, oftentimes, the forms at the pay Web sites are not even current. By going directly to the source — namely the BCIS — you'll always be guaranteed that you're getting the most-recent forms.

Seeking Professional Help

With all the questionable services and attorneys out there, how do you go about finding ethical, reliable help? If you don't know any qualified attorneys personally, stay away from the phonebook — not because there aren't any good attorneys in the Yellow Pages (there are plenty), but because telling a reputable immigration service or lawyer from a less-than-qualified one simply by looking at a Yellow Pages ad is difficult if not impossible.

A good place to start is with friends or family members who have already successfully gained lawful immigrant status. Ask for recommendations from people you already trust.

Another good way to find a qualified reputable attorney is to call the Immigration Lawyer Referral Service at 800-954-0254. The free service is part of the American Immigration Lawyers Association (AILA), a national association made up of over 8,000 attorneys and law professors who practice and teach immigration law. Nonprofit and *nonpartisan* (meaning they have no political affiliation), AILA provides its members information, legal services, and continuing legal education that keeps them current with immigration law changes. AILA's members represent tens of thousands of people throughout the United States seeking lawful permanent residence, often representing foreign students, entertainers, athletes, and asylum seekers on a *pro bono* (free-of-charge) basis. AILA can help you find an attorney in your area who is currently a member in good standing of the state *bar association.* (In this case the word *bar* refers to a legal organization — it has nothing to do with cocktails, or steel beams . . . yet another example of how English can be a confusing language to master. Not to worry, you can find tips for improving English in Chapter 17.)

Knowing the warning signs to watch out for

Recognizing the warning signs that indicate you may be dealing with an unethical attorney or immigration service is critical. Keep in mind the following, and if any of these items apply to your situation, take it as a sign to investigate further and make sure you're getting the qualified help you need from a reputable representative and at a reasonable price:

- **Beware of any services that can't or won't give you an honest estimate, in advance, of the cost of their services.** Ideally, you should be asked to sign a written agreement (called a *retainer*) that specifies the service the attorney or representative will provide, how much it costs, how payment is to be made, and how to terminate the agreement.
- **Never give money to anyone who asks for money to influence, or *bribe,* an immigration official, even if that person claims to know someone who can help you in this way.** It is never a good idea to take bribes. The world can be a cruel place and there have been operators who will take your money and then leave it to you to sort it out with the BCIS.
- **If something sounds too good to be true, it usually is.** According to AILA, you should beware of notaries, consultants, service bureaus, travel agents, or anyone else who promises a quick, easy solution to your immigration problems. One of the key words here is *promise.* Anyone who absolutely *guarantees* to get you a visa, green card, or other immigration benefit after you pay him or her a designated fee should seriously raise your suspicions.
- **Beware when dealing with lawyers from other countries who do not know U.S. laws and are not licensed to practice in the U.S.**

If you aren't sure whether the person offering you immigration services is a lawyer or an accredited representative, ask to see the accreditation letters or state bar admission certificate. If you're still not sure, call the state bar association. You can usually find the number for your state bar association in the front of your local telephone book. An Internet search under "state bar associations" will bring up lots of sites with links to the various state bar associations. ***Remember:*** In the United States, practicing law without a license is illegal.

Consulting an immigration attorney

Because United States immigration law is so complex, with countless exceptions to every rule, a good attorney can really help your chances by thoroughly analyzing your unique case and circumstances and recommending the best way for you to obtain legal immigration status. A good immigration attorney is worth his weight in gold, because he stays current with the latest changes in immigration law — something very difficult for a layperson without legal training to do. A good attorney also has the experience to work every possible angle and advantage to help you gain legal permanent immigration status. Other ways an attorney can help your case include the following:

- Determining the best way to pursue your immigration goals
- Explaining all the immigration benefits for which you may be eligible

- Properly completing and submitting your immigration forms and documents
- Representing you in court or in discussions with the BCIS
- Filing appeals if necessary

Don't be afraid to shop around for an immigration attorney, asking many questions in the process. Try to visit or talk with an attorney personally before making a final decision to hire him or her.

Before you make an appointment to talk with a lawyer, always ask if there is an initial consultation fee. Although charging an initial consultation fee is a common practice, you want to be sure you know in advance what you'll have to pay. For instance, attorneys referred by AILA agree to charge no more than $100 for an initial half-hour consultation.

Try to get an idea of how knowledgeable your potential attorney is about current immigration law. Get his or her opinion on your particular case, including its strengths and weaknesses. Your lawyer should be able to tell you how much his or her services cost, giving you an honest estimate of how much it will cost to represent your case. The attorney should also agree to keep you informed of any additional costs that come up during the immigration process.

If for any reason you're not satisfied with the attorney, or with his or her qualifications or answers to your questions, keep looking. In immigration, as in love, you have to shop around!

Reaching for a helping hand: Nonprofit immigration organizations

Local nonprofit immigration assistance services are very low cost or even free, as long as you're able to meet the particular organization's low-income eligibility requirements.

Before working with an immigration organization, meet with them and ask for references to make sure that they have a good reputation. Find out whether an attorney, a counselor, or an accredited representative will handle your case. Be aware that many accredited representatives offer only limited types of assistance, so make sure you feel comfortable that the agency has the skills to help in your unique circumstances.

The Executive Office for Immigration Review (EOIR) provides listings of competent free immigration help throughout the country. The agency created the *pro bono program* in April 2000, to help improve access to legal advice and counseling for low-income aliens. The program also gives many people, who may not otherwise have it, access to legal representation in immigration court and during appeals. To find listings of agencies in your geographical area, visit the EOIR Web site at `www.usdoj.gov/eoir/probono/states.htm`.

Seeking out low- or no-cost immigration assistance

Many churches and religious organizations offer low- or no-cost immigrant assistance, so asking your clergyman to see if any programs may be available to help you is always a good idea.

Be sure to check at any nearby law schools as well, because they often offer immigration clinics where supervised students hone their immigration law skills while helping low-income aliens realize their immigration dreams.

Taking advantage of free immigration help from the government

Although the government won't provide someone to represent you in immigration proceedings, it does offer a lot of free information to help you in your quest for citizenship.

As we discuss in earlier chapters, the Internet is the best way to get the latest and most up-to-date information and forms. Start at the BCIS Web site (`www.immigration.gov`).

Many government agencies are still trying to catch up with the recent changes that abolished the Immigration and Naturalization Service (INS). In reading print or online materials from some agencies, you may still encounter them referring to the INS. A general guideline is to substitute the BCIS for INS when you see it in print. There may be exceptions to this rule, but in the majority of cases, the BCIS is the agency that you will most frequently interact with.

You can order forms by calling the BCIS toll-free in the U.S. at 800-870-3676, 24 hours a day. If you call Monday through Friday between 8 a.m. and 6 p.m. (no matter which time zone you're in), you can even ask questions of a real live person.

The BCIS offers a wonderful free publication called *A Guide to Naturalization,* which covers a wide variety of topics concerning immigration and naturalization. The BCIS also offers the booklet in Spanish, Chinese, Vietnamese, and Tagalog. Access it free from the BCIS Web site (`www.immigration.gov/graphics/services/natz/guide.htm`), or call the toll-free number and request publication M-476 (in the language of your choice).

Taking citizenship test-prep classes

Some people opt to take classes to help them prepare to take the citizenship English and civics tests. Although taking a class isn't necessary or required (you may study on your own), many people find the classroom environment helps them stay focused on the subject at hand and accomplish their goals in a reasonable time period. Another advantage of attending citizenship preparation classes is that the class forces you to interact with others, which in turn will improve your communication skills.

Check adult-education centers in your area to find low- or no-cost citizenship test-prep classes. These classes are often held after hours at high schools, community colleges, community centers, or churches. Look for flyers or ask questions at any of these locations to find classes near you.

Taking a General Educational Development (GED) test-prep class will not only help you prepare to take your citizenship test, but it will also earn you the equivalent of a U.S. high-school diploma — a minimum educational requirement for many jobs. Look for GED prep classes in the same places you look for citizenship classes.

Chapter 8

Troubleshooting Immigration Glitches

In This Chapter

- Communicating with the BCIS
- Avoiding worst-case scenarios
- Appealing BCIS decisions

Like dealing with any government agency, dealing with the BCIS involves *bureaucracy* — a complex set of procedures that you must follow exactly in order to successfully complete the immigration process. As frustrating as it may be, following rules and protocol — even when dealing with the worst-case immigration scenarios like denials, rejections, or even removal from the country — is important.

Communicating with the BCIS

If you have immigration-related questions or need more information or clarification about the specific procedures and protocols you need to follow, a good place to start is the BCIS's National Customer Service Center (NCSC). Call 800-375-5283 or 800-767-1833 (TTY). The toll-free service, available in English and Spanish, dispenses automated information 24 hours a day, 7 days a week. Through the automated system, you can order forms, get information about basic eligibility, and get instructions for filing and filling out forms.

Filling out immigration forms incorrectly can cause them to be sent back for further clarification, or worse, to be denied. If you have any questions about how to properly complete forms, getting help *before* sending them in is best.

If you need more than basic information and want to speak with a live person for help or clarification, call the NCSC Monday through Friday during these hours:

- **From Alaska:** 8:00 a.m. to 5:00 p.m. local time
- **From Hawaii:** 8:00 a.m. to 4:00 p.m. local time
- **From Puerto Rico and the U.S. Virgin Islands:** 9:00 a.m. to 6:00 p.m. local time
- **From anywhere else in the United States:** 8:00 a.m. to 6:00 p.m. local time

Note: In Guam, live assistance is only available Tuesday through Saturday from 6:00 a.m. to 11:00 a.m. local time.

Because of higher call volumes on Monday, the best times to call the NCSC for personal assistance are Tuesday through Friday. A phone with an automatic-redial function will help you to get through with less frustration.

If you live outside any of the preceding locations, contact the nearest U.S. embassy or consulate for immigration-related customer service.

What if you lose your Certificate of Naturalization?

You can get a new Certificate of Naturalization by filling out and submitting an Application for Replacement of Naturalization/Citizenship Document (currently Form N-565) along with the proper fee. You can get this form from the BCIS Web site or by calling their forms line at 800-8780-3676.

Be aware that getting a new Certificate of Naturalization can take up to year. That's why we always suggest you get a U.S. passport as soon as you receive your Certificate of Naturalization — a passport also serves as evidence of citizenship.

Registering changes

When it comes to your immigration goals, neglecting the simplest tasks can have serious consequences. Be sure to tell the BCIS each and every time you change your address. If the BCIS doesn't have your current address, you can easily miss important correspondence. Without this information, you may miss crucial appointments that will put an end to your immigration dreams. The BCIS must always know how to get in touch with you. Not keeping them informed of your current whereabouts is a misdemeanor and a removable offense.

If your naturalization application is currently *pending,* or being processed, you can call the NCSC toll-free number at 800-375-5283 to report address changes.

If you haven't yet applied for naturalization and your address changes, you must submit a change of address form, AR-11 to the BCIS change-of-address processing center. Mail the form to BCIS, Change of Address, P.O. Box 7134, London, KY 40742-7134. If you're sending the form via commercial overnight or fast freight services, send it to BCIS, Change of Address, 1084-I South Laurel Rd., London, KY 40744.

Writing to your local immigration office when your address changes is also a good idea (check your local telephone book or go to `www.immigration.gov` for the address). When you write the address on your envelope, be sure to write the words *Attention: Change of Address* underneath the immigration office address. In your letter, be sure to include

- Your name as it appears on any immigration forms or applications
- Your A-Number
- Both your old address and your new address, indicating clearly which one is which

Although the BCIS does not require you to send your change-of-address form via certified, registered, or receipt mail, doing so is still a good idea. That way you'll have proof you sent the notice, in case it ever gets lost in the mail or in BCIS processing.

Changing appointments

The BCIS takes its appointment schedule very seriously. Unless it is a dire emergency, do not miss your appointments for interviews, fingerprinting, or any other immigration processing. Missing appointments can get you disqualified from the immigration benefits you're seeking.

If an emergency arises and you absolutely cannot make your appointment, be sure to contact the BCIS to request to have your appointment rescheduled — and do it as soon as you know about your conflict. Call the NCSC, which will pass along the information to the local BCIS field office, which makes the final decision. Our experience suggests you should also send a letter directly to the local field office, clearly indicating on the envelope that you're writing to request a rescheduled interview (and send it certified mail, return receipt). Be aware there is no guarantee you'll get another chance.

Filing a complaint

What if you think you've been treated unfairly by a BCIS employee? You do have recourse, and filing a complaint will not affect your eligibility for naturalization.

The first step is to try to speak with the offending employee's direct supervisor. If the supervisor doesn't handle the complaint to your satisfaction (or if for some reason you're never able to speak with the supervisor), the next step is to write a letter to the director of your district office (call the office to get the person's name and address or go to the BCIS Web site).

If you still don't get satisfaction, you can get a preaddressed complaint form (currently Form I-847), that you can fill out and send to BCIS headquarters in Washington, D.C. Order the form through the BCIS forms line at 800-870-3676, or download it from `www.immigration.gov`.

If you have a legitimate complaint, be sure to file it in a timely fashion. Many people, knowing that filing a complaint may slow the immigration process, neglect to file one in the hopes that their case will be looked upon favorably. If you wait an undue length of time before raising your concerns in an official matter, the government may want to know why you didn't raise the complaint sooner.

Dealing with Rejection and Appealing BCIS Decisions

What if the BCIS denies your application for lawful permanent residence or naturalization? Don't panic. It's not over yet. You can appeal your case and, in many instances, you may reapply. In immigration proceedings, two separate government agencies share the appellate review authority:

- **The Administrative Appeals Office (AAO),** which is part of the Bureau of Citizenship and Immigration Services (BCIS), a division of the Department of Homeland Security (DHS)
- **The Board of Immigration Appeals (BIA),** which is under the jurisdiction of the Executive Office of Immigration Review (EOIR), which is part of the United States Department of Justice (DOJ)

Immigrant visa rejections

If you get a denial notice, read it carefully — it contains information about your right to appeal the decision and how to go about doing so.

Working and traveling during the citizenship application process

Of course, because you must be a lawful permanent resident in order to apply for citizenship, working during the naturalization process is okay. Travel should not be a problem either, as long as it doesn't interfere with your continuous residency requirements. If you leave the United States for more than six months, you will, in most cases, disrupt your continuous residence. Consult with your attorney before leaving the country for any extended periods of time before gaining citizenship.

Of course, if you are applying for lawful permanent residence, you aren't allowed to work unless you have an employment authorization document, which you can apply for as soon as a visa is available for your classification and you file your form I-485 (Application to Register Permanent Residence or to Adjust Status).

You, or most likely your immigration attorney, will file a *brief,* or explanation, that supports the reasons for your appeal. After reviewing your case, the appellate authority for your particular case — either the AAO or the BIA — will decide to change the original decision, uphold the rejection, or send the case back to your local immigration office for further action.

In some cases, you may also file a *motion to reopen* or a *motion to reconsider* your case. This means that you're asking the office to reconsider their decision. In order to file either of these motions, you must have compelling reasons to do so:

- In order to successfully file a *motion to reopen,* you must provide affidavits and documents that prove new facts in your case that didn't come into play during your original hearing.
- In order for an immigration office to *reconsider* its decision, you must prove that the decision was based on an incorrect application of the law or BCIS policy.

Needless to say, we can't recommend strongly enough that you get the help of a qualified immigration attorney in these cases, because you're dealing with highly complex issues.

The right to appeal immigration decisions comes with strict time deadlines. Read your denial notice carefully and make sure to file your appeal before the deadline or you will *forfeit,* or lose, the right to appeal. Make sure you also include the proper fees or, again, you may lose your chances. In most cases:

- You have 30 days to appeal the denial of a petition or application. Increase that to 33 days after the date of the decision if you received the notice by mail.
- If you're appealing a revocation of an approved immigrant petition, you must file the appeal within 15 days of the date of the decision or within 18 days of the date of the decision if the decision was delivered by mail.

If an attorney or other representative is filing the appeal, he or she should include a Form G-28 — or if it is an appeal to the BIA, an EOIR-27.

The person who submitted the original visa application or petition is the only one who may file an appeal. The beneficiary of a visa petition may *not* appeal a decision, unless the beneficiary is also the petitioner. For instance, if you live abroad and your potential U.S. employer filed an immigrant visa petition on your behalf, your employer must file the appeal (you cannot do so yourself).

Naturalization rejections

If you are denied naturalization, you can go through an administrative review process. Your denial letter will explain how to request a hearing with an immigration officer and will include the form you need to file the appeal — a Request for Hearing on a Decision in Naturalization Proceedings (currently Form N-336).

The denial letter will also tell you the date on which you may reapply for citizenship. If your application was denied because you failed the English or civics test, you may reapply for naturalization as soon as you want.

Reapplying for naturalization is just like starting the entire naturalization process all over again. You must:

- Complete and submit a new Application for Naturalization (Form N-400)
- Pay the required fee for applying again ($260 as of this writing)
- Make a new appointment and get refingerprinted
- Submit new photographs

Demonstrating Good Moral Character

As we discuss in previous chapters, to become a naturalized U.S. citizen (and in some cases even to become a lawful permanent resident), you must demonstrate that you possess good moral character.

Aggravated felonies committed on or after November 29, 1990, and murder represent permanent bars to naturalization. Other crimes constitute *temporary bars,* meaning you must wait a designated period of time before applying for citizenship.

Your Application for Naturalization form will ask you about crimes. Reporting all crimes on your record — even crimes that have been *expunged* or removed from your record — is important. If you neglect to inform the BCIS about a crime and they find out about it later, they can use it as grounds to deny your naturalization application — even if the crime itself was not serious enough to originally deny your case. Worse, some crimes can not only jeopardize your eligibility to naturalize; they can cause revocation of permanent resident status and removal from the U.S.

After you file your naturalization application, the information in it is fair game for the BCIS (and the Bureau of Immigration and Customs Enforcement, or BICE), even if you ask to withdraw your application (a request that the BCIS can deny).

If you have any crimes in your record, consult an immigration attorney for help with your case — preferably *before* you file. (Chapter 7 shows you how to find a reliable attorney.)

So what other things may result in a BCIS denial on grounds of lack of good moral character? If, within the five- or three-year period of permanent residence prior to naturalization, any of the following apply to you, you may have something to worry about:

- You've committed any crime against a person with intent to harm.
- You've committed any crime against property that involves fraud or evil intent.
- You've committed two or more crimes for which the combined sentence was five years or more.

- You've violated any controlled-substance law of the United States, any state, or any foreign country.
- You've been confined in jail, prison, or a similar institution for which the total confinement was 180 days or more during the past five years (or three years if you're applying based upon your marriage to a United States citizen).
- You've lied to gain immigration benefits.
- You've participated in prostitution (either working as a prostitute or hiring one).
- You've been involved in illegal alien smuggling into the U.S.
- You've engaged in *polygamy* (marriage to more than one person at a time).
- You've earned your income principally from illegal gambling, or were convicted for two or more gambling offenses.
- You have been a habitual drunkard.
- You've failed to pay court-ordered child support or alimony payments.
- You had an extramarital affair that destroyed an existing marriage.
- You committed unlawful acts not mentioned in this list, but which otherwise adversely affect your good moral character.

If you've recently been ordered deported or removed, you aren't eligible for citizenship. If you're currently in removal proceedings, you may not apply for citizenship until the proceedings are complete and you've been allowed to remain in the country as a lawful permanent resident.

Avoiding Removal

Even if you have been legally admitted to the United States, on a temporary or permanent basis, under certain circumstances you can still be *removed,* or forced to leave the country. Granted, this is the worst-case scenario, and we hope you will never have to deal with this situation, but nonetheless, you should be aware of the reasons for removal and what you can do if you ever find yourself facing it.

After you become a naturalized citizen, you will no longer need to worry about removal, because you have the same rights as a natural-born United States citizen. Your citizenship can only be revoked under extreme circumstances, such as a treason conviction.

Prior to the immigration law changes of 1996 (IIRAIRA), the process of removing an alien already in the country was known as *deportation.*

Understanding the reasons for removal

The reasons for removal are many, but most people who face forced exile from the United States fall into one of these categories:

- Entering the country illegally
- Violating the terms of admission
- Working in the United States without permission

- Having criminal convictions
- Being a member of certain prohibited organizations (such as a terrorist organization)
- Becoming a public charge within five years of entering the U.S.

Appealing removal decisions

Removal is a serious and complicated subject. After you're forced to leave the country, chances are good you won't be allowed back into the U.S. for at least five years — unless you get a waiver, which is not easy.

Do not attempt to contest removal on your own — whether before the immigration court or on appeal. Seek out the services of a qualified attorney or immigration organization. (Chapter 7 shows you how to find a good lawyer or other representation — even if you have little or no money.)

Beware of additional sanctions for failing to depart the U.S. following a final order of removal. You continue to accrue unlawful presence, which can result in additional bars to reentry and ineligibility for future immigration benefits. You also run the risk of facing a permanent bar to entering the U.S.

Part III
Understanding U.S. Government

"I don't know why they call it a green card when it takes so much red tape to get one."

In this part . . .

In order to pass the civics portion of your naturalization interview, you'll be asked to demonstrate a basic understanding of the United States government and how it works. But more than just fulfilling a test requirement, finding out about the U.S. government will put you in touch with what it truly means to be an American and the benefits, freedoms, and responsibilities that go with it. Our government is a government "of the people," but how can you participate if you don't understand how things work? This part will familiarize you with our three-branch system of government; the duties and limitations of the executive, legislative, and judicial branches; as well as the structure and powers of state and local governments.

Chapter 9

Guaranteeing Our Freedom: The Declaration of Independence and the Constitution

In This Chapter

- Forming a new nation
- Recognizing the importance of the Declaration
- Understanding the Constitution
- Getting familiar with the Bill of Rights
- Identifying the amendments to the Constitution

The two most important documents in the United States are the Declaration of Independence and the Constitution. These two documents form the foundation of the U.S. government. The events that led up to their creation were the same events that transformed 13 British colonies into the most powerful country in the world.

If you understand the Declaration of Independence and the Constitution and the history behind them, you'll understand the principles of the U.S. government and you'll know why Americans take their freedoms so seriously. You'll also be prepared for a big part of the civics portion of your citizenship test. In this chapter, we introduce you to both documents, filling you in on their meaning and importance.

Announcing the Birth of a New Nation: The Declaration of Independence

At the time it was written, the Declaration of Independence served as an official notice to the world that a new, independent nation, the United States of America, was born. Like a birth announcement for a new baby, the Declaration notes the exact day when formal separation from England took place: July 4, 1776. We celebrate Independence Day in the U.S. every July 4, to mark this important anniversary.

In addition to establishing the U.S. as a new nation, the Declaration of Independence outlines the specific reasons the American colonists wanted to form a free country, separate and independent from England.

Leading up to the Declaration: The colonists' complaints

Between 1689 and 1763, the British kings had allowed the American colonies a lot of freedom. They didn't do this because they were a particularly nice guys — their energies were just needed elsewhere, because England was at war with France at the time. When the war between France and England ended, King George III turned his attention back toward the American colonies. Because the war had left England with a lot of financial debt, King George III thought getting extra revenue from the colonies was a good idea. And, as you may have guessed, the colonists didn't think George's idea was as good as George thought it was.

Of the many grievances the colonists had with the king, the most important problems that led them to declare their freedom and fight the Revolutionary War were the following:

- **Taxation without representation:** Even though England required the colonists to pay hefty taxes to the British government, the colonies were not allowed to send representatives to the legislature to vote on those taxes or fight for their interests.
- **Quartering:** Colonists were required by British law to house British soldiers in their homes.
- **Land policy:** England restricted the colonists to only settling land located east of the Appalachian Mountains.
- **Trade restrictions:** England forced the colonist to pay high taxes for trading with any country other than England. Of course, England also expected to pay less money for goods than the colonists would have made by trading with the rest of the world.

  Needless to say, King George III did not believe in free trade. In fact, trade restrictions had been the cause of several violent confrontations between the colonists and the British. The most famous of these were the Boston Massacre (in which five colonists were killed by British soldiers) and the Boston Tea Party (in which colonists protesting a tax on imported tea dumped all the tea on board ships in Boston Harbor into the sea). These demonstrations only provoked harsher penalties and more taxes from the king.

Sowing the seeds of government: What the Declaration says

It took Thomas Jefferson 17 days to write the original Declaration of Independence. Benjamin Franklin and John Adams then helped Jefferson revise his first draft. They sent their masterpiece to the Continental Congress on July 2, 1776, and after two days of debate and more changes, the final draft of the Declaration of Independence was adopted.

Seeking the actual documents

Each year, more than a million visitors flock to the Rotunda of the National Archives in Washington, D.C., to view the Declaration of Independence, the Constitution, and the Bill of Rights. As we write this, the National Archives and Records Administration (NARA) is undergoing extensive renovations that are not expected to be complete until September 2003. In the meantime, you can view the documents online at www.nara.gov. Check the NARA Web site for the latest updates on reopening dates before planning a visit, or call 866-325-7208.

Visiting Independence Hall

The Constitution and the Declaration of Independence really come to life when you visit Independence National Historical Park in downtown Philadelphia, Pennsylvania. The Park spans approximately 45 acres and includes about 20 buildings open to the public. You can tour Independence Hall, where both the Declaration of Independence and the Constitution were created and where much of our country's most important early events took place. The room is restored to look just as it did in 1787, including original chairs and inkstands.

Congress Hall was the home of the U.S. Congress from 1790 to 1800 and was the location of President George Washington's second inauguration and President John Adams's inauguration. One block to the north of these buildings is the Liberty Bell, which was rung from the belfry of Independence Hall to celebrate the historic events of July 4, 1776.

Administered by the National Park Service, Independence National Historical Park is open every day from 9 a.m. to 5 p.m. Hours for some buildings are extended on weekends in the spring and throughout the week in July and August. Some buildings may be closed on January 1, Thanksgiving, and December 25. Admission to the park is free. For more information, write to Independence National Historical Park, 313 Walnut St., Philadelphia, PA 19106, or call 215-597-8974 or 215-597-1785 (TTY). You can also visit the park's Web site at www.nps.gov/inde/.

A total of 47 revisions were made to the Declaration of Independence before it was presented to the Continental Congress. After voting for independence on July 2, 1776, Congress then continued to improve the document, making 39 additional changes before its final adoption on July 4.

The first part of the Declaration declares the break with England and the reasons why the colonists thought they were justified in taking this important action. The second part of the Declaration lists the colonists' complaints against England's King George III. The Declaration of Independence concludes that, because of the king's oppressive acts, the colonies had the right to declare themselves free and independent states.

Aside from the long list of grievances with King George III, Jefferson made two key points in the Declaration of Independence that he said were "self-evident":

- **That "all men are created equal" and have been given by God certain rights — namely, the right to "Life, Liberty, and the pursuit of Happiness" — that no one can take away.** This means that anyone who lives in the United States has these rights, regardless of whether he or she is a U.S. citizen.
- **That a government exists only by the consent of the governed.** This means that if the citizens of a country feel that their government is not carrying out their wishes, they have the right and the duty to change or do away with that government.

The principles Jefferson set forth in the Declaration of Independence were the ideals the Founding Fathers later incorporated into the Constitution and the Bill of Rights.

Recognizing the Supreme Law of the Land: The Constitution

The most important document in the United States is the U.S. Constitution, which was signed by the delegates to the Constitutional Convention on September 17, 1787. The Founding Fathers wrote the Constitution to be a "rulebook" of how our new nation was expected to operate. After fighting so hard to win their freedom in the Revolutionary War, the Founding Fathers wanted to ensure that this nation could never come under tyrannical rule again. They needed a system of government where the citizens had a say in their government at the local, state, and national levels. For this reason, the Constitution was written to protect the essential "self-evident" rights that Thomas Jefferson wrote about in the Declaration of Independence. The Constitution doesn't *give* Americans their freedoms, but rather acts to guarantee or protect those freedoms.

The U.S. Constitution has lasted for over 200 years, through many changes in the country and the world. The Constitution is known as the "supreme law of the land" for these reasons:

- No other laws may contradict any of the principles set forth in the Constitution.
- No person is exempt from following the laws set forth in the Constitution. For that matter, the government itself must also adhere to the principles of the Constitution.
- The Constitution guarantees the rights and freedoms of all people living in the U.S., whether they are U.S. citizens or not.

Keeping it simple: What the Constitution says

Through the years, the Constitution has been the subject of countless debates. To this day, legal experts fight over the constitutionality of certain laws. People disagree over how to interpret the Constitution when it comes to important issues like gun control, the place of religion in government, and even the immigration and naturalization process. Politicians argue about the Founding Fathers' intent when they wrote the document.

Even though many scholars and legal experts have studied it, the Constitution is essentially quite simple, based on the following principles:

- **Popular sovereignty:** The U.S. is a government by the people, for the people. The ultimate political authority does not reside in the government or in any single government official; instead, the ultimate political authority rests with the people. The people have the right to change or abolish their government or to amend their Constitution, and no one can take that right away from them. The Founding Fathers thought this principle was important to protect Americans from ever coming under tyrannical rule, like they had been under King George III.
- **Rule of law:** The U.S. government is guided by a set of laws rather than by any individual or group of people, and the government possesses only the powers that are specifically granted to it in the Constitution. This means that if something isn't in the Constitution, the government doesn't have the authority to do it. Designed to protect individual rights and liberties, the rule of law calls for both individuals and the government to obey the law. In other words, the government is as accountable to the law as any individual. The rule of law prevents any one person or political group from gaining enough power that they can overpower the rights of others.
- **Separation of powers and a system of checks and balances:** The Constitution establishes that no part of the U.S. government has final authority. The Founding Fathers wanted to make sure that no one branch of government could ever dominate over the other two branches. Although the separation of powers between the executive, legislative, and judicial branches is one of the basic laws of the Constitution, there are many places in which the responsibilities and powers of government branches intentionally overlap. This is known as the system of checks and balances, because one branch is always checking and balancing the activities of the others.

- **Federalism:** The Constitution created a *federal* system of government, meaning that the government's power is shared between the national government and the individual state governments. The Founding Fathers wanted to make sure that the federal government could never grow strong enough to overpower the will of the individual states. To avoid problems, the Constitution specifically withholds various powers from the states, the central government, or both, giving the federal government final power over some matters and state and local governments the last word on others.
- **Judicial review:** Although the Constitution makes no specific references to the power of the Supreme Court to check abuses of the legislative and executive branches, by the early 1800s the court had been called upon to review the constitutionality of both federal and state laws and acts. The right to hold laws unconstitutional actually goes back before the signing of the Constitution; some colonial judges had invalidated state laws on the grounds that they violated that state's constitution. Through practice, the Supreme Court has become the chief interpreter of the Constitution. The court's job is to examine laws that are challenged on the basis of being unconstitutional. If the Supreme Court finds the law in question to be in accordance with the Constitution, the law stands. If, on the other hand, the Supreme Court rules that the law goes beyond the powers granted to the government by the Constitution, then it cannot be considered a law, because it goes against the supreme law of the land. The court's implied powers became more official in 1803 with the historic *Marbury* v. *Madison* decision, in which the Court assumed the authority to declare acts of Congress and the president unconstitutional.

Understanding the constitutional articles

The original body of the United States Constitution consists of seven articles or sections, which each discuss a different aspect of the government, or rules for how the country is to be run. The following list gives an overview of those articles:

- **Article I:** Establishes the legislative branch of the U.S. government (the House of Representatives and the Senate) and provides rules for how representatives and senators are to be elected, their duties, and the limits of their powers in government.
- **Article II:** Establishes the executive branch of the U.S. government (the presidency), outlines the requirements for holding office, and provides details on how the president is to be elected and the scope of presidential power, including *impeachment* (the process of removing a president from office).
- **Article III:** Establishes the judicial branch of the U.S. government with the forming of the Supreme Court and outlines its judiciary powers.
- **Article IV:** Deals with matters of the individual states, including how new states can be admitted to the union, the government's guarantee to states, and rules for how the states should legally interact with one another.
- **Article V:** Establishes the procedure for amending or changing the constitution (see the nearby sidebar "Changing the Constitution" for more information).
- **Article VI:** Outlines the legal status of the Constitution. This includes the law of the land and the oath of service, which binds legislators, executives, and judicial officers of the U.S. Article VI also outlines the responsibilities and procedures for paying off financial debts the states accumulated before the signing of the Constitution.
- **Article VII:** States that ratification by a minimum of nine states is enough to legally establish the Constitution between those states.

Checks and balances

The executive, legislative, and judicial branches of government check and balance each other in many ways. For instance, the president has the power to appoint federal judges, ambassadors, and other high government officials, but the United States Senate must confirm those appointments before they can go into effect. In this way, the power of the president is "checked" by Congress.

Likewise, the president has the power to *veto* or reject laws that Congress enacts. (*Veto* means "I forbid" in Latin.) Congress may, however, override the president's veto with a two-thirds vote of both houses (the House of Representatives and the Senate).

The Supreme Court retains the right to call the activities of the legislative and/or judicial branches of government unconstitutional or illegal because they violate the principles set forth in the Constitution.

Making a good idea better: The Bill of Rights

Even before the U.S. Constitution was ratified, people began talking about how to improve it. The Founding Fathers believed they had written the document in such a way that individual rights required no express protection. But many people in 1789 were concerned about protecting certain freedoms and rights that the original document neglected to mention. After all, they had just fought the Revolutionary War — they knew what it was like to *not* have rights and they didn't want to give away the freedoms they fought so hard for. It was the promise of a Bill of Rights to be added to the Constitution that helped get the document ratified in the first place.

On December 15, 1791, the first ten amendments — also known as the Bill of Rights — were added to the United States Constitution, thereby guaranteeing important rights to both citizens and noncitizens alike. The Bill of Rights specifically restricts government invasion of certain individual liberties and prohibits the establishment of any official religion. Nearly two-thirds of the Bill of Rights is devoted to safeguarding the rights of those suspected or accused of crimes.

Here's an explanation of the ten amendments that make up the Bill of Rights:

- **First Amendment:** Guarantees the rights of freedom of speech, religion, press, peaceable assembly, and the right to formally complain to the government. This important amendment prevents the government from censoring citizens or the press and allows citizens to peaceably protest government policies and hold their government accountable. It also safeguards freedom from governmental religious persecution.
- **Second Amendment:** Guarantees the right of the people to keep and bear arms or weapons.
- **Third Amendment:** States that the government is not allowed to house soldiers in private homes during peacetime without the homeowner's permission.
- **Fourth Amendment:** Guarantees the right of the people to be secure in their persons, houses, papers, and effects, against unreasonable searches and seizures. In other words, the government cannot search or seize a person's property without a warrant — an official document, issued by a judge, that confirms the government has a legitimate reason to conduct the search.
- **Fifth Amendment:** States that a person cannot be tried twice for the same crime and cannot be compelled to testify against himself or herself.

- **Sixth Amendment:** Gives a person charged with a crime the right to a fair and speedy public trial by an impartial jury, to confront witnesses against him/her, and to have legal representation. This means that even if the accused can't afford a lawyer, one will be provided to him or her free of charge.
- **Seventh Amendment:** Guarantees a trial by jury in most federal civil lawsuits.
- **Eighth Amendment:** Prohibits excessive or unusual bail or fines or cruel and unusual punishment.
- **Ninth Amendment:** States that the people have rights other than those specifically mentioned in the Constitution. In other words, just because the Constitution didn't specifically mention it, doesn't mean it's not your right.
- **Tenth Amendment:** Says that any power not given to the federal government by the Constitution is a power either of the states or of the people.

Keeping up with the times: Constitutional amendments

As time passed, Congress found more reasons to amend the Constitution and adopt new rules for the country to live by. Of all the thousands of amendment proposals put before Congress, only 33 managed to obtain the necessary two-thirds approval vote. Of those 33, only 27 received approval from at least three-fourths of the state legislatures.

Here's a summary of the rest of the constitutional amendments:

- **Eleventh Amendment (adopted 1798):** Prevents citizens of a state or foreign country from suing another state in federal court.
- **Twelfth Amendment (adopted 1804):** Gives the president and vice president separate ballots in the Electoral College system. Before the adoption of the Twelfth Amendment, the candidate with the most electoral votes became the president and the candidate with the second highest number of electoral votes became the vice president. This resulted in some strained and underproductive political pairings. (Imagine if George W. Bush had Al Gore as his vice president.)
- **Thirteenth Amendment (adopted 1865):** Ended slavery in the United States.
- **Fourteenth Amendment (adopted 1868):** Guarantees the citizenship of all people born or naturalized in the United States. This amendment also deals with matters of public debt, and says that a given state's population determines the number of representatives it can send to Congress.
- **Fifteenth Amendment (adopted 1870):** Guarantees the right to vote to African Americans and former slaves.
- **Sixteenth Amendment (adopted 1913):** Gives Congress the right to collect a federal income tax.
- **Seventeenth Amendment (adopted 1917):** Guarantees the people the right to directly elect senators and sets up rules for Senate terms as well as how to fill Senate vacancies that occur in the middle of a senator's term.
- **Eighteenth Amendment (adopted 1919):** Made it illegal to produce or sell liquor in the United States. The Eighteenth Amendment holds the distinction of being the only amendment to be repealed (see the Twenty-first Amendment, later in this list).
- **Nineteenth Amendment (adopted 1920):** Guarantees women the right to vote.

- **Twentieth Amendment (adopted 1933):** Changed the date the president takes office from March to January, as well as set forth requirements for Senate assembly.
- **Twenty-first Amendment (adopted 1933):** The Twenty-first Amendment repealed the Eighteenth Amendment, which was the prohibition on liquor. (The only way the Constitution provides for repealing an amendment is to pass another amendment.)
- **Twenty-second Amendment (adopted 1951):** Established a two-term limit for the president.
- **Twenty-third Amendment (adopted 1961):** Gave residents of the District of Columbia the right to vote in presidential and vice presidential elections.
- **Twenty-fourth Amendment (adopted 1964):** Guarantees citizens the right to vote for president, vice president, and members of Congress without having to pay a voting tax.
- **Twenty-fifth Amendment (adopted 1967):** Gives the vice president power to assume the role of president if the president dies, becomes disabled, is impeached, or resigns.
- **Twenty-sixth Amendment (adopted 1971):** Gives the right to vote to citizens at least 18 years of age.
- **Twenty-seventh Amendment (adopted 1992):** Says that no law that changes the salary of senators or representatives can take effect until an election of representatives has a chance to intervene.

Changing the Constitution

The main body of the Constitution has remained unchanged since its adoption, but the constitution has been *amended,* or changed. Amendments are the government's way of keeping up with the times and allowing laws to change with the country's needs and circumstances. Article V offers two ways to propose amendments to the Constitution:

- **A vote of two-thirds from both houses of Congress — the Senate and the House of Representatives — is enough to propose a new constitutional amendment.**
- **Two-thirds of the state legislatures can ask Congress to call a national convention to propose amendments.** Although this is a legal and legitimate way of proposing amendments, up to this point in U.S. history, this method has never actually been put into practice.

After an amendment has been proposed, it must be *ratified,* or accepted, by three-fourths of the state legislatures before it can actually become part of the Constitution. In theory, an amendment can also be ratified by special ratifying conventions in three-fourths of the states, although this method has only been used once — to ratify the Twenty-first Amendment, which repealed the *prohibition* (ban) on alcohol.

Chapter 10

Understanding the United States Federal Government

In This Chapter

- Looking at the organization of the U.S. government
- Meeting the members of the executive branch
- Making laws with the legislative branch
- Recognizing the role of the judicial branch

In order to pass the citizenship test, you'll need a basic understanding of the United States government. If you've read Chapter 9, on the Declaration of Independence and the Constitution, you already understand the most important principles that shaped the U.S. federal government. The Founding Fathers, in an effort to protect the freedoms they fought so hard for in the Revolutionary War, wanted to make absolutely sure the federal government could never grow strong enough to overthrow the will of the people. They thought long and hard about how best to create a structure of government that would serve the population of the U.S. without limiting their freedom.

In this chapter, we cover the three branches of government, their duties, and the important people responsible for running them. You'll see how the various branches share duties and check and balance each other to ensure fairness and control government power. The United States government is a huge entity that affects the lives of not only American citizens, but also of people throughout the world. Understanding how it functions is the first step toward getting involved in this government "of the people."

Seeing How the U.S. Government Works

Self-government — a government for the people, by the people — is a cornerstone principle of the United States Constitution. Nearly everything the Founding Fathers put into the document was designed to protect U.S. citizens from ever having to worry about the government or any branch of the government. It was also designed so that no one individual could ever have the opportunity to overpower the will of the majority. The brilliant insight the Founding Fathers displayed when structuring the United States has allowed the Constitution to last more than 200 years, despite the many changes and transitions the world has gone through during that time.

The rights and duties of U.S. citizens

Thomas Jefferson wrote in the Declaration of Independence that "all men are created equal" and "are endowed by their Creator with certain unalienable Rights" — namely the right to "Life, Liberty, and the pursuit of Happiness." The Constitution also guarantees everyone living in the U.S. freedom of speech, religion, press, and other important rights outlined in the Constitution's Bill of Rights.

Jefferson's other key point in the Declaration was that a government exists only by the consent of the governed. If the citizens feel that their government is not carrying out their wishes, they have the right and the duty to change or do away with that government.

In order to protect the government that guarantees their inherent rights, all Americans have important duties to their country, including the following:

- **Voting:** Being a good U.S. citizen begins at the voting booth. Through their votes, citizens can and do have the power to change their government. If an elected official doesn't live up to a majority of his or her constituents' expectations, those constituents can choose not to reelect that official to another term in office. (*Constituents* are the people who live in an elected official's district or districts.) Citizens also have the power to elect different representatives, change laws, or even change the constitution itself, if a majority of the citizens agrees.

  Not only do good citizens need to vote, they need to be informed voters. Being confused about the issues and candidates is easy if you get all your political information from paid political ads that tell only one side of the story. Becoming educated is time consuming, but the stakes are high enough to merit getting the real facts from a variety of sources, such as newspapers, radio and television news sources, Web sites, and perhaps most important, the words of the candidates themselves.
- **Serving on juries:** The government may call upon citizens to serve on a jury. Jurors perform an essential role in sustaining the U.S. system of justice, so jury duty is an important responsibility of every U.S. citizen. The right to a trial by a jury of your peers is guaranteed in the Constitution, and a jury's fair and honest decisions help protect U.S. citizens' fundamental right to justice for all.
- **Obeying laws:** Everyone needs to obey the laws of the community, state, and country in which he or she lives, as well as support the Constitution of the United States.
- **Paying taxes:** All persons living in the U.S. are expected to pay income and other required taxes, honestly and on time, as outlined in the Sixteenth Amendment.
- **Defending the country:** Male citizens are required to bear arms for the armed forces or otherwise perform services for the government when required in times of war or crisis. Service is only required if a draft is reinstated. The U.S. military converted to an all-volunteer system in 1975, but Congress retains the right to reinstate the draft should the country ever need additional military personnel.

The system of checks and balances

Problem: How to structure a sound, strong, central government, while simultaneously ensuring that no individual or group within that government could ever become powerful enough to overpower the will of the states or the majority of its people.

Solution: A structure of three separate governmental branches, each with its own distinct powers, that operate independently of each other while at the same time interact with each other.

Voting 101: Who, where, and when

Although there are slight variations in voting laws from state to state, all states require voters to be U.S. citizens at least 18 years of age. The states have varying requirements in regard to convicted felons; some do not allow convicted felons to vote, and others do, providing they have paid their debts to society. Most states also require voters to be of sound mental health. For state-by-state voting eligibility details, visit `www.fec.gov/pages/Voteinst.htm`.

You can obtain a voter-registration application from local election officials in your county, or through registration outreach programs sponsored by groups like the League of Women Voters. You can also register to vote at state Department of Motor Vehicles (DMV) or drivers' licensing offices, at state offices that provide public assistance or programs for the disabled, and at armed-forces recruitment offices. Some states also offer registration opportunities at public libraries, post offices, unemployment offices, and public high schools and universities.

In the U.S., presidential elections are always held on the first Tuesday after the first Monday in November. In non-presidential years, national elections may be held to elect senators and representatives. State and local elections vary, so be sure to keep up with current events in your local community.

The three-branch system of government outlined in the U.S. Constitution accomplishes three important things:

- It divides the duties and responsibilities of the federal government.
- It keeps the federal government from ever gaining enough power to overthrow the will of the individual states.
- It constantly checks and balances the division of governmental power.

The power of any one branch cannot grow too large, because the three branches of government are constantly looking over each other's shoulders. Some examples of how governmental power in the United States is checked and balanced include the following:

- Congress (legislative branch) has the power to impeach the president (executive branch) and federal court justices and judges (judicial branch), if Congress deems it necessary.
- Although Congress (legislative branch) has the power to pass bills to become law, the president (executive branch) has the power to veto those bills.
- The Supreme Court (judicial branch) can declare Congressional laws (legislative branch) or presidential actions (executive branch) unconstitutional.

Identifying the Duties and Functions of the Executive Branch

Comprised of the president, the vice president, the executive departments, and independent agencies, each part of the executive branch has specific powers and duties, outlined in the following sections.

Understanding how political parties influence the U.S.

A political party is a group of people who have similar ideas about how the government should be run. Political parties distribute information about their candidates and the party platform (views on important issues). Because there is strength in numbers, political parties can accomplish more to further their causes working together as a group to raise funds and get the word out about their candidates. The party also works to promote its platform.

The Democratic and Republican parties are by far the largest political parties in the United States, although many other smaller parties, like the Libertarian Party, the Green Party, and the Reform Party, exist. Some candidates don't belong to any political party at all and are considered independent. You probably won't hear much about independent candidates, because it's difficult for an individual to match the economic strength of a party. Likewise, many independent candidates' campaigns get little or no media coverage.

By registering to vote under a political party, a voter can still vote any way he or she chooses on election day. In other words, if you register as a Democrat, you're under no obligation to vote for the Democratic candidate.

Like certain candidates, some voters also prefer to remain independent and not register for any political party. Depending on where you live, however, there may be advantages to registering with a party. Some states restrict voting in primary elections — the elections that determine which candidates will actually run for President — to those who have declared a party affiliation (and sometimes that party must be Democratic or Republican). Some voters get around this loophole by changing their party affiliation just to be able to vote in the primaries, then changing it back to independent for the general election. For state-by-state party requirements on voting in primary elections, visit the Federal Election Commission Web site at `www.fec.gov/votregis/primaryvoting.htm`.

The President

The president is the leader of the U.S. as well as the Commander in Chief of the military. He is responsible for directing the federal government and enforcing federal laws and treaties, conducting foreign policy, and approving or vetoing bills passed by Congress. The president also advises Congress on the nation's needs. In addition, the Constitution gives the president the power, "when appropriate," to pardon people found guilty of breaking federal law.

In order to become President of the United States, you must be a natural-born citizen, be at least 35 years old by the time you will serve, and have lived in the United States at least 14 years over the course of your life.

The Vice President

Occupying the second highest office in the U.S., the vice president stands ready to assume the duties of president if the current president dies, becomes disabled, or is otherwise unable to serve. The vice president also presides over the Senate and casts the deciding vote in cases of a tie. The office of vice president carries the same age, citizenship, and residency requirements as the president (see the preceding section).

The Cabinet and executive departments

Fifteen departments currently help in carrying out government policies that affect nearly every aspect of our daily lives:

- **The Department of State** handles matters of international diplomacy, issues visas, and manages U.S. embassies and consulates.
- **The Department of the Treasury** is responsible for printing currency and managing the country's finances.
- **The Department of Defense** manages the U.S. military and is responsible for protecting the country.
- **The Department of Justice** acts as the country's law-enforcement agency.
- **The Department of the Interior** manages publicly held U.S. lands.
- **The Department of Agriculture** manages the nation's food supply by, among other duties, helping American farmers and regulating food-safety laws.
- **The Department of Commerce** deals with issues of trade, employment, and economic growth.
- **The Department of Labor** protects America's workforce by enforcing labor laws and regulating wages and benefits.
- **The Department of Health and Human Services** advises and protects Americans on matters of health.
- **The Department of Housing and Urban Development** helps Americans find housing and regulates fair housing practices.
- **The Department of Transportation** regulates transportation safety as well as maintains and oversees the nation's transportation systems.
- **The Department of Education** manages and regulates schools and other educational institutions.
- **The Department of Energy** oversees matters of energy including conserving energy, protecting America's oil reserves, and planning for future needs.
- **The Department of Veterans Affairs** administers benefits to America's military veterans.
- **The Department of Homeland Security** protects the country against further terrorist attacks, including managing most components of immigration.

The heads of the executive departments, usually called *secretaries,* make up the president's *Cabinet,* or official group of advisors. The Cabinet guides the president on policy issues and advises him on how best to implement policies.

Although the heads of most of the departments are known as secretaries, like the Secretary of Defense or the Secretary of Agriculture, the head of the Department of Justice is known as the Attorney General.

Independent agencies

Dozens of executive branch independent agencies serve very specific and sometimes even temporary needs the government may have. Examples include the Commission on Civil Rights, the Federal Trade Commission (FTC), the National Labor Relations Board, the Federal Election Commission (FEC), the Small Business Administration (SBA), and the United States Postal Service (USPS). These agencies change according to the country's current needs and circumstances.

Understanding how and why the Electoral College elects our president

Many people are surprised to find out that the President and Vice President of the United States are not directly elected by a popular vote, but rather by members of the Electoral College — a group of elected officials from the 50 states and the District of Columbia. Confusing as it may be, our Founding Fathers had some tough choices to make when they implemented the idea of the Electoral College in the Constitution.

Some of the framers of the Constitution believed the selection of the president should be left to the U.S. Congress or each state's legislature. These plans were ultimately rejected because they unbalanced the power between the federal and state governments. Others thought the average American voter was capable of making wise choices when it came to electing the leader of the land, while still others believed the decision was far too important to leave up to the general populace.

Article II, Section I of the Constitution represents the final compromise — a system in which each state is represented by the same number of electors as the state has U.S. Senators and Representatives. This gives each state representation based upon the number of people who live there. The distribution of electoral votes among the states can vary every ten years, depending on the results of the census (the official government count of the country's population).

The Electoral College selects a president by majority vote — if no candidate receives a majority of electoral votes then it's up to the House of Representatives to choose a winner.

No constitutional provision or federal law requires electors to vote according to the results of the popular vote in their states, so a candidate can win the popular vote but lose the electoral vote, as was the case in the 2000 presidential election. Any candidate who wins a majority of the popular vote also has a darned good chance of winning the Electoral College, but there are no guarantees. To reduce the chances of this uncomfortable situation arising, some states require electors to pledge to cast their votes according to the popular vote. These pledges fall into two categories — electors bound by state law and those bound by pledges to political parties. Penalties and fines vary from absolutely nothing, to replacement by another elector, to a fourth-degree felony in New Mexico. The District of Columbia and 26 states all have some type of law governing electors; electors in the remaining states, although expected to vote according to popular vote, are not legally compelled to do so.

For this reason, the Electoral College system remains controversial to this day. Many people believe it should be abolished so that the president can be elected by a direct popular vote. However, a constitutional amendment would need to be passed in order to change the current voting system.

Understanding the Duties and Functions of the Legislative Branch

The legislative branch of the U.S. government consists of the Senate and the House of Representative, collectively known as *Congress.* The Senate and House are primarily responsible for making the laws that govern the U.S. Sometimes they work separately, although they also share many of their duties and responsibilities. You can find out a lot more about Congress by checking our *Congress For Dummies* by David Silverberg (published by Wiley).

Working together: The United States Congress

The two houses of Congress have some very specific and separate responsibilities (covered in the following sections). However, the Constitution declares that both the Senate and the House of Representatives share duties related to:

- Regulating money and printing currency
- Borrowing money on behalf of the government
- Levying and collecting taxes
- Regulating trade, both among states and with foreign countries
- Regulating the system of weights and measures
- Maintaining the defense of the nation and declaring war
- Maintaining the U.S. military
- Making laws regarding naturalization
- Establishing post offices
- Passing laws to govern the District of Columbia

The Constitution also lists some things that Congress may *never* do, specifically:

- Tax exports
- Pass trade laws that do not treat all the states equally
- Spend tax money without a law that authorizes that spending
- Authorize any titles of nobility
- Pass any law that punishes someone for an act that was legal when the act was committed
- Pass any law that takes away a person's right to trial in court

Meeting your senators

Each state sends two senators to the United States Congress. Each senator represents the whole of his or her state, not any specific district. A senator must be at least 30 years old, be a resident of the state he or she represents, and have been a U.S. citizen for at least 9 years. Elected for six-year terms, as per the Seventeenth Amendment, there is currently no limit to the number of terms a senator may serve.

Duties specifically delegated to the senate are

- Determining guilt or innocence in impeachment cases
- Confirming presidential appointments
- Ratifying treaties between the U.S. and foreign governments

Meeting your representatives

The United States census, taken once every ten years, determines the number of congressional representatives a state may send to Congress. Each state, regardless of how small its population, is allowed at least one representative. Most states are divided into districts with each member of the House representing his or her own district rather than the state as a whole. The District of Columbia (Washington, D.C.) also sends a single representative to Congress, although he or she does not vote. Currently, 435 members serve in the House of Representatives.

To qualify to be a representative, a person must be at least 25 years old, be a resident of the state he or she represents, and have been a U.S. citizen for at least 7 years.

Contacting your elected officials

Government representatives are technically employees of the people, so as a citizen, it's important to let them know how you feel about important issues. Each call, fax, letter, or e-mail sent to an elected official's office is recorded. If enough people call a representative about any given issue, it can have a big effect on the way that representative votes. Because a representative depends on his or her constituents at reelection time, he or she has a vested interest in keeping the majority of those constituents happy.

Write to the President, the First Lady, the Vice President, or the wife of the Vice President in care of the White House:

The White House
1600 Pennsylvia Ave. NW
Washington, DC 20500
Phone: 202-456-1414
(comment line for the hearing impaired: 202-456-6213)
Fax: 202-456-2461

You can e-mail them at the following addresses:

- President George W. Bush: `president@whitehouse.gov`
- Vice President Dick Cheney: `vice.president@whitehouse.gov`
- Laura Bush: `first.lady@whitehouse.gov`
- Lynne Cheney: `mrs.cheney@whitehouse.gov`

You can get information about your representative's local office in the Blue Pages of your telephone book, or by calling the U.S. House of Representatives switchboard operator at 202-225-3121 to get directly in touch with your congressional representative's office. In addition, you may choose to visit your representative's Web site to e-mail him or her (find your representative's Web site by going to `www.house.gov`). Send your representative a letter by addressing your envelope to:

Office of Representative [Name]
United States House of Representatives
Washington, DC 20510

To get in touch with your senators, you can also use the Blue Pages of your phone book, or phone the U.S. Capitol switchboard at 202-224-3121 and an operator will connect you directly with the Senate office you request. You can e-mail your senators from their individual Web sites (find your senators' Web sites by going to `www.senate.gov`). Send senators a letter by addressing envelopes to:

Office of Senator [Name]
United States Senate
Washington, DC 20510

Duties of the House include

- Introducing budget and tax bills to Congress
- *Impeaching,* or putting on trial, government officials who may have committed some crime or gross misconduct

You can really see the Constitution's system of checks and balances at work when you study the separate duties of the Senate and the House of Representatives. Although the House can impeach an official, the Senate must determine final guilt or innocence. Although the president can appoint government officials, the Senate must approve those appointments.

Passing laws

In spite of all their shared and separate duties, Congress spends most of its time passing laws. New federal laws can start in either the Senate or the House of Representatives. The procedure of getting a law passed may seem complex, but it's all part of the system of checks and balances designed to keep the country fair and democratic. Before a law can pass, a lot of people have the chance to discuss it, ask questions about it and its impact, and change or amend it if they think that's necessary.

The process begins when a senator or representative introduces a bill that he or she wants to become law; the only exception is that only representatives are allowed to introduce tax or budget bills. Of course, long before the bill is introduced in Congress, citizen activists and political groups have usually been hard at work to gain support for their causes, bringing the issue to their representatives' attention.

Understanding the Duties of the Judicial Branch

Made up of the system of federal courts, the judicial branch of government interprets the laws of the United States. Federal court duties include

- Explaining the meaning of the Constitution, the laws of the United States, and its treaties
- Settling legal disagreements between citizens of different states
- Settling disputes between or among two or more states
- Settling legal questions between the states and the federal government
- Settling legal disputes between individuals and the federal government
- Settling disagreements between states and foreign governments and/or their citizens
- Naturalizing U.S. citizens

Making sense of the federal court system

The entire federal court system makes up the judicial branch. The court system is *hierarchical,* meaning that each court has greater power than, and can overturn decisions made by, the court below it.

The courts in the federal court system include the following:

- **The Supreme Court:** The highest court of the land. A Supreme Court ruling constitutes the final decision on a case.
- **Circuit courts of appeals:** The country's 11 circuit courts routinely hear appeals from lower courts when their participants believe the lower courts' decisions to be unjust.
- **District courts:** The lowest of the federal courts, district courts determine rulings for people accused of breaking federal laws.
- **Special courts:** Congress has also established some special courts that have very specific and limited jurisdiction: Court of Claims, Customs Court, Court of Customs and Patent Appeals, and Court of Military Appeals.

Consulting the ultimate constitutional authority: The Supreme Court

Nine judges (or *justices,* as they're called when talking about the Supreme Court) preside over the highest court of the land. One of the justices, known as the *Chief Justice,* acts as the court's leader. The Supreme Court can overturn decisions made by lower courts as well as declare state or federal laws *unconstitutional,* or against the supreme law of the land. If a majority of the justices feel a law disagrees with the Constitution, it must be abolished. The Supreme Court's decision is final.

Most of the Supreme Court's cases are *appellate* cases, meaning the participants are *appealing* a decision made by the lower courts that they believe to be unfair. The only cases that actually originate in the Supreme Court are cases involving foreign diplomats.

Chapter 11

Looking at State and Local Governments

In This Chapter

- Understanding the roles of government
- Governing at the state level
- Making sense of local governments

The United States is a *federalist* union, which means that national, state, and even local governments share power. Although some differences exist, the three levels of government represent a *republican* form of government. In a republican government, the supreme power lies with the citizens, who have the power to elect their representatives. Obviously, a government like this cannot work without the involvement of an active, informed citizenry, and likewise, citizens have a duty to interact with their government at the local, state, and federal levels.

State and local elections can greatly impact the day-to-day lives of the people who live within their jurisdictions — sometimes in more profound ways than the federal government. You're more likely to have more personal interaction with your local or state government — state governments are smaller than the federal government and they have fewer people to interact with, and local governments are even smaller than state governments. The smaller the government entity, the quicker and more efficiently it can respond to the specific needs of its people.

In this chapter, we familiarize you with how state and local governments work in the U.S., and tell you how you can get involved and be informed about the government actions that directly affect the area where you live. We also get you ready to answer possible questions about your state and local government during your naturalization test.

Looking at State Governments

The United States Constitution gives a great deal of governmental power to the individual states and ensures that the federal government can never grow so strong that it overpowers the will of the states. (For more details on the Constitution, see Chapter 9.)

Even though there were only 13 states when the U.S. was formed, the Founding Fathers knew the union would grow. In order for the states to work productively with the federal government, it was important that each state had the same form of government. (For more information on how the federal government is structured, see Chapter 10.)

It helps to think of state governments as the "little brothers" of the federal government — like brothers, they look a whole lot alike. Here are some ways that the federal government and state governments are similar:

- **All state governments are based upon a constitution.** Each state has its own state constitution.
- **All state governments consist of three branches — the executive, legislative, and judicial branches.** The three branches of state government check and balance each other's powers, just like the three branches of the federal government do.
- **Through their interactions, federal and state governments check and balance each other's powers.**

Identifying the state government structure

Most states, even the ones that provide citizens the opportunity for direct democracy (meaning that individual citizens can petition to put initiatives on election ballots), are *representative democracies,* which means that elected officials make the laws and governmental decisions. Although minor details and legal technicalities vary from state to state, all 50 state governments are comprised of an executive branch, a legislative branch, and a judicial branch, just like the federal government. See Table 11-1 for a comparison of federal and state government roles.

If you're interested in the particular details of your state's government structure, `www.constitution.org` has a link to the full text of each individual state's constitution.

Table 11-1 Federal versus State Governments

Federal Government	State Government
President	Governor
Vice president	Lieutenant governor
Presidential cabinet (the attorney general and the various department secretaries)	Governor's advisors (the attorney general, secretary of state, treasurer, comptroller or auditor, and others who attend to the practical business of running a state)
House of Representatives	House of Representatives*
Senate	Senate*
Federal court system	State court system

** Forty-nine states have bicameral (two-house) legislatures, usually consisting of a Senate and a House of Representatives (there are slight state-to-state differences in what the houses are called; for example, in New York it's call the State Assembly). Nebraska's unicameral (single-house) legislature is the one exception.*

The executive branch

The similarities to the federal government continue even within the three branches of state government. The state level counterpart to the president and his cabinet are the governor and his or her group of advisors. A lieutenant governor stands ready to serve in case the governor dies or becomes incapacitated.

Depending on the state, the governor's advisors may be elected officials or they may be people appointed by the governor. Advisors include a secretary of state, an attorney general, a treasurer or comptroller, as well as other advisors who work on specific issues such as health, labor, education, or public utilities.

They've got you covered: The National Guard

Authorized by state law to serve as a state's *militia,* or citizens' army, the National Guard stands ready to serve their state's governor in times of statewide emergencies and disasters as well to enforce the state's laws in times of crisis such as riots or civil unrest.

Regionally based and recruited, the National Guard is under control of the state government only during peacetime. The guard does double duty by simultaneously being prepared to serve the federal government in wartime emergencies and other matters of national security. To show its appreciation, the federal government provides 90 percent of the National Guard's funding, although this number only amounts to 8 percent of the total U.S. Department of Defense budget.

The requirements for becoming governor vary slightly from state to state, but most require candidates to be U.S. citizens of a certain age (usually 30 or older) and to have been a resident of the state a designated amount of time. Some states restrict the number of terms a governor may serve; others don't. In either case, a governor's term in office is usually two or four years.

A governor's duties mirror the president's, just at the state level instead of the national level. These duties include

- Advising the state legislature on needed laws
- Serving as the head of the state's National Guard, which stands ready to serve and protect the people of the state in times of emergency or crisis
- Calling special sessions of the state legislature
- When appropriate, pardoning or reducing the sentences of people convicted in state courts

The state executive branch carries out the laws passed by the state legislature, but unlike the executive branch of the federal government, the state's executive branch also has the power to propose new laws to the state legislature.

The legislative branch

Every state except Nebraska has a state *bicameral,* or two-house, legislature — usually a house of representatives and a senate, just like the federal government. (Nebraska makes do with just one house in its legislature.) Each state determines its own legislative structure and requirements for holding office. Most state senate terms cover four years, and the typical house of representative term spans two years, although the term lengths vary from state to state. Some states base representation on population, others determine the number of representatives by geographic area. Some states have representatives who only represent a specific district, or area, of the state; other states have representatives who represent the state as a whole.

The main purpose of the legislative branch is to create and carry out laws. The procedure for proposing and passing new laws closely resembles that of the federal government — the senate or house of representative proposes, debates, and passes a bill to the governor for final approval.

The judicial branch

Just like its federal counterpart, the state judicial branch is comprised of a system of courts and judges who decide both *civil cases* (those that deal with a citizen's interaction with the government) and *criminal cases* (where a citizen is accused of breaking the law and committing an actual crime).

Discovering your state representatives

As a potential U.S. citizen, you could be asked to name your state senators and representatives during your citizenship interview. You can find out who your state representatives are by calling your state capitol building switchboard. Find out about county and city governments by contacting your main governing offices like city hall or the county seat. Visit `www.congress.org` for information about representatives on the federal, state, and local levels throughout the country, including the area where you live.

Another good source for finding out about your elected officials is your local newspaper, which often (though not always) includes addresses for state and local representatives. Some telephone books have a Blue Pages section that references important government contact information. With or without Blue Pages, most phonebooks list government contact numbers in a convenient location.

State court duties differ somewhat from federal courts in that their jurisdiction only covers state and local laws. State courts explain state laws and how they should be applied in practice, settle disagreements between citizens, determine guilt or innocence in breaking state laws, and, when appropriate, declare state laws unconstitutional.

Serving the people: The responsibilities of state governments

Because the United States Constitution delegates to the individual states any authority not specifically granted to the federal government, your state government provides many important components that help make living in the U.S. great, including:

- Maintaining a police force to protect the lives and property of the people
- Regulating and maintaining transportation within the state
- Providing for public education
- Regulating business within the state

In addition, the federal and state governments work together as partners on some programs and services, often in the form of the state receiving federal funding and aid for specific programs such as:

- Health care
- Public assistance for those in need
- Improvements in living conditions
- Improvements in working conditions

Just because the states have lots of power doesn't mean they can do whatever they want. Article VI of the United States Constitution says that any state or local law can be called *unconstitutional,* or against the supreme law of the land, if it contradicts our nation's most important document (the Constitution).

The Supreme Court has most often exercised its authority to call state laws unconstitutional in order to protect civil rights. For instance, in 1996, it struck down a Colorado law that deprived persons of protection against discrimination based on sexual orientation under state and local laws.

Knowing citizens' responsibilities to their states

Just as the states exist to protect and serve the people who live within their borders, citizens have the duty to support their state by obeying state laws, paying state taxes, becoming informed about important issues and elections, and exercising their right to vote in all state and local elections.

Understanding state constitutions

State governments operate under the authority of their respective state constitutions — the set of rules for how the state government will conduct itself. (When Americans have a good idea, they stick with it.) Likewise, state constitutions closely resemble the U.S. Constitution and are made up of four sections:

- **The preamble:** The preamble declares the purpose for the constitution and ensures that the governmental authority comes from and rests with the people of the state.
- **The bill of rights:** State constitutions typically duplicate much of the U.S. Constitution's Bill of Rights (see Chapter 9), listing fundamental rights like freedom of speech, freedom of religion, and protection against unlawful search and seizure. In addition, the states sometimes guarantee other rights not specifically set forth in the U.S. Constitution. Examples include specific mention of rights for crime victims, accepting or abolishing the death penalty, equal rights for women, or provisions that protect workers from losing their jobs if they don't belong to a union.
- **An outline for the structure of government:** The outline for the structure of government establishes not only the structure of state government, but also the structure for local governments within the state. State governments represent the needs of their citizens to the federal government. In order to effectively serve its population, the state government must be able to productively interact with local governments within the state. The state constitution details the procedures for how state and local governments should work together as well as how new local governments can be created.
- **Methods for changing the constitution:** Just like the federal government, the states need to keep up with the times, so each state constitution outlines a procedure for amending or changing its constitution in order to best meet the changing needs of the people.

Making Sense of Local Governments

Local governments take their form from the detailed guidelines set forth in a state's constitution, but they're usually not based upon a constitution themselves. Different types of local governments include

- County government
- City government

- Township government
- Village government

In order for a new local government to form, it must receive a *charter,* or official approval from the state legislature. This charter incorporates or creates the new government and county, city, township, or village, and defines its responsibilities, authorities, and governmental structure.

Counties usually operate under the jurisdiction of a board of commissioners or board of supervisors. Some counties also hire a qualified person to work closely with the board of commissioners or board of supervisors and to act as the county manager. In addition, the county may elect certain government officials, such as the sheriff or dogcatcher, who fulfill important community duties.

Most cities and towns elect a mayor, who acts as the chief executive. The mayor works together with a city council — a local version of a state legislature — to pass the laws that govern the city. In some cities, an elected commission does double duty as both the executive and legislative branches of government. In still others, an elected council hires a city manager who works in conjunction with the council to run the city.

The duties of local governments include providing services like police and fire protection; insuring the safety of drinking water; collecting trash; maintaining schools, local courts, and jails; and keeping official records of births, deaths, and marriages. In addition, local governments build and maintain local streets and roads and provide transportation services that benefit residents, such as building bridges or tunnels or providing commuter services.

The citizens of a city or county can have a huge impact on the way their local government runs, because they have much greater access to their elected officials at this level of government. Ordinary citizens are invited and encouraged to share their views at city council meetings, school board meetings, county planning meetings, and other official hearings. They can also influence local public policy by starting and circulating petitions, calling and writing to local politicians, and even running for office themselves.

The requirements and terms for city officials vary widely, so check the rules in your local area.

As a potential U.S. citizen, you're likely to be asked not only about public office holders, but also about your involvement in your local community. A good way to show you participate in your local community is to show membership in local charity or civic organizations by showing proof of volunteer efforts, as well as by providing items that show involvement in the community such as library cards or receipts for enrollment in adult education classes.

One type of civic activity you should *not* have engaged in in the U.S. before becoming a citizen is voting.

Part IV
Exploring U.S. History and Culture

The 5th Wave
By Rich Tennant
George Washington: Father of the Country and first US President. Originator of the White House Cabinet; established Congress's right to tax US citizens and re-wrote existing boating regulations to increase the number of people allowable in a row boat from 5 to 12.

In this part . . .

As part of your citizenship test, you'll need to demonstrate a basic knowledge and understanding of U.S. history. In this part, we cover the people, places, and events that shaped the United States of America — from before it ever became a country, all the way to the present. American history is a fascinating topic. You can make finding out about it fun, and get involved in your subject — read as much as possible, watch educational television programs about historical events and people, perhaps even try to visit some famous historical sites and landmarks to really make history come alive.

In this section, we also delve into the subject of American culture — things like holidays and celebrations, important American symbols, and honored American heroes. You may be asked about any of these subjects during your naturalization interview, but just as importantly, these are key components of living as an American in the U.S.

Chapter 12

U.S. History in a Nutshell, Part I: Pre-U.S. to World War I

In This Chapter

- Understanding Columbus's new discovery
- Fighting for freedom in the Revolutionary War
- Defending the new nation
- Dividing the nation: The Civil War
- Expanding westward
- Industrializing America

Your journey through the fascinating history of the United States of America begins here, starting before there ever was a United States. Hold on tight — we cover a lot of territory in a very small amount of space in this and the following chapter. But don't worry, you'll find out more than you need to pass your citizenship test — you only have to show a *basic* understanding of U.S. history.

Before We Were the United States

Long before we were a country, the land that is now the United States was considered *undiscovered* by the more civilized nations of Europe and Asia; however, tribes of natives lived in various parts of the land — tribes as different from each other as the terrain of the land that they called home.

Going along with Columbus on his voyage

Christopher Columbus, the man credited with "discovering" America, was actually looking for China when he landed on what is now part of the Bahamas, off the coast of what is now the United States, in 1492. King Ferdinand and Queen Isabella of Spain, who footed the bill for Columbus's expensive journey, wanted to trade with the Far East — India, China, Japan, and the Spice Islands. Unfortunately, making a journey from Europe to Asia in the fifteenth and sixteenth centuries was dangerous, expensive, and time consuming. Realizing that the world was round, Columbus convinced the Spanish monarchs that he could sail west around the world to reach the Far East in a more timely and less costly manner, compared to sailing around Africa or trekking over land.

But Columbus miscalculated, believing the globe to be significantly smaller than it actually is. When he landed on the islands in the Bahamas, he believed he was near the Indies — and so he called the native people living there *Indians.*

Although there is some disagreement between scholars about exactly where in the New World Columbus first set foot on land, it is widely believed that on the morning of October 12, 1492, he landed at a Bahamas island that he named San Salvador. In his journeys, he visited many other islands, naming them as went, including Hispaniola, Santa Maria de la Concepcion, Fernandina, Isabela, and Las Islas de Arena.

Despite not achieving his goal of finding an easier, faster way to reach the Far East from Europe, Columbus's discovery of what was a New World to the Europeans forever changed the course of history.

Christopher Columbus's three ships, the *Nina,* the *Pinta,* and the *Santa Maria,* were actually quite small, about 49 to 118 feet in length (between 15 and 36 meters). They collectively carried Columbus and his crew of about 90 men to the New World.

Migrating to the New World

As soon as news of Columbus's discovery spread, explorers from around the world, including England, France, Holland, Italy, and Spain couldn't wait to set sail for the New World. Throughout each of their journeys, the early explorers created maps and kept detailed journals of their voyages, which in turn helped other explorers who came later.

An Italian explorer by the name of Amerigo Vespucci was the first to declare the New World a continent in its own right. The land was named *America* in Vespucci's honor.

New settlers soon began to populate America. Some came to seek their fortunes through the trade opportunities the land offered. Others came to escape religious or political persecution in their native countries. Still others came to teach and convert to their religion the Native Americans who were already living in the New World.

The British and French claimed most (but not all) of North America, while the Spanish dominated South America, where they found gold and riches.

The Spanish settlement at St. Augustine, Florida, holds the honor of being the oldest permanent settlement in North America. Britain established its first colony at Jamestown, Virginia.

Finding out about the American colonies

Before they united into a nation of states, they were 13 British colonies. But the philosophy and ideals that would inspire the yet-to-be-born nation of the United States of America were already firmly in place.

Some colonies were settled by groups with specific interests in mind, such as the Pilgrims (see the nearby sidebar, "Seeking religious freedom: The Pilgrims") and the Puritans. Others, known as *proprietary colonies,* formed when the king bestowed large pieces of land to certain members of the nobility. These colony "owners" made money by renting and/or selling their land. Still other colonies were born when residents of one colony traveled in search of better land and economic opportunity.

Seeking religious freedom: The Pilgrims

The Pilgrims, in 1620, were the first group of settlers who came to America seeking religious freedom.

Even before their ship, the *Mayflower,* landed at Plymouth Rock in what is now Massachusetts, the Pilgrims outlined the kind of government they wanted in a document called the Mayflower Compact. The Pilgrims wanted to form a democracy where the people voted on the laws they lived by and the government that regulated them. The Mayflower *Compact* (constitution) established the basis of written laws and legal forms of government in the new land.

The Pilgrims were ill prepared for their first winter in the new land and only about half of them survived. With help from friendly Native Americans, the remaining Pilgrims learned how to hunt, fish, and farm in order to survive in the harsh new environment.

In addition to setting forth principles of government that were later incorporated into the United States Constitution, the Pilgrims gained fame for starting the holiday of Thanksgiving, which is celebrated every year on the fourth Thursday of November. On this day, Americans celebrate with a great feast and give thanks for their blessings. (See Chapter 14 for more on Thanksgiving.)

Generally speaking, democracy thrived in the New World. In the charters that established the colonies, the King of England gave the colonists most of the same rights citizens living in England enjoyed. Some colonies employed *representative assemblies* — elected officials who determined the laws for the colonies — to govern their citizens. Others believed in a more direct form of democracy where voters would gather at town meetings, vote on the laws of their town, and elect representatives to the colonial assemblies. Today, most of our government depends on representatives, although some examples of *direct democracy* still exist at the local level in a few tiny towns. Although rare in today's modern world, the laws of some small U.S. towns are still determined though votes taken at local town meetings.

Still, the colonies could not be considered completely democratic. Their laws exercised significant restrictions on who was allowed to vote or hold a representative office — namely male landowners. In some instances voters were also compelled to meet certain religious qualifications. In addition, the King of England and his representatives still maintained a lot of control. With the exception of Connecticut and Rhode Island, king-appointed governors retained the power to *veto,* or override, any laws passed by the continental assemblies. The governor also had the power, or *jurisdiction,* to appoint certain government officials.

Recognizing the lucky thirteen

If you read Chapter 16, you'll come to see that the number 13 has special significance to Americans. After all, 13 British colonies pulling together to unite for greater good and freedom forms the foundation of our nation. In respect and honor, our flag sports 13 stripes — one for each of the original colonies (listed here in order of their admission to the United States):

- Delaware
- Pennsylvania
- New Jersey
- Georgia
- Connecticut

- Massachusetts
- Maryland
- South Carolina
- New Hampshire
- Virginia
- New York
- North Carolina
- Rhode Island

Revolutionary Times

During much of the time between 1689 and 1763, the English found themselves at war with the French over differences in the ways the two countries settled and colonized the new land. The American colonists became accustomed to a lot of freedom, because England's monarchs were too preoccupied with matters of war to give much thought to them. The colonists enjoyed a relatively democratic self-government and more or less free trade with Europe. However, all that was about to change.

Understanding the events leading to the Revolutionary War

At the time, the French occupied most of the land that is now Canada, while England controlled most of what is now the United States. However, both countries claimed rights to the land that is now Virginia, and war broke out over the disputed land. Because the French allied themselves with many of the Native American people who were already living here, the war became known as the French and Indian War. It lasted from 1754 to 1763.

George Washington, who would later become the first President of the United States, heroically fought for the British during the French and Indian War.

Although France and its allies dominated most of the war's earlier battles, England took stock, reorganized, and sent additional troops. The war ended with the 1763 Treaty of Paris, in which France lost her colonies and England took control of most of North America.

After the French and Indian War, England's King George III turned his attentions back toward the American colonies. Burdened with a large financial debt, he intended to take full advantage of England's colonial properties by

- Allowing the colonists to only trade with England by forcing them to pay high taxes if they traded with other nations
- Selling the colonists goods manufactured in England at inflated prices
- Strictly enforcing existing tax laws as well as imposing new taxes
- Establishing restrictions and limitations on settling new lands
- Requiring colonists to *quarter,* or house, British soldiers in private homes, as well as provide them with food and basic supplies

Meeting the real American natives

The Native Americans, the people whom Columbus had mistakenly named *Indians,* represent the only true *native* people of this land. The remainder of the U.S. population can trace their heritage to immigrant roots.

The various tribes of Native Americans differed greatly in the way they interacted with the new visitors to their land. Some tribes demonstrated friendship and a willingness to interact with the newcomers, while others exhibited hostility, to the point of even launching violent attacks against the Europeans. The possibility of such attacks was a real-and-present danger for early American settlers.

Throughout the early history of America, the native people were defeated and pushed toward the west. Their bows and arrows proved no match for the guns the new settlers brought with them, and the native people lost great expanses of their land. Also, the Europeans brought diseases with them that the native people were ill equipped to fight — their immune systems had never before been exposed to such challenges. Large numbers of Native Americans died as a result.

Anticipating that the colonists wouldn't like the new policies, England passed several laws to help strictly enforce their power over the colonies, including the following:

- **The Navigation Acts (1600s):** The Navigation Acts restricted the colonists to only trading with England. Because other countries would have been willing to pay substantially more for the same goods, the colonists felt this was unfair.
- **The Writs of Assistance**: These general search warrants gave British government officials the right to search any ship or building — including private homes — for smuggled goods, at any time, for any reason.
- **The Stamp Act (1765):** The Stamp Act compelled colonists to buy official government stamps to be affixed to legal documents like wills and land transfers, and even public documents like newspapers.
- **A Royal Proclamation on Land Policy (1763):** This law prohibited colonists from settling any land west of the Appalachian Mountains, which England reserved for Indian use. Colonists who had already settled in these territories were required to return to the East.
- **The Tea Act of 1773:** The Tea Act imposed a special tax on imported tea and gave the East India Company a monopoly on the tea trade in America. The act made it illegal for the colonies to buy non-British tea and forced them to pay a three-cent-per-pound tea tax. The Tea Act so angered the colonists that some of them, disguised as Indians, boarded ships in Boston Harbor and dumped all the tea in their holds into the ocean. The Boston Tea Party, as the rebellious protest came to be known, represents one of the most famous turning points in early American history.
- **The Repressive Acts of 1774:** The British Parliament enacted the Repressive Acts to punish the citizens of Massachusetts for the Boston Tea Party. So restrictive were this series of British laws that the colonists started referring to them as the *Intolerable Acts.*

The Repressive Acts refer to several laws that allowed the British to exercise control over the colonists, including

  - The Boston Port Act, which closed Boston Harbor until colonists repaid the East India Company for tea lost during the Boston Tea Party.
  - The Massachusetts Government Act, which stated that members of the Boston Assembly would no longer be elected by the citizens of Boston but rather appointed by the king. The colonists rebelled by electing their own officials who met at a different location.

- The Administration of Justice Act, which took away the colonial courts' power to arrest British officers.
- The Quartering Act, which required colonists to house British soldiers and provide them with food and basic supplies.

As bad as all these laws were, what most angered the colonists was taxation without representation. While Britain forced the colonists to pay their taxes, the colonies were not allowed to send representatives to the English government to vote on those taxes and represent the colonists' interests.

Resisting tyranny: The colonists unite and fight

The colonists, a feisty bunch, did not just sit back and let England walk all over them. They rebelled by no longer buying British goods. They found homemade or homegrown substitutions wherever possible and smuggled other necessary goods into colonial harbors. In a 1774 show of unity, the colonists gathered together in Philadelphia at the first meeting of the Continental Congress. Every colony except Georgia sent representatives to this historic first meeting.

At the time, only a few of the more radical colonists were even considering breaking away from England. The main purpose of the first Continental Congress was to express colonial grievances against British policy. The colonists accomplished this by writing a Declaration of Rights that included a request for the king to repeal the Intolerable Acts. Not content to simply sit and wait for an answer, the colonists resolved to prepare *militias,* or citizen armies, should the need to fight for their rights arise. The colonies also agreed to a nonimportation agreement that officially boycotted British goods by giving local Committees of Vigilance in each colony the power to fine or arrest those who broke the agreement by buying British goods.

Britain ignored the colonists' requests and instead sent troops to Massachusetts to seize military supplies and find the men instigating the rebellion. On April 18, 1775, in the small Massachusetts village of Lexington, the British caught colonists by surprise, killing eight minutemen (members of the Massachusetts militia) and wounding others. When the British soldiers pushed on to Concord, the colonists opened fire in the "shot heard 'round the world," and started the Revolutionary War.

Answering the slavery question

To the delegates of the first Constitutional Convention, slavery — which had existed in the colonies since 1619 — was not a moral issue but rather a matter of debate about money. Generally speaking, most Southern states approved of slavery, because the practice provided low-cost labor for their plantations. Most Northern states didn't practice slavery or were undertaking measures to outlaw it. Still, there was little talk of actually outlawing slavery at the first Constitutional Convention. The Northern states' only real issue concerned how to count the slave population. The South thought each slave should count towards the number of representatives the state was allowed to send to Congress. However, it did not want to count slaves when it came to matters of taxation. Of course, the North held the opposite view. The states finally agreed to the *three-fifths compromise,* in which every five slaves would be counted as three people for purposes of determining a state's number of representatives and the amount of taxes owed. As part of the compromise, the Constitution also guaranteed the South's slave trade for at least 20 years.

At the start of the war, whether the colonists were actually fighting for independence from England or merely for their rights as British subjects remained unclear. Many factors influenced the colonists' ultimate decision to break away from England, although some remained loyal to England throughout the war.

The British brought in *mercenary* (paid) soldiers known as the Hessians from Germany to help fight their battle. This greatly angered the colonists and they looked to France for help. The French refused to help, however, unless the colonists declared independence from England.

George Washington served as Commander in Chief of the colonial military. An experienced military man — he also fought in the French and Indian War — General Washington's troops lacked the training, ammunition, and supplies of their British counterparts. Nonetheless, they could shoot more accurately, knew the land better, and had the strength of their beliefs to help them through the tough battles ahead.

Declaring independence from England

After a lot of fighting, hardship, and loss of life, the colonists were forced to conclude that England was never going to treat them any better — in fact, it seemed that stricter and harsher punishments lay ahead.

At the request of the Second Continental Congress, Thomas Jefferson wrote the original Declaration of Independence with help from fellow committee members Benjamin Franklin and John Adams. The first part of the Declaration declares the break with England and the reasons for the break. The second part of the document lists the colonists' complaints against England's King George III in order to illustrate that England had ignored the colonists' complaints. The final draft of the Declaration of Independence was adopted on July 4, 1776. (For more detailed information about the Declaration of Independence — one of the most important documents in the U.S. — see Chapter 9.)

October 19, 1781, marked the final battle of the Revolutionary War. While marching from Virginia to New York, British commander Lord Cornwallis became trapped in Yorktown on the Chesapeake Bay. While his troops waited for reinforcements, the French navy blocked their escape. After a series of battles, Cornwallis surrendered to the Continental Army, essentially ending the Revolutionary War.

Benjamin Franklin, John Adams, and John Jay traveled to Paris to write the treaty that officially ended the conflict. Signed in 1781, the Treaty of Paris defined the United States's boundaries as

- The Atlantic Ocean to the east
- The Mississippi River to the west
- The Great Lakes to the north
- Florida to the south (Florida itself was controlled by Spain at the time, so the southern border of the United States was actually the northern border of Florida)

Establishing the new nation

Suddenly the 13 original colonies became a new nation, complete with all the debts, responsibilities, and challenges that went along with winning independence from England.

Although the Declaration of Independence had established a foundation for government, each of the original 13 states operated under its own individual laws. New Americans found themselves having to make tough choices in defining their government structure and powers.

After fighting so hard to break from the oppression of British rule, many colonists naturally feared a strong central government. Yet practical concerns like the need to establish trade and foreign policy necessitated some form of centralized government.

In 1781, Congress *ratified* (adopted) the Articles of Confederation — the first national constitutional agreement of the 13 new United States. Under the Articles, the federal government retained little power, delegating most authority to the individual states. Although many early Americans liked the agreement because it prevented the federal government from growing strong enough to overthrow the will of the people, as well as opened up the West to peaceful settlement, The Articles of Confederation neglected to address many of the problems that the new country encountered, like regulating trade, dealing with foreign governments, and matters of defense.

Under the Articles, Congress lacked the authority to enforce laws. The federal government wasn't even able to collect taxes to pay basic legislative and defense expenses, not to mention the debt the colonies had accumulated during the Revolutionary War. Congress also lacked the authority to recruit troops, despite the fact that the federal government was expected to provide defense for the new country.

To make matters worse, many states began printing their own money, which undermined the value of the money produced by the federal government.

Because the Articles of Confederation required at least 9 of the 13 states to meet and agree on issues, and all 13 needed to agree on any *amendments* (changes) to the Articles, the young country soon found itself on the verge of bankruptcy. Debates erupted about whether the states should be independent entities that operated like separate countries or 13 mutually dependent states, operating as one united country.

These problems led to the calling of the first Constitutional Convention in 1787. After much debate and compromising, the Convention resulted in the drafting of the United States Constitution — the supreme law of the land and our most important historical document.

For more details about the United States Constitution, see Chapter 9. For now, know that the Constitution makes these important points:

- No other laws may contradict any of the principles set forth in the Constitution.
- No person is exempt from following the laws set forth in the Constitution, nor is the government itself.
- The Constitution guarantees the essential "self-evident" rights Thomas Jefferson set forth in the Declaration of Independence — rights and freedoms guaranteed to *all* people living in the United States, whether they are United States citizens or not.

It took a lot of debating before the delegates of the Constitutional Convention agreed upon the fine points of the new government. Large states with large populations favored a system of government where population determined representation in government. Smaller states believed each state should be delegated the same designated number of representatives. The great compromise, ratified by nine states in 1788, created the legislative branch of government, consisting of two senators from each state (regardless of size of area or population) and a number of congressional representatives determined by the state's population. The first assembly of the new U.S. government met in the country's temporary capital, New York City, in 1789.

The importance of the census

Following America's independence from England, there was an almost immediate need for a *census,* or population count, of our new nation. Article I of the U.S. Constitution requires a census to be taken every ten years. The first census, conducted in 1790, counted the population at 3.9 million people. By comparison, the 2001 census counts that number at over 281 million.

Every ten years, the U.S. government sends out census forms to the more than 105 million households in the United States. Uncle Sam wants to know how many people live in each house as well as their ages, sex, and race. It's not that the government is nosy — the sole purpose of census surveys is to secure general information. The government takes the confidentiality of census replies seriously. By law, no census taker or any other Census Bureau employee can reveal identifiable information about any person, household, or business, and schedules and questionnaires from any census cannot be released for 72 years. Even then, only the heirs or legal representative of the named individuals are allowed access to the records.

The information provided by the census guides the government's planning for U.S. needs, now as it did back in the 1700s. Through the years, the census questions evolved with the country's growth and progress. The broad profile of the people who make up this nation helps the federal government determine how to best meet the needs of its people. For instance, a town with a growing population of children will probably need more schools, but a town with a growing population of senior citizens would better benefit from reliable public transportation and senior services.

The census also plays an important role in upholding democracy, because the number of representatives a state sends to the House of Representatives in Congress is based on the state's population. For an accurate count of the state's population, the government consults — you guessed it — the census results.

You can easily see why filling out census forms is such an important citizen responsibility — if you neglect to complete your census forms, you may be helping to cheat your local community of the representation it deserves and the public services it needs.

The Census Bureau's Web site (www.census.gov) offers a fun place to surf and check out facts about your state or region or the U.S. in general. You'll also find a wealth of statistical information about the U.S. as well as census information in Spanish and a fun Census for Kids educational Web site.

Growing a nation

Our first President, George Washington, believed in the importance of uniting the 13 states to work as a strong single nation. During his two terms in office, he influenced all the presidents who later held the office by:

- Establishing the practice of consulting a presidential Cabinet of advisors (for more about the President's Cabinet, see Chapter 10)
- Setting the precedent for presidents serving no more than two terms in office, thereby preventing any single person in the government from gaining too much power
- Establishing a practice of staying neutral in foreign politics, a practice that would remain in force for more than 100 years

Washington and other Federalists like Alexander Hamilton, believed a national bank was necessary to stabilize the young country's economy. The Anti-Federalists, who became the Democratic Republicans with the birth of the political party movement in the U.S. (more on political parties in Chapter 10), feared the national bank gave too much power to the federal government. When it came to money and financing the nation, the Federalists favored a looser interpretation of the Constitution while the Anti-Federalists favored a strict interpretation that severely limited the government's powers and duties.

The two sides agreed, however, on matters of foreign policy, believing the United States should remained neutral in the conflicts between other nations, a policy that Washington stressed in his farewell address.

Democratic-Republican Thomas Jefferson and Federalist John Adams battled it out in the election to become the second president. In the election of 1796, Adams defeated his rival by only three electoral votes. Despite the fact that the two maintained a difficult and antagonistic relationship and only spoke to each other during debates, as outlined in the Constitution, the man with the second highest number of votes — in this case, Thomas Jefferson — became the Vice President.

The Twelfth Amendment gave the president and vice president separate ballots in the Electoral College system. Before the amendment's adoption, the candidate with most electoral votes became the president and the candidate with the second-highest number of votes became the vice president, resulting in some strained and counterproductive political pairings like that of John Adams and Thomas Jefferson.

John Adams had a lot of factors working against him:

- The immensely popular George Washington was a tough act for anyone to follow.
- Although the public believed in Adams's experience and qualifications, he was not well liked — the public perceived him as a snob.
- His political archrival and vice president, Thomas Jefferson, continually undermined his credibility and efforts.
- Certain members of his own political party were plotting against him.

Adams also lost popularity when he approved the Alien and Sedition Acts, as outlined in the following list. Designed to counter the growth of Jefferson's Democratic-Republican Party and never strictly enforced, the Alien Act expired in 1800 when Thomas Jefferson was finally elected President.

- **The Naturalization Act of 1798** increased the amount of time (from three to five years) an immigrant had to reside in the U.S. before becoming a citizen.
- **The Alien Enemy Act** empowered the president to imprison or deport immigrants of countries at war with the U.S. or those he believed to be dangerous to the country.
- **The Sedition Act** made it illegal to publish negative or defamatory statements about the federal government or its officials.

Warring after the Revolution

Like Washington before him, John Adams worked hard to keep the U.S. neutral in matters of foreign politics. He knew the new nation lacked the strength and resources to win a battle against any of the European nations. But Adams was really put to the test when the British violated the United States's neutral status by seizing merchant ships. Instead of going to war, Adams negotiated a treaty with the British. This in turn angered the French, who were warring with the British at the time.

Depending on their individual beliefs, Americans sided with France or Britain. In what is considered the most important accomplishment of his presidency, John Adams negotiated with both nations to keep the U.S. out of the conflict, allowing free trade with both nations to continue for a while. Eventually though, France and England set up blockades.

Britain demanded that all foreign ships first stop at British ports before continuing on to other European destinations. If the Americans managed to avoid the blockades, the ship's owner reaped high profits. When they were caught, however, the British took the ships away. Although merchants accepted these sieges as a necessary risk of doing business with warring nations, the Americans became outraged when the British began forcing American sailors to enlist in the British military forces by claiming they were deserters from the British navy.

In 1794, the French, too, began seizing U.S. vessels in retaliation for negotiating treaties with the British. Congress responded by ordering the navy to attack any French ships off the U.S. coast. A peace convention in 1800 with France's new dictator, Napoleon, ended the conflict.

President Thomas Jefferson kept the country out of war by prohibiting U.S. exports to other countries, hoping that the need for U.S. exports would force the warring nations of Britain and France to change their politics. Because merchants and anyone else whose livelihood depended on trade opposed the act, the law proved difficult for Jefferson's administration to enforce. It was replaced by other acts that forbade trade with only England and France. Eventually the United States offered to resume trading with whichever nation first changed its neutral trading restrictions. France liked the deal and changed its policies; trade between the U.S. and France resumed.

By 1812, our fourth President, James Madison, was trying to convince Congress not to declare war on England and Spain. He lost that argument, with several factors contributing to the U.S. entering the War of 1812, including the following:

- Americans were outraged over Britain's seizing ships and forcing U.S. sailors into British military service.
- The U.S. objected to Britain giving aid to the Indians attacking American settlers on the Western frontier.
- A war against Britain gave the U.S. an excuse to seize the British Northwest Territories and possibly even Canada, as well as to acquire Florida from Britain's ally, Spain.

During the War of 1812, the British managed to invade and burn most of Washington, D.C. U.S. troops, led by Andrew Jackson, seized Florida at one point, only to have the territory return to Spain as part of the 1814 Treaty of Ghent, which ended the war. In the meantime, not knowing about the peace agreement, Jackson's troops defeated the British at the Battle of New Orleans.

Although the Treaty of Ghent restored peace, it did not address the conflicts that led to the War of 1812 in the first place. But because the European nations were no longer at war, some of the issues, such as free trade conflicts simply disappeared. Still, the War of 1812 ushered in a new era in U.S. history, characterized by the following:

- A desire to settle the Western territories
- An increased emphasis on manufacturing and industry
- The end of the Federalist political party

The Civil War Years

At no time in our history was our union more threatened than during the Civil War (1861–1865) — the war in which United States citizens of the North and South took up arms against one another. In some instances, family members on opposite sides of the conflict (and opposite sides of the *Mason-Dixon line,* which divides the North from the South) actually fought each other in the war's bloody battles.

Many people believe slavery to be the issue that prompted the Civil War, but in reality a combination of factors caused the division that almost destroyed the United States:

- The election of Abraham Lincoln as President (more about Lincoln later in this chapter and in Chapter 15) divided the country.
- Different economic strengths and weaknesses led the two territories to argue over the protective tariff and the issue of slavery. The *protective tariff* placed a tax on imported goods in order to give U.S. manufacturers a market advantage. The industrial north needed the tariff to compete with otherwise lower-priced foreign goods. The agricultural South, which purchased a large amount of those goods, resented paying higher prices for the U.S.-made versions. Likewise, the South argued it needed inexpensive slave labor to compete in the international market. The North resented slavery on both moral and economic grounds.
- Different beliefs about the type of union the country should be and struggle for control of the central government greatly contributed to the Civil War. The North viewed the nation as a union of the people that could not, under any circumstances, be divided. The South, on the other hand, interpreted the union as an agreement among the states that could be broken if a state disagreed with federal law — allowing that state to *secede,* or withdraw, from the union.

Dividing the states: The Civil War

The seeds of the Civil War were planted long before the conflict ever came to battle. As far back as the drafting of the Constitution, the North and South disagreed on the issues of slavery and *tariffs* (taxes) on imports and exports. The agricultural South wanted protection against export taxes that would make goods like tobacco, rice, and indigo too expensive on the world market. The industrial North demanded protection against lower-priced imports cutting into their business.

The Continental Congress compromised by prohibiting Congress from ever taxing exports, while protecting American commerce by levying tariffs on imported goods. But the differences between the North and the South remained and, in fact, grew during the United States's early history.

Throughout the Civil War, the North and the South had differing strengths and weaknesses, which led to a long, bloody war that caused enormous loss of money, property, and human lives.

The South's strengths included the following:

- Large land areas, including long areas of coastline
- Some of the nation's best military leaders, including General Robert E. Lee and General Thomas "Stonewall" Jackson
- Ownership of most of the existing military equipment and supplies
- Enough financing and troops that they could afford to lose a few battles
- Ongoing income thanks to cotton exports
- The defensive position, which meant they only needed to keep the Northerners out of their states in order to win the war

But the North had its own strengths, too, some of which eventually overpowered some of the South's advantages:

- A bigger population — almost double that of the South — and, therefore, more troops
- A stronger navy
- Better transportation
- Enormous financial reserves, as well as the industrial capability to create their own munitions and supplies (Although the South had the advantage of owning most of the military equipment and supplies at the beginning of the war, the North's industrial strength soon turned the tables in their favor.)

Contributing factors and compromises

In the 1820s, *nationalism* (the belief in a strong, united country) gave way toward feelings of *sectionalism* (loyalty to a particular state or region). The United States unofficially divided itself into three main sections, each with its own thoughts and beliefs on how the country should be run:

- **The Northeast,** which was dependent on industry for its economy
- **The South,** which was dependent on agriculture produced by plantation owners for its economy
- **The West,** which was dependent on agriculture produced by independent farmers and ranchers for its economy

Because they didn't benefit financially from the real-estate sales, the North also opposed the government's generous land policy, which allowed settlers moving west to buy large tracts of land for bargain-basement prices.

Slavery quickly became the most emotional issue of the war. Although the North generally objected to slavery because of the unfair economic advantage it gave Southern plantation owners, a growing number of *abolitionists* (people who believed slavery should be outlawed because it was morally wrong) were starting to make their voices heard.

As more states joined the union, the slavery issue grew more heated and divisive — the North believed that new states admitted to the union should be slave free, while the South still fought for the right to own slaves. Federal politicians tried to avoid a civil war by creating compromises to the controversial and explosive issue. In the end, none of these ideas pleased either side enough to stop the conflict from growing into a full-fledged war between the states. But before the states began actually fighting with one another, they first tried the following:

- **The Missouri Compromise (1820):** Admitted Missouri to the union as a slave state, while at the same time admitting Maine as a free state. The Missouri Compromise, which kept the country's balance between free and slave states equal, declared that all territories north of the 36°30" latitude would become free states, and all territory south of that latitude would become slave states.
- **The Compromise of 1850:** Admitted California to the union as a free state, but left the remaining Mexican territories to decide the issue by the vote of the people living there, an act known as *popular sovereignty.* Still, California's admission to the union permanently upset the even balance between free and slave states in the U.S. The Compromise of 1850 also ended the slave trade, although not the practice of slavery itself, in the District of Columbia. Because this was a *compromise* (a give and take of issues on both sides) another part of the law enacted a strict *fugitive slave law,* which made it easier for slave owners to recapture runaway slaves, and took away the runaways' rights to testify or to be tried by a jury for the crime of running away.

- **The Kansas Nebraska Act of 1854:** Established the rule of popular sovereignty in the Kansas and Nebraska territories. Abolitionists and slave owners alike rushed to settle the territories, and as you may have guessed, their conflicts turned violent. The Act led to the forming of the new Republican political party, made up of groups that opposed slavery. After only two years of existence, the Republicans dominated the House of Representatives.

The number of representatives a state can send to Congress is based upon that state's population. Because more people lived in the North, this gave the antislavery Republicans the chance to gain power quickly.

Any attempts at compromise ended when the Dred Scott case reached the Supreme Court. Dred Scott, a slave who lived with his master in a free territory for five years, sued for his freedom when he was returned to his slave-state home. The Supreme Court ruled against Scott, stating that slaves were private property and not citizens, and therefore did not have the right to sue in court. The decision pleased the South and enraged the North. Republicans declared the decision could not be legally binding, and tensions between the North and the South increased.

Fighting the war between the states

South Carolina *seceded* (withdrew) from the union and demanded that all federal property in the state be surrendered to state authorities on December 20, 1860. Fort Sumpter, one of only two forts in the South still under Union control, became an important stronghold. Learning that Lincoln planned to send additional troops and supplies to reinforce the fort, Confederate General Beauregard demanded its surrender, which was refused. On April 12, 1861, the Confederate Army attacked Fort Sumpter, which surrendered two days later. Congress officially declared war on the Confederacy the very next day.

Both sides were ill prepared for the first major battle of the Civil War, the Battle at Bull Run. Confederate troops caused union soldiers en route to Richmond, Virginia, to retreat back to Washington. However, the rebels didn't realize their victory in time to follow up and take advantage of their position.

At the beginning of the war, the South dominated. The Battle of Antietam marked the turning point, when the North began to take control. Soon after the battle, on September 22, 1862, President Abraham Lincoln's Emancipation Proclamation freed all slaves in the states that had seceded. Although Lincoln had little power to actually enforce the law in the South, the proclamation provided the basis for freeing all slaves after the war.

After Northern victories in Tennessee, Union General William Tecumseh Sherman led his troops on a long, violent, and bloody invasion of the South, destroying most everything in their path including homes, farms, and railroads. Sherman's march from Atlanta and Savannah in Georgia and up through South Carolina and North Carolina, infamous for its brutality, destroyed Southern morale and spirit and became a major factor leading to the end of the war.

Although they had always dominated the West, the North's most important victory in the East came with the three-day-long Battle of Gettysburg. President Lincoln's Gettysburg Address, a speech made to dedicate the cemetery on the battlefield, inspired Americans then (as it does now) to make sure that a government "of the people, by the people, and for the people, shall not perish from this earth."

The birth of the Red Cross

Clara Barton, Superintendent of Nurses for the Union Army during the Civil War, founded the American Red Cross in 1881, treating the wounded of both sides of the conflict on the Civil War battlefields.

The American Red Cross still operates today, working closely with government agencies during times of major crises. In 1905, Congress granted a charter to the American Red Cross that required it to act "in accord with the military authorities as a medium of communication between the people of the United States and their armed forces."

Today, the American Red Cross provides humanitarian services to members of the U.S. military and their families around the world. Living and working in the same difficult and dangerous environment as our troops, the Red Cross gives comfort to soldiers and provides emergency-message services (about deaths and births, for example), comfort kits, and cards for the troops to send home to loved ones.

The Civil War's final battle raged between General Robert E. Lee for the South and General Ulysses S. Grant for the North. Equally powerful and skilled military men, Grant had the advantage of more supplies and more troops, which allowed him to capture the Confederate capital of Richmond, Virginia, before trapping Lee and his men at Appomattox Court House (also in Virginia). Lee surrendered on April 9, 1865, and the war was over. North and South once again came together as the United States of America.

Reconstructing the U.S. after the Civil War

Although arguments between the North and South still continued for years after the Civil War, nationalism won out over sectionalism. The country united and set about rebuilding its strength during a period called *Reconstruction,* which lasted from 1865 to 1877.

After the war, the Reconstruction Acts of 1867 set up five military districts, each headed by a general with absolute power, in the South. States could not be readmitted to the union until they ratified the Fourteenth Amendment and guaranteed *suffrage* (the right to vote) to blacks. Although blacks in the South had some political power, there were still a lot of people in power who would infringe upon their rights, so the federal government passed the following laws and constitutional amendments designed to help former slaves adjust to living in a free society:

- The Fourteenth Amendment to the Constitution made all blacks citizens. It also punished states that denied blacks the right to vote by reducing the number of representatives they were allowed to send to Congress.
- The Fifteenth Amendment put an end to any gray area concerning voting rights by specifically guaranteeing blacks the right to vote.
- The Freedman's Bureau provided help to former slaves in obtaining food, housing, education, and jobs.

Factories, Farmers, and Cowboys: The Industrial Revolution and the Push Westward

Following the War of 1812, the U.S. felt a strong sense of patriotism and *nationalism* (the belief that the United States was a strong, united country working for the greater good of all). In this spirit, Congress passed the Protective Tariff Act of 1816 to nurture the new industries that had sprung up before and during the war by raising the prices of British-manufactured goods, thereby giving U.S. manufacturers an advantage. Although the act represented a change in the U.S.'s free-trade policy, it was believed necessary in order to promote the growth of the nation.

The aftermath of the War of 1812 also saw a strengthening of the national bank, and for the first time, although not without controversy, the federal government spent money on transportation improvements like roads, railroads, canals, and bridges. Because the Constitution did not specifically give the government the right to spend taxpayers' money for such improvements, a great many Americans objected.

The Civil War also had a significant impact on the United States's growing industry. After the Southern states left the Union, the Northern Congress was able to pass bills on banking, homesteading, and the building of the transcontinental railroad. Had representatives from the agricultural South been present, the bills probably wouldn't have passed, but without the South's interference, Republican legislation during the Civil War opened the path to America's Industrial Revolution — a period of massive and rapid growth in manufacturing and industry, not to mention the discovery of gold in California.

At the same time, many adventurous Americans traveled west to settle the frontier, escape crowded Eastern cities and factory jobs, and seek their fortunes. The American West held great appeal for early Americans, because there was plenty of free or inexpensive land that anyone could settle and develop. "Go west, young man, and grow up with the country," New York newspaper publisher Horace Greeley advised. And the transcontinental railroad made movement of people and goods much easier. True, the settlers had to endure many hardships, and survival could be difficult, but the rewards were also great. People had to work together, which made the West a place of greater equality and social democracy than other parts of the country. In fact, the American West gave rise to the Populist political party. Although short lived, the Populists had a great impact on U.S. government, including the concept of *graduated income tax,* by which the amount of tax a person pays increases as his or her income increases, and the direct election of senators (remember the Seventeenth Amendment — refer to Chapter 9 for more information). Most important, the Populist movement showed politicians that poor people could have political power and influence, further cementing the notion of a government by and for the people.

Appreciating the importance of immigrants to a growing nation

U.S. demand for workers during the Industrial Revolution exceeded birth rates, and immigration was encouraged to fill factory jobs, build railroads, and settle the Western lands. Government policy at this time encouraged immigration, and immigrants helped the country to grow strong and rich. Between 1880 and 1930, over 27 million people entered the United States. Families often immigrated together, although men frequently came first, found work, and later sent for their families.

The U.S.A.'s national road

Constructed between 1825 and 1850, the National Road, also known as the Cumberland Road, was the first highway built by the federal government. An important overland shipping route from Pennsylvania to Illinois, the road also became a crucial connection between the North and the West.

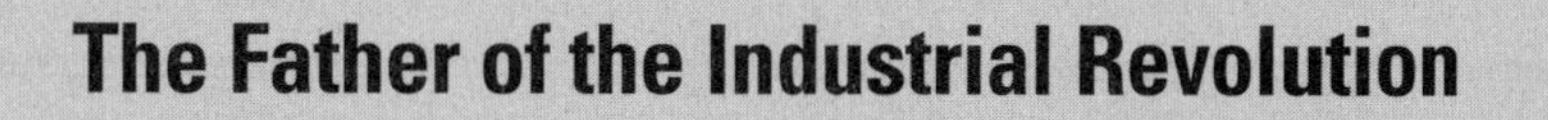

Samuel Slater, an English immigrant, brought plans to build an English-style textile factory with him to the United States in 1791. His extensive experience working in British mills helped him to construct the United States's first mill and earned him the title of Father of the American Industrial Revolution. Because the U.S. had great natural resources and the labor force to use them, the manufacturing of cotton cloth and clothing became the first major industry for the country.

By the 1880s, steam power significantly shortened the time it took to travel to the United States and immigrants poured in from around the world. Although they came seeking opportunity, life for new immigrants during the American Industrial Revolution was not easy. Immigrant workers often lived in crowded slums in industrial cities. Low wages meant wives and even children had to work to help the family survive.

In addition to jobs in factories and mines, thousands of immigrants found work on the transcontinental railroad, settling in towns along the way west. News of the California Gold Rush quickly spread throughout the world, drawing even more immigrants from both Asia and Europe.

U.S. government policy toward immigrants generally stayed friendly until the time of World War I (see Chapter 13), with the exception of the Chinese Exclusion Act of 1882. Fears and prejudice in the old West led to some Americans blaming Chinese immigrants for economic hardships and loss of jobs, despite the enormous positive impact Chinese immigrants had in helping to build the transcontinental railroad and working the mines in the West. The act was repealed in 1943 as a result of our wartime alliance with China, allowing legal Chinese immigration for the first time in 60 years, although until 1965, the quota of Chinese immigrants allowed to enter the country remained lower than that of Europeans.

Recognizing the rise of labor unions

After the Civil War, factories were rapidly replacing cottage industries and handcrafted merchandise in supplying the U.S.'s consumer needs. The growth of industry created endless opportunities for immigrants, but it also created conditions where factory owners and employers could take advantage of their workers, forcing them to work long hours in unsafe conditions for low wages.

Individually, the workers didn't have enough power to change their lot in life — if one worker complained, the employer would simply replace him or her. But by uniting as a group, workers gained enough clout to influence their employers and create better working conditions. After all, if a factory owner lost all his employees, production halted.

Labor unions used many tactics to fight for their causes, including *strikes* (in which workers would stop working until their conditions were met) and *boycotts* (in which consumers refused to buy goods until their demands were met).

Although labor unions were feared at first, they have become a respected part of the American political process, fighting for fair wages, improved working conditions, and job security for their workers. In some cases, union membership is even required in order to hold certain jobs.

Tracing your roots through Ellis Island

Ellis Island in New York served as the gateway for more than half of the immigrants entering the U.S. between 1892 and 1924. During the height of the immigration influx, as many as 10,000 people would file through Ellis Island in a single 24-hour period. It's estimated that more than 40 percent of all current U.S. citizens can trace their ancestry back to an immigrant who entered the country through the Ellis Island processing center.

If you have ancestors that came to the U.S. through Ellis Island, the Statue of Liberty–Ellis Island Foundation has made tracing your roots online easy, by cataloging Ellis Island immigration records. A simple Internet search of your family's names can instantly bring up their immigration records. Trace your family's history by visiting www.ellisislandrecords.org.

The following labor unions had a great impact on creating fair working conditions for American laborers:

- **The Knights of Labor:** One of the first successful labor unions, the Knights of Labor, founded in 1869, fought for the rights of both skilled and unskilled laborers. The union worked to reduce the workday to 8 hours at a time when the average workday lasted 12 hours; it also fought to abolish child labor. Although it enjoyed some early successes, the Knights of Labor failed by the late 1880s due to a lack of common interests between skilled and unskilled workers and the huge pool of unskilled laborers willing to replace those who fought for their rights.
- **The American Railway Union:** The American Railway Union fought for the rights of railroad workers.
- **The American Federation of Labor (AFL):** The AFL, founded in 1881, also fought for better wages and working conditions, but it only admitted skilled laborers. Because skilled workers proved harder to replace, the union enjoyed greater success than the Knights of Labor had been able to achieve.
- **The Congress of Industrial Organizations (CIO):** The CIO organized workers according to the industry they worked in rather than their level of skill. CIO strikes proved successful, because they effectively shut down the entire industry involved.
- **Company unions:** In addition, many small unions called *company unions* formed when the employees of a particular company united to fight for better wages, working conditions, and hours.

The AFL and CIO merged in 1955 to create one of the most powerful labor unions in our nation's history, the AFL-CIO.

The Addition of New Territories: The Incredible Expanding Country

By the early 1800s, the United States had a strong, secure government, and Americans were eager to push westward and settle the land. In 1823, the Monroe Doctrine declared that Europe should not interfere in the affairs of the Western Hemisphere and that any attempt at interference by a European power would be seen as a threat to U.S. security. In a show of unity and support for the new independent nations in South America, the doctrine also declared to the world that the Western Hemisphere was closed to further colonization, stating that independent New World nations could not be recolonized by Europe.

Important American inventions of the Industrial Revolution

Although the influence of people, especially immigrants, was integral to the growth of the Industrial Revolution, several important inventions also contributed to the rapid industrialization of the United States:

- Eli Whitney was instrumental in the success of America's cotton mills with his invention of the **cotton gin,** which separated cotton fiber from seeds 50 times faster than by hand. Whitney also developed a manufacturing system using standardized identical and, thus, interchangeable parts. Before this important industrial contribution, each part of a given machine was designed only for that single purpose, making replacement parts nearly impossible to obtain. Standardized parts made ordering replacement parts from manufacturers easier, making repairs simple and inexpensive. Whitney first used the system to make muskets for the U.S. government.
- Elias Howe's invention of the **sewing machine** further advanced the clothing industry.
- Robert Fulton designed and built America's first **steamboat,** the *Clermont,* as well as the first practical **submarine,** the *Nautilus.*
- The Boston Associates, a group of Boston businessmen, built the first **power loom.** The power loom was able to make cloth so cheaply that American women began to buy it rather than make it by hand.
- One of the U.S.'s most important inventors, Thomas Edison, gave us the **light bulb, electric battery, phonograph, mimeograph,** and **moving pictures.**
- Samuel F. B. Morse constructed the first **electromagnetic system** in 1844, when he built a line from Baltimore to Washington, D.C. Within ten years after the first telegraph line opened, 23,000 miles of wire crisscrossed the country, making railroad travel safer, and allowing businessmen to conduct their operations more efficiently and profitably.
- With his invention of the **telephone** in 1876, Alexander Graham Bell took communications to an even higher level.
- Christopher Sholes revolutionized written communication with his invention of the **typewriter.**
- George Washington Carver, a black chemist, invented many new uses for a variety of agricultural crops such as peanuts, soybeans, and sweet potatoes. Carver came up with 325 products from peanuts alone, including **food products, household items, shampoos, cosmetics, dyes, paints and stains,** and many more. These products offered Southern farmers alternatives to growing cotton and contributed to rural economic development.
- John A. Roebling pioneered the development of **suspension bridges** and designed the Brooklyn Bridge, although he unfortunately died before his masterpiece was completed.
- Louis Sullivan designed the first **steel-skeleton skyscraper.**
- Joseph Glidden solved the problem of how to fence in cattle on the Great Plains, where lumber was scarce, with his invention of **barbed wire.**

In addition, several land acts in the early 1800s lowered the price of land, making it easier for prospective settlers to acquire it and encouraging people to move west. The vast territories of open land and rich natural resources led Americans to believe it was the destiny of the American people to grow rich and prosper. This belief in *Manifest Destiny* led American politicians and settlers to push west, acquire new lands, and extend the American way of life far beyond its earlier boundaries. With this newfound strength, stability, and sense of purpose, the United States began acquiring new territories and adding new states to the union:

- **The Louisiana Purchase:** As a result of a European war, France gained control of the area around the Mississippi River and the port of New Orleans in 1802. Surprisingly, Napoleon decided to sell the Louisiana Territory to the United States a year later for only $15 million. Overnight, the size of the country doubled, expanding the borders to what is now Santa Fe, New Mexico, and Pikes Peak, Colorado, in the west and north to the current U.S.-Canadian border. With the purchase of the Louisiana Territory, the French government lost the last of its holdings in North America.

- **The Florida Purchase:** After losing part of Florida to the United States in the War of 1812, Spain decided to sell the rest rather than risk losing the entire territory in another war. The U.S. paid $5 million for Florida in 1819. This was an important acquisition for the country, because pirates and smugglers, not to mention runaway slaves and hostile Seminole Indians, had formerly used the territory as a hideout, knowing that, under Spanish rule, they were safe from the arms of U.S. law.
- **Annexation of Texas:** The Florida Purchase recognized that Spain still held the land rights to Texas. However, soon after the purchase, the Mexicans revolted, winning their independence from Spain and gaining control of Texas. The Mexicans, eager to settle the land, welcomed U.S. settlers with the understanding that they would become Mexican citizens. The American Texans, however, didn't completely agree with this arrangement, and skirmishes started. The Mexican government tried to prevent further immigration into Texas, but the Texans rebelled and declared their independence from Mexico in 1836. The Battle of the Alamo, in which the Texans were defeated by Mexican General Santa Anna, so angered the Texans that Sam Houston, commander in chief of the Texas territory, led his troops to defeat Santa Anna and form the Lone Star Republic. Houston then asked the U.S. to *annex* Texas, or add it as a new state to the union. The U.S. didn't immediately agree, however, due to political differences having to do with slavery. The Texans then began to look toward France or England for help. Because having France or England so close to the U.S. was unacceptable to our government, Congress agreed to annex Texas as a state in 1845.
- **The Mexican Cession:** Even after the annexation of Texas, U.S.-Mexican relations remained strained. Losing Texas angered the Mexicans, and a war over the territories west of Texas to the Pacific Ocean took place from 1846 to 1848. Americans living in what is now California established the California Bear Flag Republic. The United States's goal was to add territory to the country, not necessarily to defeat the Mexicans. The Treaty of Guadalupe-Hildago in 1848 ended the war with Mexico. For a purchase price of $15 million, Mexico officially gave up disputed areas of Texas as well as all the territory west of the Louisiana Purchase to the Pacific Ocean.
- **Oregon Country:** The United States and Great Britain had both claimed rights to the land in the northwestern part of the country, known as the Oregon Country. During the War with Mexico, President James Polk agreed to an offer with England to divide the territory — the northern part in what is now Canada would belong to England, while the southern part would remain the property of the United States.
- **Gadsden Purchase:** In 1853, the $10 million Gadsden Purchase completed what is now the continental United States by adding a small piece of property in Southern California. Although the property may seem expensive compared to land areas like the Louisiana Purchase, it did provide a convenient railroad into what is now the state of California.
- **Alaska:** In 1867, the territory that is now our largest state, Alaska, was thought of as a barren wasteland, populated only by a few Native American tribes. When then Secretary of State William Seward offered to pay the Russians $7.2 million for the land, people thought he was crazy, sarcastically referring to the purchase as "Seward's Folly" or "Seward's Icebox." Those thoughts quickly vanished in 1896 when gold was discovered in Alaska. Today, the state is one of the country's richest stores of natural resources, including fish, timber, oil, and gold.
- **Island Territories:** In February 1898, an explosion from a mine in the Bay of Havana crippled the United States warship *Maine.* The incident sparked a war with Spain that the U.S. easily won by April of the same year. A peace treaty was signed in which the United States received Puerto Rico, Guam, and the Philippine Islands (now an independent country). As a result of the same treaty, Cuba received its independence.
- **Hawaii:** Although Queen Liliuokalani of Hawaii had previously given the U.S. naval rights to Pearl Harbor in 1887, Hawaiian settlers overthrew her regime in 1893 and asked the U.S. to annex Hawaii as a state. Hawaii officially joined the United States in 1898 and became a territory in 1900, but it would take until 1959 before the islands became our 50th state.

Chapter 13

U.S. History in a Nutshell, Part II: World War I to the Present

In This Chapter

- Making sense of World War I and World War II
- Keeping warm during the Cold War
- Fighting for freedom: The civil-rights movement
- Dividing the nation: The Vietnam War
- Looking at recent U.S. history

After surviving the hardships of the Civil War (see Chapter 12) industry was thriving in the U.S., attracting thousands of immigrants seeking better opportunities and more freedom.

But although things were good here, trouble was brewing in Europe. Wars between European nations began to break out. True to the Constitution, the U.S. tried to remain neutral in the battles raging among many European countries. Most Americans believed the complicated political alliances between the various battling nations caused the war. A period of neutrality known as *isolationism,* continued for over 100 years — from the end of the War of 1812 until the U.S. declared war against Germany in 1917.

President Woodrow Wilson issued an official Proclamation of Neutrality stating that the United States would not favor one side over another. This neutral stance allowed the U.S. to continue trading with all sides. However, all that was about to change.

The World War I Years

The circumstances that led to World War I (1914–1918) had been building for quite some time due to various European nations making enemies of some countries while forming *alliances,* or friendships, with others. National rivalries and conflicts over control of colonies, along with economic competition and an arms race, all contributed to the world going to war.

Table 13-1 outlines where European loyalties were at the beginning of the conflict.

Table 13-1 European Alliances

Country	*Allied With*
Austria-Hungary	Germany and Italy
Britain	France
France	Russia and Britain
Germany	Austria-Hungary and Italy
Italy	Germany and Austria-Hungary
Russia	France and Serbia
Serbia	Russia

Understanding the causes behind World War I

Although conflicts and territory disputes had been raging in Europe for years, most historians see the assassination of Archduke Francis Ferdinand, an heir to the Austrian-Hungarian throne, as the single incident that set the wheels of World War I in motion. The resulting chain of events forever changed the course of history.

On June 28, 1914, while on a visit to Sarajevo, Bosnia, the Black Hand, a radical, militant Serbian political group, assassinated Archduke Ferdinand.

Austria-Hungary carefully considered its reaction to the killing. Looking for an excuse to go to war and squash the rebellious Serbs, the Austrian-Hungarians decided, three weeks later, to issue an official Ultimatum to Serbia. The document blamed the Serbian government itself for the assassination and accused them of trying to undermine the Austrian-Hungarian government. The Ultimatum to Serbia challenged Serbia's *sovereignty,* or governmental authority.

Austria-Hungary expected Serbia to reject the Ultimatum's harsh terms, thereby giving them a reason to launch a war against the small country. Although Austria-Hungary was aware of Serbia's alliance with Russia, they never expected the larger country to get involved in so small a conflict. They were wrong. By enforcing the Ultimatum, Austria-Hungary began the unlikely chain of events that ended with the entire world being at war.

Dissatisfied with Serbia's response to the Ultimatum, Austria-Hungary declared war on Serbia on July 28, 1914. A month later, Russia sent troops to help her ally, Serbia.

Austria-Hungary

The *dual monarchy* (a government ruled by a king or queen, and in this case one for each country) of Austria-Hungary controlled a large empire, populated by people of many nationalities: Austrians, Hungarians, Czechs, Slovaks, Serbs, Croats, and Romanians. Despite its ethnic diversity, only Austrians and Hungarians had the right to rule. Of course, the other groups desired political independence from such an unfair rule.

The area of Serbia particularly gave the monarchy trouble because it served as the heart of a nationalist political party. The Austrian-Hungarian empire believed if it could gain control over the Balkans, and thereby Serbia, its political control problems would be over.

Germany saw the Russian involvement as an act of war against its ally Austria-Hungary. It declared war on Russia on August 1, 1914. France responded by declaring war against Germany and, therefore, against Austria-Hungary. Germany, looking for the quickest route to France's capital city, Paris, invaded neutral Belgium. On the same day, Britain, in order to uphold an old treaty to defend Belgium, and to aid its ally France, declared war on Germany. Of course, Britain's colonies, including Australia, Canada, India, New Zealand, and the Union of South Africa also offered financial and military support to the cause.

In the United States, President Woodrow Wilson officially declared the United States neutral in the conflicts in Europe, and the U.S. continued trade with all sides.

Italy, although technically allied with Germany and Austria-Hungary, avoided the conflict on a technicality — the terms of its official alliance only promised military aid in the case of *defensive* war. Because Austria-Hungary attacked Serbia, this was an *offensive* war, and Italy at first declared neutrality. They did join the conflict a year later, allied with France, England, and Russia.

The United States finally entered the war on April 6, 1917, as a result of Germany's submarine warfare, which threatened America's commercial shipping industry. Before long, countries the world over, from Asia to South America were involved in the conflict.

World War I is also known as The Great War.

Winning the Great War

The United States managed to stay neutral in the European war from 1914 until 1917, but remaining neutral eventually became impossible. Germany's use of its new submarines to attack both military and merchant-marine ships angered Americans. Although they didn't necessarily want to enter a war, they would if they felt it could help the greater good of the world.

Most Americans already sympathized with the Allies — England, France, Italy, and Russia. Germany's aggressive acts of unrestricted warfare on nonmilitary ships were the final straw — the United States felt they had a moral obligation to help.

Prior to the United States entering the war, Germany had the upper hand. State-of-the-art war machinery like tanks, airplanes, and submarines created a new way of fighting and the Allies were losing the long, hard struggle. U.S. involvement brought fresh troops and more supplies — enough to turn things around and for the allies to triumph. Germany unconditionally surrendered on November 11, 1918.

After they entered the war, Americans did so with commitment and enthusiasm. Congress authorized the Selective Service Acts to begin drafting young men for battle. People bought savings bonds in order to raise funds for the war effort, and industry changed its focus from producing items for consumers to making items needed for war — weapons, ammunition, uniforms, and military supplies. Ordinary citizens pitched in by conserving resources such as oil and gasoline and by giving up items they normally enjoyed. For instance, each week had a "meatless" day. On this day, people were asked to give up meat so more food could be sent to the troops.

Safeguarding the future: The Treaty of Versailles

President Woodrow Wilson had a 14-Point Plan for peace that he outlined in a speech given to Congress on January 8, 1918. Wilson believed enacting his 14 points would form the foundation for lasting peace. After the war, Wilson and leaders of England, France, and Italy tried to negotiate a peace treaty based upon these important political ideals:

- No secret treaties or alliances
- Freedom of the seas
- Freedom of international trade
- Reduction of armaments
- Fair settlement of colonial claims
- *Self-determination* (the right of the people of a country to determine what type of government they want)
- The establishment of a League of Nations (see the nearby sidebar)

Although the allies did not agree with all of Wilson's ideas, some were incorporated into the Peace Treaty of Versailles, signed on June 18, 1919. However, the Treaty was much harsher and more restrictive than Wilson ever intended.

The German government was given three weeks to accept the terms of the massive treaty. The Treaty of Versailles took away significant German territory holdings, including some 7 million people, as well as all of Germany's overseas possessions. The region of Alsace-Lorraine was returned to France. Belgium expanded its borders to the east into formerly German territory. Furthermore, the treaty limited the German army to a maximum of 100,000 men, and restricted the navy to no more than 6 warships under 100,000 tons each. It prohibited the Germans from using heavy artillery, gas, tanks, aircraft, and submarines. It also called for Germany to pay *reparations,* or money, to the Allies in excess of £6,600,000,000 (about $10.4 billion U.S.) for the damage caused by the war. Perhaps most unfair, Germany was expected to formally accept *all* the blame for the war, in a portion of the treaty known as the War Guilt Clause.

The Treaty of Versailles is an enormous and complicated document, consisting of over 400 articles and numerous annexes. In addition to limiting German power and redistributing territories and boundaries, the treaty created new countries, including

- Czechoslovakia
- Estonia
- Finland
- Hungary
- Latvia
- Lithuania
- Poland
- Yugoslavia

The Treaty of Versailles remains controversial to this day. Many people then, as now, thought the terms far too harsh. After all, how could Germany be expected to accept *all* the responsibility? Furthermore, the money demanded in reparations proved an unreasonable amount. Many historians blame the treaty for establishing the groundwork that led to World War II (more on that later in this chapter).

Surviving the Great Depression

After World War I, Americans wanted life to get back to normal — peaceful times and an American policy of isolation and neutrality in foreign affairs. The economy had thrived during the war and in the period immediately following, known as the *Age of Normalcy.* But by the end of the 1920s, the economy was on a downslide. The efficiency of American industrialization was largely responsible:

- The U.S. produced more goods than it could sell.
- Due to high tariffs, sales of American goods to foreign countries were down.
- Because of low working wages, Americans were unable to purchase many of the goods they were producing.
- Many Americans lost jobs due to new machinery that automated a lot of the tasks that used to be done by hand.
- The high investment returns of the Industrial Revolution led many people to speculate and overinvest in the stock market.

Tough economic times caused people to become scared and quickly sell their stocks, which in turn caused the stock market crash that occurred on October 29, 1929, known as Black Tuesday. Businesses, including over 5,000 banks, failed. Factories shut their doors. By 1932, over a quarter of the U.S. workforce was out of work, and many of those who were employed were forced to accept reduced wages for their labor.

In 1932, as a result of the economic hardships of the Great Depression, the United States saw a significant change in the way its government functioned. Franklin D. Roosevelt became our thirty-second president with the promise to help the "forgotten man" (the common working man). Before his presidency, as the governor of the state of New York, Roosevelt had spent government money to give aid to those hurt by the Depression. His presidential campaign had three key points collectively known as the *New Deal:*

- **Relief:** Relief efforts provided government jobs or other financial assistance to the unemployed, as well as mortgage loans designed to prevent home- and landowners from losing their property.
- **Recovery:** Designed to help put people back to work, recovery efforts gave aid to farmers and business owners (in other words, the employers).
- **Reform:** Reform efforts sought to increase people's confidence in the economy and to prevent another Depression from ever happening. They protected bank deposits and other investments and regulated businesses and banks.

Roosevelt's policies represented a significant expanding of the government's role, which some saw as a movement against the principles of the Constitution. Nonetheless, people were in a panic about money. They believed in Roosevelt's policies and his optimism about the United States. He won the presidential election by a landslide.

The League of Nations

The forming of the League of Nations, a precursor to today's United Nations, was one of the most important points of the Treaty of Versailles. Those countries that ratified the treaty became members of the League, agreeing to settle any disagreements through negotiations. Supporting diplomacy, economic cooperation, and peaceful solutions to international disputes, the League optimistically sought to eliminate the need for war.

But the United States never actually *ratified* (officially accepted) the Treaty of Versailles. Many senators longed to go back to the U.S. foreign policy of isolationism. Ironically, even though it was part of President Woodrow Wilson's 14-Point Plan, the United States Senate refused to ratify the treaty because it would mean joining the League of Nations. The senate favored going back to a neutral position in foreign matters, as outlined by President George Washington.

Economic depressions in Europe

World War I left Europe burdened with overwhelming debt. Not only did the European governments need to repay bills accumulated during the war, but they were often left with the task of having to rebuild areas left ruined by the war's destruction. The United States's wartime allies France and Great Britain owed money to privately owned American companies as well as to the U.S. government. To make matters worse, trade and industry failed to thrive after the war, creating mass unemployment.

Instead of working together, the difficult conditions caused many European countries to place high tariffs on imported goods in order to protect domestic trade. Political instability followed. In addition, new countries were constantly threatened by the growing strength of communist Russia. Italian citizens overthrew their government and Germany hoped for a revision of the Treaty of Versailles. The aftereffects of the war weakened even France and England, the two countries that truly favored the Treaty of Versailles.

Despite the controversy, Roosevelt's measures helped the economy, at least in the short term, and people's confidence began to rise. Soon, the government employed over 5 million people to build highways, public buildings, dams, and parks. The U.S. slowly climbed out of the Depression, and by 1939, over ten years after it had begun, the Great Depression was finally over.

The World War II Years

Conditions in Europe in the early 1930s set the stage for World War II (1939–1945):

- Economic depressions increased fear and distrust, allowing extreme political groups and dictators to gain power.
- The countries that were part of the Treaty of Versailles had such a desire for peace that they neglected to properly prepare for military defense.

As soon as he gained power, Adolf Hitler began working on his dream of Germany dominating Europe by planning to conquer more territory. In October 1933, Germany withdrew from the League of Nations, claiming the Treaty of Versailles had left them militarily weak. Over the next few months, the German army grew three times as large as it had been under the conditions imposed by the treaty.

World War II officially began when Hitler's troops invaded Poland, without a Declaration of War, on September 1, 1939. Using new military techniques like mechanized and air warfare, the Germans quickly crushed the unprepared Polish defenses.

The attack prompted Poland's allies, Great Britain and France, to declare war on Germany. Other League of Nations members soon followed suit.

Choosing sides: The Axis and the Allies

Germany banded together with Italy and Japan to create the most important *Axis powers.* The countries the United States eventually went to war with had several things in common:

- All eventually adopted some form of dictatorship government that gave the state supreme authority.
- All were ambitious, fighting for expansion of territory at the expense of neighboring countries.

- All used an intolerance of communism as a way to gain support for their early actions from conservative groups.

The Allied countries — France and England at first, then later the Soviet Union, the United States, and many other smaller countries — opposed the Axis countries.

At first, the United States did not want to get involved in Europe's problems. Congress passed several Neutrality Acts before the war started. The acts stated that if a war in Europe began, the United States would not sell war goods or make loans to any country involved in the conflict. Regardless of public policy, most Americans sympathized with the Allied forces.

When war actually did break out in 1939, Congress passed yet another Neutrality Act. This one allowed the U.S. to sell war goods to countries involved in the conflict, providing those countries paid cash and picked up the goods themselves. Congress knew that the only countries who were in the position to take advantage of the arrangement were France and England. The Neutrality Act allowed the United States to unofficially help the Allies, while technically remaining neutral.

As the war went on, American sympathy for the Allies grew, and by 1940 most people in the U.S. favored some sort of intervention. Congress passed the Selective Service Act, which allowed the government to start drafting men to enter the military. The United States further helped Britain's war efforts by lending or leasing them goods needed for the war with the understanding that the items would be returned when the war was over. As Britain found itself in a tough financial position, the Lend-Lease Agreement allowed them to continue their fight without immediately having to pay for the cost of supplies. The U.S. also suspended trade with Japan, making it clear to the world that Americans clearly sided with the Allies, even though they had not officially entered the war.

Hitler's rise in Germany

Many Germans did not agree with the politicians who signed the *armistice* (peace agreement) that had brought World War I to an end on November 11, 1918. Because Germany had not actually been invaded, some people refused to accept that the German army had actually been defeated. General unrest about the conditions of the Treaty of Versailles also prevailed. For one thing, the amount of reparations required were unrealistic and, in fact, the German government gave up trying to pay them after only one year.

A lot of German citizens, including one by the name of Corporal Adolf Hitler, believed Germany had become Europe's scapegoat — unfairly blamed for all the negative effects of the Great War. The hatred felt for the Treaty of Versailles created a perfect environment for extremist political parties to thrive, including the German Workers' Party and the National Socialist, or Nazi, Party.

As the leader of the Nazi Party, Adolf Hitler possessed the skill of inspiring and mobilizing his followers. Hitler was appointed Reich Chancellor of Germany in 1933 and, after the 1934 death of the German president, he also assumed the title of *Führer* (leader).

In Hitler's Germany, individuals had no freedom of protest. Politics were completely under the control of the Nazis, and elections, both local and national, were abolished. It was under Hitler's leadership that Germany started World War II and under his orders that the atrocities of the Holocaust — including the murder of an estimated 6 million Jews and about 5 million other civilians — were committed.

Hitler didn't deal well with defeat. Instead of admitting he was capable of mistakes, he accused those around him of betrayal and tried to blame others. Despite early dominance in World War II, by 1943 it became clear to many German officers and government officials that Germany was destined to lose the war. Statesmen, government officials, and allies suggested Germany negotiate a peace agreement with England and the United States, but Hitler firmly rejected the idea. Eventually, several of Hitler's officers contemplated overthrowing the dictator. His colleagues planned numerous assassination attempts on his life, although none was successful.

When Soviet troops entered Germany near the end of the war, Adolf Hitler opted to commit suicide rather than risk capture by his enemies.

Mussolini's rise in Italy

In 1910, Benito Mussolini, a man who gained infamy in his later role as a ruthless fascist Italian dictator, became secretary of a local Socialist Party. His political views at this early stage of his career were almost the exact opposite of what they would later become. At the outbreak of World War I, Mussolini strongly opposed Italy's getting involved, but a few months later he suddenly changed his mind and abandoned the Socialist Party and his job as editor of a socialist newspaper.

Fascism (a harsh, controlling form of central government, usually headed by a dictator) became an organized political movement in 1919 when Mussolini founded the *Fasci de Combattimento.* Fascist types of government remove potential sources of opposition, and Mussolini found ways to manipulate political powers and alliances after being elected to the Italian Parliament in 1921. Within a year of taking office, he dissolved all political parties except his own and become a *dictator* (a ruler with absolute power). Italy turned into a police state, but Mussolini was so skillful at *propaganda* (manipulation of the press to further his own causes) that he had little opposition. Under his dictatorship, laws were rewritten and Italy's parliamentary system of government was destroyed.

When World War II began, Mussolini waited to declare his allegiance until he was more sure of who would win. In 1940, he finally attacked Greece and was promptly defeated.

Hitler, inspired by Mussolini's prior achievements, sought a close relationship with Italy. But following military defeats on all fronts, and the Allied occupation of Sicily, Mussolini's own political associates turned against him, and he was dismissed from power and arrested. His German allies rescued him a few months later, and he set up another fascist state in Northern Italy. In 1945, with the end of the war near and Allied troops approaching, Mussolini tried to escape to Switzerland, but he was captured and executed by Italian patriots.

The U.S. under attack: Pearl Harbor

On Sunday, December 7, 1941, a day that President Roosevelt said would "live in infamy," the Japanese unexpectedly attacked the United States military base at Pearl Harbor in Hawaii.

The United States declared war on Japan the next day. Within a few days, Germany and Italy declared war on the United States. The Allies had gained another powerful partner and the Axis countries a formidable enemy.

At first, the Axis countries prevailed in the war in the Pacific, with Japan conquering the Philippines, Burma, the Netherlands East Indies, and many other Pacific islands. The United States lacked significant military forces in the area, although Australia and China helped.

The first Allied naval successes against Japan were scored in the battles of the Coral Sea and Midway. U.S. bombers forced Japan into retreat, eliminating a big part of Japan's carrier fleet in the process.

"Relocating" citizens: Japanese interment in World War II

On February 19, 1942, President Franklin Roosevelt, fueled by a Congress caught in the grips of anti-Japanese hysteria, signed Executive Order 9066, effectively suspending the civil liberties of both American citizens of Japanese ancestry and legal resident aliens from Japan. Japanese Americans found themselves, on the government's orders, being rounded up and sent to interment camps, officially called *relocation camps.*

In the name of national defense, Roosevelt's order permitted the military to bypass constitutional safeguards guaranteed to American citizens.

In an effort to be "politically correct," Order 9066 never specifically mentioned people of Japanese ancestry. Instead, its broad wording might also be taken to include those of German or Italian descent. In reality, though, only a few thousand "enemy aliens" of German or Italian descent were ever arrested, most immediately after the bombing of Pearl Harbor. And although no German or Italian citizens were rounded up and herded into interment camps, over 100,000 people of Japanese ancestry were.

The camps were overcrowded and provided poor living conditions. People lived in simple barracks-style buildings, with heat, plumbing, or cooking facilities. Because food was short during the war, it was strictly rationed in the camps. Fortunately, families were generally kept together.

Eventually, the government agreed to allow internees to leave the camps if they enlisted in the U.S. military. Not surprisingly, the offer wasn't met with much enthusiasm, and only about 1,000 internees enlisted.

Two and a half years after signing Executive Order 9066, Roosevelt rescinded the order during his second term in office. The last interment camp was closed by the end of 1945.

Today, the sad history of the Japanese interment camps reminds us that no citizen should ever be denied the basic rights guaranteed to him or her in the Constitution, regardless of how unusual the circumstances.

Fighting Germany and Japan

France, although fighting valiantly, was quickly overpowered by Germany, and signed an *armistice,* or peace agreement, with Germany in June 1940. Under the leadership of Winston Churchill, Britain resisted, despite constant German bombing attacks that left many of England's important cities devastated.

When Germany had the bad sense to invade the Soviet Union in June of 1941, England gained a powerful ally. The 1943 German defeat at Stalingrad allowed the allied Soviet army to advance from the east. Germany remained on the retreat for the remainder of the war and Italy unconditionally surrendered in September 1943.

Pearl Harbor statistics

According to U.S. Army statistics, the Japanese attack on Pearl Harbor could be broken down into two waves:

- The first attack consisted of 183 aircraft that included 40 torpedo planes, 49 level bombers, 51 dive-bombers, and 43 fighters.
- The second wave consisted of 170 planes that included 54 level bombers, 80 dive-bombers, and 36 fighters.

The attack also included 4 heavy-aircraft carriers, 2 heavy cruisers, 35 submarines, 2 light cruisers, 9 oilers, 2 battleships, and 11 destroyers.

Over 2,400 U.S. personnel were killed.

Officially ending interment

Interestingly enough, Order 9066 was never officially removed from the books until 1976, when President Gerald Ford, in a show of bicentennial-celebration goodwill, officially repealed it on February 19, 1976.

Then in 1988, almost 50 years after the camps closed, Congress passed the Civil Liberties Act of 1988 (also known as the Japanese American Redress Bill), admitting that "a grave injustice was done" and mandating payment of $20,000 in reparations to each victim of interment. Reparations were sent with a signed apology from the President on behalf of the American people.

By 1944, the Allies had developed their air warfare skills, destroying many German cities and undermining industry and transportation throughout the German-controlled portions of Europe. The efforts of the Air Force also allowed allied ground forces to regain control of most of France and Belgium. The famous D-Day invasion of Normandy, France, in June 1944, began a massive effort to regain German-occupied territory of Europe, and led to the ultimate defeat of Adolf Hitler. Germany surrendered by May 1945.

Despite substantial Allied military victories in the Pacific, the Japanese refused to unconditionally surrender. Our new President, Harry S Truman, made the difficult decision to use the new atomic bomb to convince them. On August 6, 1945, the U.S. dropped the first atomic bomb on Hiroshima, Japan. An estimated 70,000 people were killed, but still the Japanese would not surrender. The U.S. dropped a second bomb on Nagasaki on August 9, 1945. Unable to sustain further losses, Japan surrendered on August 10, 1945, on the condition that Emperor Hirohito retain at least nominal power. World War II was officially over.

Calculating the effects of World War II

The scope of World War II, being even greater than World War I, left many aftereffects. Europe and Japan had to deal with bombed-out cities that were formerly populous centers of industry. The Axis countries of Germany, Italy, and Japan suffered nearly complete devastation. Even England and France lost large parts of their former empires, knocking them off the list of the world's leading superpowers.

The losses motivated countries to work together to overcome their hardships. The idea of an international organization again gained favor. In fact, Allied forces were working to set up the United Nations (UN) even before the war was over. Still in existence today, the UN works to promote peace by providing a forum where countries can come together to discuss peaceful solutions to problems and conflicts. It also provides educational and economic aid to countries in need.

The Allies also recognized the importance of free trade in order to avoid a depression like the one that followed World War I. They made tariff agreements that kept the flow of goods open between international communities.

The Cold War Years

With countries like England, France, and Germany sustaining devastating losses of people, property, and progress after World War II, the world was left with two main superpowers:

- The United States of America, with a democratic government
- The Soviet Union, with a communist government

Dominance in the arms race (by the 1950s, both superpower countries had nuclear bombs) and economic struggle for world power created these two superpowers.

The Soviet Union emerged a superpower after World War II despite sustaining the highest losses of any country involved in the war — 7.5 million military personnel and 15 million civilians.

The U.S. and the Soviet Union both believed their system of government worked best. Despite unifying efforts in Europe and the work of the United Nations, the world began to take sides. The U.S. *allied,* or joined forces with, Western Europe, while the Soviet Union maintained control over much of Eastern Europe.

Fighting communism: The Cold War between the world's superpowers

The Cold War (1947–1991) between the United States and the Soviet Union was not actually a war in the traditional sense. No guns or ammunition were used, and no actual battles were fought. Instead money and trade were the weapons the two sides used to win their victories.

These years represent the United States's further distancing from neutral foreign policy — a change that exists to this day. The 1947 Truman Doctrine declared that the U.S. would support any nation threatened by communism. In addition, under the Marshall Plan, the United States provided massive economic aid to Europe to help revitalize the failing European economies and to help prevent the spread of communism. The U.S. also helped to found and fund the International Monetary Fund and the World Bank — both of which lend money to developing nations in order to help them avoid communist influence.

In 1949, the alliance between the U.S. and Western Europe became formal with the forming of the North Atlantic Treaty Organization (NATO). NATO's policy was to limit, or *contain,* the Soviet Union to the areas where it already had influence. Members in the organization also vowed to defend each other if ever attacked.

To counter NATO, the Soviets enacted the Warsaw Pact, which formed a military organization with the nations of Eastern Europe. The Warsaw Pact sought to promote a peaceful coexistence of the world's powers, but also to defend member nations if necessary.

Battling communism in Asia: The Korean War

After World War II, Korea was divided into a northern zone governed by the Soviet Union and a southern zone helped by the U.S. Eventually, the Soviets withdrew, leaving a communist government in the North. In June 1950, North Korea attacked its Southern neighbor without warning.

At a meeting not attended by the Soviets, the United Nations voted to send troops to help South Korea defeat the intruders — the first use of UN military forces to enforce international peace. Initially, the UN army — comprised of mostly South Koreans and Americans — were smaller and less prepared than the North Koreans, who were supported by the Chinese. Eventually, other countries sent reinforcements and the North Koreans and Chinese retreated. Korea remained divided at the end of the Korean War, and it remains divided to this day.

Important historical milestones of the Cold War

For many people, the fight against communism became a fight of good versus evil. So passionate was the belief that the United States must do anything it could to fight communism, that that belief gave rise to fanatics. In 1950, Senator Joseph McCarthy asserted that the U.S. State Department had been "infested" with communists. A special Senate committee investigated his sensational claims and found them false. Nonetheless, McCarthy continued a tireless anticommunism crusade. Many important public figures were *slandered* — their reputations destroyed by lies of communist involvement. Televised hearings in 1954 changed public opinion. After the public got a look at McCarthy's ruthless tactics, a public outcry led to his official *censure,* or reprimand, in Congress. Further investigations halted.

The Cold War spawned many of the world's recent important historical events:

- **The Geneva Summit (1955):** A meeting in Geneva, Switzerland, between the Soviet Union (led by Nikita Krushchev) and the United States (led by President Dwight Eisenhower), as well as France and Britain. The meeting discussed how the countries could achieve a peaceful coexistence, learning to compromise in order to live together.
- **The Eisenhower Doctrine (1957):** Spawned by troubles in the Middle East, President Eisenhower proposed and obtained a joint resolution from Congress authorizing the use of U.S. military forces to aid any country that appeared likely to fall to communism.
- **Castro's Revolution in Cuba (1959):** Rebels led by Fidel Castro overthrew the corrupt government of Juan Baptista, turning Cuba into a communist country.
- **The Bay of Pigs (1961):** The Bay of Pigs Invasion was an unsuccessful attempt by American-trained and -supported Cuban exiles to overthrow the communist government of Fidel Castro. Landing at the Bay of Pigs in Southern Cuba, the brief military action ended in complete failure, with the counterrevolutionaries easily captured or killed by Castro's army. The failure seriously embarrassed new President John F. Kennedy and his administration.
- **Cuban Missile Crisis (1962):** The missile crisis was the closest the world has come to nuclear war up to this point in history. After the U.S. discovered the Soviets were building missile launch sites in Cuba, the U.S. announced a quarantine of Cuba. The quarantining effectively served as a *blockade* of Cuba, but the U.S. government was careful to never call it this, because a blockade is an official act of war.

  The confrontation led to the brink of war, the fate of the world depending on the ability of John F. Kennedy and Nikita Khrushchev to reach a compromise. Khrushchev ultimately backed down, agreeing to dismantle the launch sites, and the crisis was over.
- **Richard Nixon's visit to China (1972):** President Nixon's weeklong visit broke down longstanding barriers in U.S.-China relations. Nixon established a trade policy and recognized the People's Republic of China, even agreeing to support China's admission into the United Nations.
- **SALT I Agreement (1972):** President Richard Nixon and new Soviet Premier Leonid Brezhnev engaged in Strategic Arms Limitations Talks, resulting in limiting the amount of antiballistic missiles the two countries could hold. This led to a lessening of tensions between the U.S. and the Soviet Union.

Desegregating America: The Civil-Rights Movement

The fight against communism abroad wasn't the only problem the United States had to deal with after World War II. Domestic unrest that started during the Civil War was coming to a head.

President Lincoln's Emancipation Proclamation freed the slaves during the Civil War (for more on the Civil War, turn to Chapter 12).

Nonetheless, blacks in 1950s America, especially in the South, still suffered from *discrimination,* or unfair treatment based upon their race. Some states limited the right to vote for blacks. Schools, buses, trains, and public businesses like theaters and restaurants were often *segregated,* or separated into facilities for blacks and whites.

The fight for civil rights actually began during World War II when President Roosevelt established the Fair Employment Practices Committee, which prohibited discrimination practices on the basis of race, creed, color, or national origin, by the United States defense industry. His successor, President Harry S Truman furthered the cause by founding the Committee on Civil Rights, which stated that discrimination based on race or religion prevents the American ideal of democracy.

The Supreme Court chimed in on the fight in 1954 in a landmark ruling that stated "separate educational facilities are inherently unequal" *(Brown* v. *Board of Education of Topeka, Kansas).* This historic decision meant that segregation in schools was declared unconstitutional or against the supreme law of the land. The court ordered the schools to be desegregated.

American blacks finally had official government support in their fight for equality, but it was a constant struggle, especially against prominent Southern government officials who continually blocked civil-rights legislation. Even the court's order to desegregate schools was tested. In 1957, President Eisenhower had to send U.S. Army units to Arkansas to safely escort black children to a previously all-white school.

Reverend Martin Luther King, Jr., the most famous civil-rights leader, believed blacks could change society through nonviolent means (see Chapter 15 for more information on King). Blacks began to organize. Peaceful demonstrations and boycotts led to the desegregation of buses, restaurants, restrooms, and other public places. In 1963, about 250,000 participants, blacks and whites — the largest gathering of people to that date — marched on Washington, D.C., to demand civil rights. To guarantee equality for blacks, the federal government passed Civil Rights Acts in 1957, 1960, 1964, and 1968.

The Twenty-fourth Amendment, which outlawed taxing voters at presidential or congressional elections, passed in 1964 as another way to remove barriers to black voters. But evidence of continuing interference with attempts by African American citizens to exercise their right to vote, prompted Congress to pass the Voting Rights Act in 1965, with amendments added in 1970, 1975, and 1982. Considered to be the single most effective piece of civil-rights legislation Congress ever passed, black voter registration saw a marked increase soon after its passing. In order to battle unfair voting processes, the acts:

- Ended the use of literacy requirements for voting in six Southern states and in many counties of North Carolina.
- Prevented changes in voting procedures from being legally enforceable in those jurisdictions until they were approved by either a three-judge court in the District of Columbia or by the Attorney General of the United States.
- Gave the U.S. Attorney General authority to appoint federal voting examiners to ensure that legally qualified persons were free to register for federal, state, and local elections, and to assign federal observers to oversee elections.

Fighting the Vietnam War

During the time of President Eisenhower, the United States began to provide economic and military aid to the tiny country of South Vietnam.

TECHNICAL STUFF

What's in a name?

In discussions of the Vietnam War, you'll often hear the term Viet Cong. This was the name given to guerilla fighters on the Communist side. The North Vietnamese Army (NVA), on the other hand, were regular troops.

In the mid-nineteenth century, the French had established tentative control over the southernmost provinces of Vietnam. French rule in Vietnam was always troubled, with the country's natives resisting French domination. When the French expanded to central and northern Vietnam, they were met with an aggressive resistance movement. But the rebels were no match for France's large military force, and they were ultimately subdued. France began to exploit Vietnam's resources. Not surprisingly, the Vietnamese people felt exploited under French rule:

- Huge tracts of land in southern Vietnam were turned over to French settlers and Vietnamese collaborators.
- Vietnamese contract workers in mines and rubber plantations could be fined or even jailed if they tried to leave their jobs.
- Educational opportunities generally declined under French rule.
- Political rights and participation by the Vietnamese remained strictly under French control.
- The French used force to squash any protests, driving many Vietnamese into exile.

One of the most prominent Vietnamese rebels was Ho Chi Minh, known for organizing the League for Vietnamese Independence (abbreviated in Vietnamese as *Viet Minh*) in 1941. During World War II, the French lost their hold over Vietnam when they surrendered to Germany, and Japan assumed control of the country. The Viet Minh worked behind Japanese lines to supply information on Japanese troop movements to America's Office of Strategic Services (OSS). In return, they received some arms and supplies from the OSS and began building a small guerrilla force. When Japan surrendered to the United States, the Viet Minh were the most powerful political force in Vietnam.

On September 2, 1945, hoping his wartime allies would help restrain the French from trying to dominate Vietnam again, Ho Chi Minh proclaimed Vietnam a free and independent country.

Although the United States didn't necessarily approve of French tactics, a growing concern over Communist power in Asia led them to support the French war effort. Vietnam was soon under French control again, and the Viet Minh resumed their fight for independence.

The 1945 Geneva Conference brought a temporary end to fighting by dividing Vietnam at the 17th parallel.

Eisenhower believed the U.S. should support any country that was threatened by communism. Vietnam was a country divided:

- The northern part of Vietnam, led by Ho Chi Minh was communist.
- The southern part of Vietnam, led by Ngo Dunh Diem, who became Prime Minister of South Vietnam as the defeated French forces left, was fervently anticommunist.

When Kennedy succeeded Eisenhower as President, aid to South Vietnam increased. In 1964, when the North Vietnamese allegedly attacked two American destroyers, Congress passed the Gulf of Tonkin Resolution that gave then President Lyndon Johnson the authority to do whatever he thought was militarily necessary to protect our country. Suddenly the United States was at war with the tiny country of North Vietnam, a war that would last from 1964 until 1973.

Many Americans did not think the U.S. should be involved in this war. Bitter antiwar protests broke out throughout the country. President Richard Nixon campaigned on the promise to withdraw from Vietnam honorably. After his election, Nixon continued peace talks, which had been going on throughout the war, but with little result.

The war finally ended with the 1973 Paris Peace Agreement. Everyone involved compromised, and Vietnam returned to being a divided country.

Despite the Paris Peace Agreement, fighting between the South Vietnamese and the communists continued. In early 1975, North Vietnam launched an attack on its southern neighbor. This time the U.S. Congress denied South Vietnam's requests for aid. On April 30, 1975, North Vietnamese troops marched into Saigon, and the South Vietnamese resistance collapsed. Vietnam was formally reunified in July 1976, and Saigon was renamed Ho Chi Minh City, after the leader of North Vietnam.

U.S. casualties in Vietnam during the era of direct U.S. involvement (1961–1972) were more than 50,000 dead. The war divided the U.S. along political lines as well — those who opposed the war and those who believed the U.S. should fight. It made people again examine the Founding Fathers' beliefs in American neutrality in foreign conflicts, although we have never again been able to return to those earlier ideals.

Understanding the U.S. Today

Although popular interpretations of the Constitution have changed over the years, Americans still look to their most important document when creating laws and deciding the best way to run the country. Changes in public sentiment along with complicated international politics have forever changed the United States's policy of neutrality in foreign affairs. Nonetheless, our government's system of checks and balances still ensures against any one person or group gaining so much power that they can overthrow the will of the people.

The U.S. currently finds itself fighting a war the Founding Fathers could have never conceived — not against an aggressive country, but rather against unknown groups of terrorists.

In recent years, the United States has had to grow and adapt to new challenges, especially in the area of international relations.

The only president never to be elected

Gerald R. Ford holds the unusual honor of being the only United States President to never have been elected. How is this possible? When Richard Nixon's Vice President, Spiro Agnew, resigned, Nixon selected Gerald Ford up to the Vice President spot. When Nixon resigned, after the Watergate scandal, Ford became the nation's new President.

Important recent historical events

Several important historical events have taken place from the Vietnam War through the present:

- **The fight for women's rights (1966):** The National Organization for Women (NOW) was founded to "to take action" to bring about equality for all women, including equal rights with men, equal employment opportunities, equal pay for equal work, divorce-law changes, and legalized abortion. To this day, NOW remains a major political force, with over 500,000 members.
- **The U.S. wins the moon race (1969):** Neil Armstrong became the first man to walk on the moon on July 20, 1969.
- **Arab oil embargo (1973):** To try to put pressure on the United States to take a pro-Arab political stance, the Organization of Petroleum Exporting Countries (OPEC) — an international oil *cartel* or organization controlled by an Arab majority — joined together and imposed an *embargo,* or suspension of trade, on all U.S.-bound oil. The U.S. began to realize how dependent it was on foreign oil, and saw the need to do something about it.
- **Building of the Alaska pipeline (1975):** An above-ground pipe 4 feet in diameter, the pipeline is used to pump oil from the fields of northern Alaska to a tanker station in Valdez Bay where it is put aboard ships for transport to the continental U.S., thereby reducing some of the need for foreign oil.
- **The Watergate Scandal (1972):** Five men were arrested for breaking into the Democratic National Committee's executive quarters in the Watergate Hotel on June 17, 1972. Further investigation showed that President Nixon himself might be involved. Although he withheld them at first, the Supreme Court ordered Richard Nixon to turn over tape recordings of the plans for the cover-up of the scandal. Senate hearings began in 1973, and Nixon finally admitted his involvement. When his *impeachment trial* began — a trial that could remove him from office if he was found guilty — he decided to resign instead.
- **Panama Canal Treaty (1978):** Passed by President Jimmy Carter, the treaty called for the gradual return of the Panama Canal to the people and government of Panama by 1999.
- **Iran hostage crisis (1979):** The overthrow of the Shah of Iran by Islamic rebels led to a steady decline in U.S.-Iran relations. In protest of the U.S. admitting the exiled Shah to America for medical treatment, a crowd of Iranians seized the U.S. embassy. About 90 people were inside, 52 remained in captivity until the end of the crisis 444 days later. At first, President Carter tried economic sanctions, then diplomatic negotiations, all of which failed. A rescue effort, attempted in April 1980, also failed miserably and resulted in the deaths of eight U.S. soldiers. Carter's inability to resolve the situation was a contributing factor in his defeat in his bid for reelection. Ironically, the hostage crisis was finally resolved the day Carter left office and Ronald Reagan was inaugurated. With the assistance of Algerian intermediaries, the United States had negotiated a deal to have the hostages released in exchange for the release of almost $8 billion in Iranian assets.
- **Economic growth and the digital revolution (1990s):** The 1990s in the United States saw a time of great economic growth and birth of the digital revolution. Just as the Industrial Revolution fueled a period of economic growth, so did the birth of the Internet and digital revolution in America in the 1990s. Like the Industrial Revolution, it also led to wild speculation, overinvesting in the stock market, and an economic recession that followed (although not nearly as bad as the Great Depression).

Trouble in the Middle East: The Gulf War

Iraq's invasion of Kuwait on August 2, 1990, began a conflict that included the United States, England, Egypt, France, and Saudi Arabia, along with a coalition of 27 other nations. Iraqi President Saddam Hussein defended the attack by claiming that overproduction of oil in Kuwait had cost the Iraqi economy millions of dollars. He also accused the Kuwaitis of illegally pumping oil from Iraq's Rumaila oil field.

The United Nations placed a trade embargo on Iraq, setting a deadline of January 15, 1992, for a peaceful withdrawal of Iraqi troops from Kuwait. Saddam Hussein stood his ground and refused to leave. In response, the U.S.-led coalition of nations launched Operation

Desert Storm, a massive air war that destroyed much of Iraq's military *infrastructure,* or foundation. The main coalition ground forces invaded Kuwait and Iraq on February 24 and in only four days, defeated the Iraqis, freeing the people of Kuwait. Despite victory, both sides sustained enormous losses.

Worst of all, Saddam Hussein, a brutal dictator, retained power in Iraq. Although he agreed to coalition peace terms on paper, in reality he took great efforts not to comply with the terms, especially on the issue of UN weapons inspections. Continued resistance to weapons inspections led to the coalition resuming bombing raids against Iraq.

As of this writing, the United States again finds itself at war with Saddam Hussein and Iraq over the issue of weapons inspections. The outcome is yet to be determined.

The U.S. today

On September 11, 2001, The United States experienced its worst attack since the Japanese attack on Pearl Harbor in World War II. New York's World Trade Center and the Pentagon building in Washington were hit by commercial airliners, hijacked by Middle Eastern terrorists.

This center of world commerce, along with the headquarters of United States military operations, provided prominent political targets for the terrorists. Thousands of lives were lost; calculating the loss to the U.S. economy is impossible because the results are still being felt.

For the first time, the U.S. finds itself in a war against not a country, but against terrorists who know no borders. The search for Osama Bin Laden, the man believed responsible for planning and executing the attacks, continues, and the United States is ready to fight.

Chapter 14

Celebrating U.S. Holidays and Observances

In This Chapter

- Letting freedom ring: Independence Day
- Commemorating the nation's heroes
- Discovering more reasons to celebrate

Americans love to celebrate, and throughout the year they find many reasons to do just that. Some of the celebrations, like the Fourth of July (also known as Independence Day), are joyous. Others, like Memorial Day, serve as solemn reminders of the sacrifices that formed our nation while celebrating the freedom we hold so dear. Still other American holidays, like Halloween, are just for fun.

For the purposes of passing your citizenship test, concentrate on knowing about the patriotic or government holidays and celebrations. But to live your life in the U.S. to the fullest, check out the traditions, joys, and memories that come with celebrating all the events in this chapter.

Celebrating Freedom: Independence Day

Independence Day is the national holiday commemorating the signing of the Declaration of Independence by the Continental Congress on July 4, 1776, in Philadelphia, Pennsylvania. Also known simply as the Fourth of July, Americans use this day to get together with friends, family, and other members of their communities to celebrate their patriotism.

Because it comes in July when the weather in most of the country is warm and sunny, many people celebrate with picnics and barbecues. Parks as well as backyards across America are filled with the scent of burgers on the grill. American flags fly, and you can see red, white, and blue everywhere — from the decorations in shop windows to the clothing of many revelers.

On the Fourth of July, you'll find most U.S. communities sponsor large displays of brilliant, noisy fireworks — reminiscent of the guns and bombs of the war for independence. Check your local newspapers around the holiday to find a fireworks display near you. Community Fourth of July festivities, which usually include patriotic music, entertainment, and, of course, fireworks, provide fun for the entire family and are usually free of charge or very low cost.

Honoring America's Heroes

Many of America's holidays honor her heroes — the men and women who made this country what it is today. Taking part in observances that celebrate America's heroes is a good way to find out about the most important people in American history.

As of this writing, some citizens groups are lobbying to create a national holiday to remember the victims of the terrorist attacks of September 11, 2001. Although on the surface, designating a day a national holiday may seem like a great idea, it's not as simple as it looks. Holidays have a *huge* financial impact on taxpayers, because they give all federal employees a paid day off from work. Countless groups lobby Congress to honor their heroes with a holiday. Elected officials must walk a delicate political balance when choosing who does and does not merit their own special day, and new holidays are very rarely added.

Presidents' Day

Each year, Americans celebrate the third Monday in February as Presidents' Day, a day that honors the accomplishments and contributions of all the past U.S. presidents. But it wasn't always so. Prior to 1971, citizens celebrated George Washington's birthday as a federal holiday in February; Abraham Lincoln's birthday, although never designated a federal holiday, was officially celebrated in several states. All that changed in 1971, when President Richard Nixon renamed the holiday and broadened its scope to honor *all* our past presidents. However, most citizens still think of the day as honoring Washington and Lincoln.

You usually won't find any major celebrations or parties going on for Presidents' Day, but it does give many folks a much-needed day off from work. It has also become a day when many merchants offer special sales.

If you want to celebrate two of our most important presidents in their own right, George Washington was born on February 22, 1732, in Westmoreland County, Virginia, and Abraham Lincoln was born on February 12, 1809, in Hardin County, Kentucky.

Martin Luther King, Jr., Day

Each year on the third Monday of January, the U.S. celebrates and honors the life, work, and dream of slain civil-rights leader Dr. Martin Luther King, Jr.

When to celebrate?

Sometimes holidays in the U.S. can be confusing, because only four American holidays are still celebrated on the same calendar day every year:

- New Year's Day (January 1)
- Independence Day (July 4)
- Halloween (October 31)
- Christmas (December 25)

Other holidays occur at the same time each year, but not necessarily on the same date:

- Thanksgiving is observed on the fourth Thursday in November.
- Easter varies each year, depending on the time of the full moon.

Most other national holidays were changed so they can be celebrated on a Monday. This comes as a result of the Uniform Holidays Bill, signed in 1968. The bill gives federal employees three-day weekends on Presidents' Day, Memorial Day, Veterans' Day, and Columbus Day, regardless of on which day of the week the holiday actually falls.

TECHNICAL STUFF

What's the difference?

A lot of people, including many American citizens, don't understand the difference between Memorial Day and Veterans' Day. Memorial Day honors and remembers the military men and women who *died* in service to their country. Veterans' Day is set aside to honor *everyone* who honorably served in the military, living or dead, in times of war or peace.

The newest of our federal holidays, Ronald Reagan signed the legislation that created the holiday in 1983. Despite the challenges that creating a new national holiday presented to them, the Southern Christian Leadership Conference (SCLC) felt so strongly about Dr. King's message of nonviolent social change that they worked diligently on the cause of starting a national holiday in his honor. They created one of the largest petition drives in history — gathering over 6 million signatures — and submitted them to Congress in 1970. The group applied continuous pressure during a long, hard, 15-year lobbying effort. It finally paid off when the country celebrated the first Martin Luther King, Jr., Day in 1983.

Many communities hold parades and other programs celebrating the life and work of Dr. King. Check your local newspapers for information on programs near you.

Columbus Day

Columbus Day honors explorer Christopher Columbus, who "discovered" the New World on October 12, 1492 (see Chapter 12 for more about Columbus and his discovery).

Because Columbus is widely believed to be of Italian descent, many Italian American organizations hold Columbus Day celebrations and parades in the explorer's honor.

For years, October 12 was celebrated as Columbus Day, but like so many other holidays, that changed with the Uniforms Holiday Bill, when the holiday moved to the second Monday in October.

Labor Day

Celebrated on the first Monday in September, Labor Day honors the contributions workers have made to the strength and prosperity of the U.S. Unlike most other holidays that celebrate victories of war, or fallen heroes, Labor Day honors the common man and woman.

Leading union officials, industrialists, educators, and government officials often give Labor Day addresses. Check your local newspaper for schedules. Aside from that, Americans typically look to the day as a paid holiday, with little thought to the actual meaning behind it.

Memorial Day

Celebrated on the last Monday in May, Memorial Day honors our deceased military heroes — men and women who have died defending their country.

Parades and football

For many Americans, it just isn't Thanksgiving Day without watching the annual Macy's Thanksgiving Day Parade. The famous New York City department store has sponsored the enormous parade every year since 1927. Larger-than-life helium character balloons proudly fly in the sky high above New York's crowded streets, and the sounds of marching bands fill the air. You and your children can always count on a guest appearance by Santa Claus. If you can't get to New York to actually attend the Macy's Thanksgiving Day Parade, you can always watch it live on television. Check your local listings on Thanksgiving morning.

Football fans also have much to give thanks for on Thanksgiving, because it is one of the biggest days of the year for both college and professional football. You won't be able to flip through your TV channels from noon till night on Thanksgiving Day without seeing a football game, football discussion, football highlights, or any number of other football-related programming.

And for the record, we don't mean soccer, we mean American football — the kind with the giant men who run into each other and tackle over an oddly shaped ball with pointy ends.

The holiday began in 1866 in Waterloo, New York, when drugstore owner Henry Welles had the idea to set aside one day to honor the Northern Civil War soldiers who were buried in the town's cemetery. On the morning of May 5, the townspeople decorated the graves of the soldiers with flowers, wreaths, and crosses. At roughly the same time period, another ceremony called Decoration Day took place in Waterloo, honoring soldiers who survived the war. Veterans marched through town to the cemetery to decorate the veterans' graves with flags. By 1882, Decoration Day became known as Memorial Day, and the tribute extended to military personnel who had died in all previous wars. In 1971, President Richard Nixon declared Memorial Day a federal holiday to be celebrated on the last Monday in May.

National cemeteries throughout the land host Memorial Day remembrance ceremonies. Your local newspapers are a good source of information about Memorial Day activities in your area.

Veterans' Day

The holiday we now celebrate as Veterans' Day originally went by another name. In 1938, Congress declared November 11 a day to be dedicated to the cause of world peace and to be known as Armistice Day. In 1954, after World War II, Congress amended the Act of 1938 by substituting the word *Veterans'* for the word *Armistice,* at the urging of several veterans' service organizations. Armistice Day celebrated World War I veterans. The new holiday, Veterans' Day, sets aside time to honor *all* veterans.

The real Veterans' Day is always observed on November 11 and the Veterans' Day National Ceremony, like most Veterans' Day observances around the country, is still celebrated on November 11. Federal employees, on the other hand, get a paid holiday for Veterans' Day — a Monday or a Friday, depending on which day of the week November 11 falls.

Celebrating Other Important American Holidays and Observances

Not all American holidays are patriotic or commemorate heroes. Some, like Christmas, have religious meaning. Others, like New Year's Day, mark the passing of time. But all holidays give reason to take time to appreciate the important things in life and to connect with friends and family.

Thanksgiving

On the fourth Thursday in November, Americans throughout the land traditionally sit down with their closest friends and family to a huge feast and give thanks for their blessings. Turkey serves as the traditional main course for this dinner that draws its origins from the Pilgrims who landed at Plymouth Rock in 1620.

The Pilgrims were the first group of settlers who came to America seeking religious freedom. Unprepared for their first harsh winter in what is now Massachusetts, only about half survived. Friendly Native Americans helped the remaining Pilgrims learn how to hunt, fish, and farm. The following year's harvest was so successful that the Pilgrims and Native Americans sat down to a huge feast.

Because giving thanks would have called for a day of fasting and prayer to the devoutly religious Pilgrims, the first Thanksgiving was likely much different than the holiday we celebrate today. For starters, it lasted three days! It was, in essence, a huge potluck dinner with the various guests bringing food that could be shared with all. It can be assumed that it was held in the great outdoors, because the colonists didn't have buildings large enough to accommodate the large number of people who attended. (If you've ever spent an autumn in New England, you know this can be a chilly proposition.) Turkey was probably on the menu, as was pumpkin or squash in one form or another. One entrée that hasn't stood the test of time is venison (deer), a staple of the 90 or so Native Americans invited to the dinner. The dinner also probably included ducks, geese, and even swans. Games, races, and demonstrations of skills with bows and arrows and muskets added to the festival atmosphere.

But the Pilgrims never repeated their feast. Customs of celebrating an annual day of Thanksgiving after the autumn didn't get national recognition until the late 1770s when it was suggested by the Continental Congress during the American Revolution. New York officially adopted Thanksgiving Day as an annual custom in 1817, and many other states soon followed suit. But it wasn't until 1863 that President Abraham Lincoln appointed a national day of Thanksgiving. Since then, each president has issued a Thanksgiving Day proclamation.

Today most Americans celebrate by getting together with loved ones for a special dinner, and spending a little time reflecting on their blessings.

Christmas

Each year, Christians around the world celebrate the birth of Jesus Christ on December 25, known as Christmas. Although Christian Americans still observe the holiday's religious roots, Christmas in the U.S. has also taken on a more *secular* (or nonreligious), festive quality, making it a favorite holiday of children and revelers, not to mention storeowners. Undoubtedly the biggest holiday in the U.S., the whole country seems to celebrate at this time of year.

Who is Santa Claus?

The fanciful story of Santa Claus is based on Saint Nicholas. Dutch immigrants brought their Christmas traditions of Saint Nicholas with them when they came to America in the seventeenth century. Although their St. Nick was a kind man who left treats for children, he didn't much resemble the fat man in the red suit we know today. The American image of Santa Claus comes from a combination of images from the poem "A Visit from St. Nicholas" (also known as "The Night Before Christmas"), written in 1822 by Dr. Clement C. Moore, and a series of Christmas drawings for *Harper's Weekly* magazine by cartoonist Thomas Nast. It was there that the fat, rosy-cheeked, bearded Santa made his debut, and Americans have envisioned him that way ever since.

Christmas involves different traditions for different ethnic groups. Even individual families have developed their own special Christmas traditions over the years. Common ways to celebrate in the U.S. include the following:

- **Christmas gifts:** Americans celebrating Christmas typically give each other gifts, so expect televisions, radios, and newspapers to be flooded with Christmas-focused advertising in the months leading up to the holiday.
- **Christmas trees:** A tradition with pagan origins and popular in Europe for centuries, the first recorded sighting of a Christmas tree in the U.S. came in 1830s Pennsylvania; a local church there erected the tree as a fundraising effort. Christmas trees were generally not thought of kindly in early America, because many people saw them as pagan symbols. By the 1890s, however, Christmas ornaments were being imported to the United States from Germany, and Christmas trees were in high fashion. With the advent of electricity, Christmas trees began to appear in town squares across the U.S. and the traditional "lighting of the tree" quickly became the official symbol of the beginning of the holiday season. Although Europeans generally favored smaller trees — about 3 to 4 feet in height — Americans like to do things big, and it's not uncommon to see decorated trees proudly stretching from floor to ceiling.
- **Christmas lights and decorations:** Many Americans decorate the outside of their homes with lights for the holidays. In some neighborhoods, decorating has become a friendly competition, with one home trying to outshine the next. Local newspaper or television news will probably let you know which neighborhoods in your area are worth visiting to view Christmas decorations.
- **Nativity scenes:** The true meaning of Christmas is not lost in all the festivities. Among Christmas decorations, you'll see statue replicas of the night when Christ was born in a manger. Local churches usually stage live reenactments as well.
- **Santa Claus:** Fat, jolly, bearded, and clothed in a bright red suit, Santa Claus is a mythical figure who travels in a sleigh pulled by flying reindeer on Christmas Eve, leaving gifts for children all over the world.

In many communities, public displays of Christmas decorations also include references to the Jewish holiday of Hanukkah and the African American celebration of Kwanzaa. Look for the nine-candled menorah symbolizing Hanukkah and the seven-candled Kwanzaa kinara. Like Christmas, gift giving is one of the main ways of celebrating Hanukkah and Kwanzaa.

Trees and lights are not the only things on display during the holidays — so are our constitutional rights. Holiday displays sponsored by government entities are bound by the First Amendment's separation of church and state, which the Supreme Court has interpreted to preclude displays of a strictly religious nature. Trees and lights are fine, but nativity scenes are suspicious, unless they are part of a broader display featuring nonreligious decorations as well.

New Year's

New Year's is the great equalizer holiday. Regardless of cultural background, ethnicity, religion, or economic stature, the death of one year and the birth of a new one are cause for revelry.

January 1 marks the official first day of the New Year, but most Americans celebrate the night before, on New Year's Eve, with parties. At the stroke of midnight, everyone toasts the coming year and (usually) kiss the people around them, wishing each other a happy New Year.

Some communities sponsor New Year's "First Night" celebrations, which provide alcohol-free family fun and entertainment. Check your local area for festivities you may be able to join.

Celebrating religious freedom

Depending on where you live, you may encounter people celebrating other religious holidays and observances. The U.S. is composed of a collection of immigrants of different ethnic races and religious beliefs, and the right to freedom of religion is guaranteed in the Constitution. Especially in big cities, where large communities of ethnic immigrants tend to live in one area, you will encounter neighbors, friends, and coworkers who celebrate Jewish, Muslim, Hindu, or Buddhist holidays.

Easter

Easter is the Christian celebration commemorating the resurrection of Christ from the dead, after his crucifixion on Good Friday. Although Easter is perhaps the most serious Christian holiday, much like Christmas it has also taken on a more secular and festive nature in recent times. Immigrants coming to America brought their own Easter traditions with them. For instance, nearly every Christian culture has some type of special celebratory Easter bread. Many Easter traditions, like the Easter Bunny (who, much like Santa Claus, comes at night, leaving small treats for children), and brightly dyed Easter eggs have their roots in ancient pagan traditions. Every year the White House hosts an Easter egg hunt, where children are invited onto the White House lawn to look for the colored eggs, collecting them in their Easter baskets. Although not a federal holiday, Easter is used by many school districts as a gauge for setting their spring break.

Since the year A.D. 326, Easter has been celebrated on the first Sunday after the first full moon on or after the vernal equinox of March 21. Easter can come as early as March 22 or as late as April 25. It coincides (roughly) with the Jewish celebration of Passover (calculated by the Jewish lunar calendar) — and with good reason: Jesus's Last Supper preceding his death on Good Friday was a Passover *Seder* (a ceremonial meal commemorating the Jews' exodus from Egypt).

Recognizing Other Celebrations in the U.S.

Americans have lots of other reasons to celebrate — reasons having nothing to do with wars or heroes or events that helped shape our nation. In fact, none of the following days are actually official holidays at all. Children still go to school, people still attend to their jobs — but that doesn't stop Americans from celebrating.

Valentine's Day

Celebrated on February 14, Valentine's Day in the U.S. has two sides. For adults, it's a time to celebrate romance and to appreciate their husbands, wives, boyfriends, and girlfriends. Romantic gifts like flowers and candy are traditionally exchanged, and it is one of the most popular days of the year for couples to marry. Schoolchildren also celebrate the day by exchanging small greeting cards, brightly decorated with hearts, cupids, and silly jokes, with other classmates in a show of friendship. Valentine's Day is the second most popular occasion for sending greeting cards, surpassed only by Christmas.

Until the mid-1800s, the cost of sending mail was beyond the means of the average person, and the recipient, not the sender, was expected to pay the cost of mailing. It wasn't until the advent of the penny post that the modern custom of sending Valentine's Day cards really gained critical mass.

Mardi Gras

Unless you live in the Southern states of Alabama, Mississippi, Texas, and Louisiana, you may never encounter a Mardi Gras celebration. But if you do go to the South a couple of months before Easter, be prepared for parties, parades, and celebrations. Mardi Gras, also known as *Fat Tuesday,* is the celebration leading up to the Christian period of Lent. Mardi Gras season — also know as *carnival* in many Latin communities — officially begins on Twelfth Night, or the Christian Feast of the Epiphany, and concludes on Shrove Tuesday, just before Ash Wednesday and the beginning of Lent. Traditionally, it is a time of feasting and celebrations before the onset of the upcoming sacrifices. In the old days, and to many Christians today, this mostly meant the giving up of meat for the period of Lent (hence the name Mardi Gras, which is French for *Fat Tuesday*). Although there is an actual Mardi Gras day, the folks in the South really love to celebrate, and you'll find parades and festivities going on throughout the entire Mardi Gras season. Check local newspaper listings for details.

St. Patrick's Day

Irish immigrants brought St. Patrick's Day, celebrated on March 17, to the United States. Although the day officially honors Patrick, the patron saint of Ireland (who, legend holds, rid the Emerald Isle of snakes), in popular culture it has evolved into a time of parties, merriment, and sometimes even parades, especially in Irish neighborhoods.

Mother's Day and Father's Day

Mother's Day is celebrated on the second Sunday in May, and Father's Day is celebrated on the third Sunday in June. They are days that Americans set aside to honor their mothers and fathers (and even grandmothers and grandfathers). Cards, small gifts, and a day off from household chores are traditional ways to make the day special for moms and dads.

Halloween

Celebrated on October 31, Halloween has its origins in the Catholic Church, coming from a contraction of the words *Hallowed Eve.* The Christian All Souls Day celebration centers on prayer and remembrances for the dead. When these mixed with ancient pagan traditions, the eventual result became a celebration for children. Children dressed as ghosts went from door to door asking for treats, or else a trick would be played on the owners of the home (hence the phrase *trick or treat*). When millions of Irish immigrated to the United States in the 1840s, the tradition followed them.

Today in the U.S., Halloween is a time when people dress up in costumes, and spooky entertainment like ghost stories and horror movie are everywhere. The tradition of children going door to door and trick or treating still exists in some communities, but safety concerns have eliminated the activity in most large cities. Community-sponsored Halloween events are a safer and more practical way to celebrate with your family. Check your local newspapers for community Halloween activities in your area.

Chapter 15

Important American Heroes

In This Chapter

- Creating a new nation: Our Founding Fathers
- Elevating women: Susan B. Anthony
- Fighting for civil rights: Abraham Lincoln and Martin Luther King, Jr.

The U.S. would be nothing without her heroes. Americans owe their national heroes a debt of gratitude, because their contributions helped shape this nation into the strong, freedom-loving, democratic country it is today. These ambitious people saw problems and were not afraid to get involved and work to create change and a better world for us all.

Finding out about these people will also provide you with a stronger understanding of American history and better prepare you to take your citizenship test.

Meeting the Founding Fathers

Without the influence of her Founding Fathers, the U.S. might still be a British colony, or at least have some kind of international association with Britain, such as membership in the Commonwealth of Nations. But these freedom fighters had a bigger vision — a vision of a free and independent democratic society. Although many more men than those listed here were instrumental in the forming of our nation, George Washington, Benjamin Franklin, Thomas Jefferson, James Madison, and Alexander Hamilton represent the most important and influential of our Founding Fathers.

George Washington

The man who became the first President of the United States was born February 22, 1732, in Westmoreland County, Virginia, to a family of planters. Washington's love of farming remained consistent throughout his life, although he became much better known for his military and political accomplishments.

Washington was commissioned a lieutenant colonel in 1754, where he fought the first fights of what grew into the French and Indian War. At the Second Continental Congress in 1775, Washington was elected Commander in Chief of the Continental Army.

From 1759 until the start of the Revolutionary War, Washington managed his lands around his home in Virginia, called Mount Vernon. He also served in the Virginia *House of Burgesses,* the colony's seat of government.

After the war, Washington planned to retire, but he was troubled by the problems the new nation faced being governed by the Articles of Confederation (you can find out more about the Articles in Chapter 9). He soon began to work toward establishing a Constitutional Convention.

After ratifying the Constitution, the delegates unanimously elected Washington the first President of the United States. He took the oath of office on April 30, 1789, standing on the balcony of Federal Hall on Wall Street in New York City with John Adams serving as his Vice President.

By the end of his first term in office, Washington was disappointed that two political parties were developing in the United States. In his farewell address, he urged his countrymen to forego political-party spirit and geographical distinctions between the states. He also warned against long-term foreign alliances; the United States was largely able to maintain a position of neutrality in foreign affairs until World War I. Despite his personal beliefs, Washington never infringed upon the policy-making powers the Constitution gave Congress.

After leaving office, Washington retired to Mount Vernon, his beloved home. Unfortunately, he was only able to enjoy it for about three years. George Washington died of a throat infection on December 14, 1799.

Benjamin Franklin

An inventor, statesman, and philosopher, Benjamin Franklin was one of the most influential of our Founding Fathers, despite the fact that he never held the presidential office. A printer by trade, Franklin's book *Poor Richard's Almanac* became the best-selling book in the colonies, selling over 10,000 copies a year. In addition to publishing the *Pennsylvania Gazette,* he helped establish newspapers in New York, Connecticut, and two islands in the West Indies.

At 81, Franklin was the oldest delegate to the Constitutional Convention. During the fight for independence, he traveled to Europe to represent the colonies, negotiating with the French to help the colonial cause by securing guns, ammunition, and other provisions for the army as well as volunteer troops. He also helped negotiate the peace treaty with England after America won its independence from England.

Franklin had many inventions to his credit including:

- Swim fins
- Bifocal eyeglasses
- Glass harmonica
- Watertight bulkheads for ships
- Lightning rod
- Odometer
- A style of wood stove that came to be known as the Franklin stove

Franklin's experiments led to the discovery that lightning is actually a form of electricity (and not a punishment from God, as was thought at the time). He was knocked unconscious several times during his experiments, which entailed flying a kite in an electrical storm with a piece of metal at one end and a metal key at the other. His experiments with lightning led him to invent the lightning rod, which protected buildings from lightning fires and damage, and opened the door for many important advances in electricity that came later. Although he received much recognition for his inventions, Franklin didn't profit from them, choosing instead to give them freely to the world.

Benjamin Franklin is the only Founding Father to have signed all five documents that established American independence: the Declaration of Independence, the Treaty of Amity and Commerce with France, the Treaty of Alliance with France, the Treaty of Peace with Great Britain, and the Constitution of the United States of America.

Thomas Jefferson

Thomas Jefferson, our third president, was born on April 13, 1743, in Virginia, but even before he became the Commander in Chief, he made major contributions to the country. With the help of Benjamin Franklin and John Adams, Jefferson wrote the original Declaration of Independence (you can find more on this in Chapter 9) at the age of 33. He was elected to Congress in 1783 and succeeded Benjamin Franklin as minister to France in 1785. George Washington chose Jefferson as his Secretary of State in 1789. But this was the dawn of political parties in the U.S. Sharp differences between Federalist Alexander Hamilton and Democratic-Republican Thomas Jefferson prompted Jefferson to resign his position a few years later. Sympathetic toward the French Revolution, Jefferson also opposed a strong central government, believing most of the power of government should remain with the states.

Jefferson ran for president in 1796, losing by three votes.

Before the adoption of the Twelfth Amendment, the candidate with most electoral votes became president, and the candidate with the second highest number of votes became vice president. Jefferson became Vice President under his opponent John Adams.

By the time Jefferson became president, the revolution in France was over. He was able to cut taxes and reduce the national debt, as well as acquire the Louisiana Territory from Napoleon, probably the most notable act of his administration. But war between England and France was raging in Europe, with both countries interfering with American merchant ships. In an attempt to keep the United States neutral in the European conflicts, Jefferson placed an *embargo* (a government order prohibiting shipping) on merchant ships. The embargo was wildly unpopular, ending Jefferson's presidency on a low note.

After retiring to Monticello, his mountaintop home, Jefferson founded the University of Virginia. He died on July 4, 1826.

James Madison

Our fourth president, James Madison, was born in 1751 in Virginia. Perhaps more important than his role as president, however, was the impact he had on preparing and ratifying the country's most important document, the Constitution. Madison didn't just prepare the Bill of Rights; his influence had a great impact on getting the Constitution ratified in the first place.

Madison believed a strong central government would provide the order and stability needed to make our young country strong. The Federalist Papers, which he authored with Alexander Hamilton and John Jay (see Chapter 9), convinced many colonists of the importance of ratifying the Constitution. He also helped frame the Bill of Rights and enacted the United States's first revenue legislation. The development of the Republican, or Jeffersonian Party, evolved out of his leadership, which opposed Hamilton's financial proposals.

Madison became president while Thomas Jefferson's unpopular embargo acts were still in force, but in 1810, Congress authorized trade with both England and France, providing they accepted the U.S.'s neutral foreign policy. Napoleon pretended to accept the conditions and Madison declared that the U.S. would trade with France, but not with England — a decision that led to the U.S. entering the War of 1812. This decision was strongly opposed by the Federalists.

Our young country was not prepared for war and sustained great losses. The British even managed to invade and burn most of Washington, D.C., setting fire to the White House and the Capitol. But a few notable military victories made many Americans believe that the War of 1812 had been successful. An increase in nationalism followed, resulting in the end of the Federalist political party.

Even after he had retired from political life, James Madison, the Father of the Constitution, continued to speak out against states' rights, which threatened to undermine the strength of the federal union. He died in 1836.

Alexander Hamilton

Born a British subject on the island of Nevis in the West Indies on January 11, 1755, Alexander Hamilton was a highly influential and controversial figure in the early formative years of the United States. He first traveled to Boston near the beginning of the Revolutionary War. Hamilton quickly established a reputation for patriotism, writing newspaper articles and pamphlets and delivering speeches attacking British policies. His military accomplishments and bravery in fighting the British brought him to the attention of General George Washington, and he served four years as Washington's personal secretary and aide.

Hamilton began his legal and political career after the war, and remained politically active for the rest of his life. He served in Congress from 1782 to 1783, was elected to the Continental Congress, and founded the Bank of New York in 1784.

Hamilton fought for the adoption of the Constitution, writing about 75 percent of the Federalist Papers — the remaining 25 percent was penned by James Madison and John Jay.

The Federalist Papers remain an important commentary on the Constitution to this day, because they illustrate the thoughts and frame of mind of two of our most important Founding Fathers, Madison and Hamilton.

Hamilton holds the honor of being the United States's first Secretary of the Treasury under our first president, George Washington. He was largely responsible for securing credit for the new nation. He advocated the need for a private bank that promoted public interests, patterned after the British model of national finance. Although many questioned the constitutionality of such a national bank, Hamilton argued the authority to create such a system was implied in the Constitution; Washington agreed. Hamilton is largely credited with creating the financial stability the U.S. needed in order to grow into the powerful country it is today.

A brilliant and ambitious man, Hamilton was known to frequently overstep his authority. Hamilton and Jefferson entered into a bitter conflict over the question of foreign affairs. When the French Revolution turned into a war against all of Europe, Hamilton called for a U.S. policy of strict neutrality.

Even after he resigned his position of Secretary of the Treasury and returned to practice law in New York in 1795, he remained one of George Washington's chief advisors. Hamilton even wrote Washington's farewell address.

TIP

A history lesson in your pocket

Want to get a quick overview of some of America's most important heroes and landmarks? Just look in your wallet. The paper currency of the U.S. is decorated with American history's most important faces, symbols, buildings, and events:

- **$1 bill:** George Washington, also known as the Father of Our Country, is on the front of the $1 bill. The Great Seal of the United States (see Chapter 16) adorns the back.
- **$2 bill:** Thomas Jefferson is pictured on the front of the seldom used $2 bill. (For some reason, this denomination of currency never gained wide popularity with the public, even though it was first made back in 1776.) The back of the bill depicts the signing of the Declaration of Independence.
- **$5 bill:** Our sixteenth president, Abraham Lincoln decorates the front of the $5 bill. A picture of the Lincoln Memorial in Washington, D.C. covers the bill's back.
- **$10 bill:** Alexander Hamilton, the U.S.'s first Secretary of the Treasury, is found on the $10 bill. The U.S. Treasury Building is pictured on the reverse.
- **$20 bill:** Andrew Jackson, the national hero who defeated the British in the Battle of New Orleans during the War of 1812, and our seventh president, is on the front of the bill. The White House, home of the president in Washington, D.C., is on the back.
- **$50 bill:** Ulysses S. Grant, a Civil War hero and our eighteenth president, decorates the front of the $50 bill. The United States Capitol building adorns the back.
- **$100 bill:** Benjamin Franklin is pictured on the $100 bill. Independence Hall, the Philadelphia location of the signing of the Declaration of Independence, is pictured on the back.

After George Washington's death, the leadership of the Federalist Party became divided between John Adams and Alexander Hamilton. But Hamilton was too arrogant, opinionated, and uncompromising to become popular enough to actually win the office of president. While Adams was in office, Hamilton constantly sought to undermine his authority. In 1800, on the eve of the presidential election, Hamilton wrote a bitter attack on President Adams. Although he intended the pamphlet to be private — only meant for the eyes of a few high-ranking government officials — Aaron Burr, one of Hamilton's political and legal rivals, published it. This made the feud between the two men even worse, and Hamilton made it his duty to prevent Burr, whom he thought had poor character, from ever gaining political power. Hamilton's influence with other Federalists cost Burr elections for the presidency and the governorship of the state of New York.

In retaliation, Burr challenged Hamilton to a duel. In the duel, which took place on July 12, 1804, Burr shot and killed Hamilton, who was only 47 years old. It was reported that Hamilton never intended to fire at his enemy. Nonetheless, Burr had fired, and one of the nation's most influential men was gone.

Freeing the Slaves: Abraham Lincoln

Our sixteenth president was born on February 12, 1809, to a poor family in Hardin County, Kentucky. Despite his humble beginnings, Lincoln was ambitious. He worked and studied hard throughout his life.

Lincoln served eight years in the Illinois state legislature. He ran for state senator in 1858 against Stephen Douglas. Although he lost this election, his spirited debates against Douglas earned him national attention and the 1860 Republican nomination for president.

The first Republican president, Lincoln helped grow the party into a strong organization and even managed to get most Northern Democrats to support the Union cause during the Civil War. In 1863, his Emancipation Proclamation declared all slaves to be free (see Chapter 12).

A great speaker, Lincoln is perhaps most famous for his Gettysburg Address, given November 19, 1863, on the battlefield near Gettysburg, Pennsylvania. The address, one of the more famous American speeches ever, officially dedicated the cemetery at Gettysburg and honored the soldiers who died in the fight. More important, the Gettysburg Address brought better understanding of the Civil War to many Americans and confirmed again that "government of the people, by the people, for the people, shall not perish from the earth."

Lincoln won reelection in 1864, as the Civil War was coming to an end. In an effort to rebuild the damage done by the war, Lincoln encouraged the South to lay down arms and rejoin the Union. His efforts were not popular with everyone. On Good Friday, April 14, 1865, Lincoln was assassinated while attending a play at Ford's Theatre in Washington. It is thought that Lincoln's assassin, actor John Wilkes Booth, was trying to help the cause of the South. In fact, his terrible deed had the opposite effect, and the entire country united in grief for the slain President.

Giving the U.S. a New Deal: Franklin Delano Roosevelt

Born in 1882 at Hyde Park, New York, Franklin Delano Roosevelt (often referred to as FDR), like his fifth cousin Theodore Roosevelt (our twenty-sixth president) before him, went into politics. He was elected a New York state senator in 1910 and was the Democratic nominee for vice president in 1920.

FDR was elected our thirty-second president in November 1932, while the country was feeling the terrible effects of the Great Depression (see Chapter 13). Unemployment reached record numbers and nearly every bank was closed. In response to the desperate times, Roosevelt enacted changes that had been previously unheard of in American policy.

The Constitution severely limited the areas where the government could get involved. The tough financial times of the Depression made people interpret the Constitution more loosely, and the scope of constitutional powers has not been taken as literally since.

Roosevelt proposed, and Congress enacted, a program designed to bring recovery to business and agriculture, as well as relief to the unemployed and to those in danger of losing farms and homes. Although popular with the people, Roosevelt's policies drew strong criticism, especially from bankers and businessmen. Roosevelt responded to the criticism by creating more new programs, including Social Security, which supplements American citizens' retirement incomes. He also enacted stricter controls over banks and public utilities, and America's wealthy saw an increase in their federal tax bills under FDR.

Roosevelt also prompted legislation to enlarge the Supreme Court, in order to increase support for his New Deal policies — the Supreme Court had previously been less than receptive. Although he lost the bid for more justices, a revolution in constitutional law followed, after which the government was legally allowed to regulate the economy.

Women on currency

Susan B. Anthony's image was chosen to decorate the new U.S. dollar coin in 1979, making her the first woman to be depicted on US currency. The coins proved unpopular with the general public, however, probably because they were so close in size to the quarter.

The Anthony dollar was replaced in 1999 with another dollar coin, this one depicting the image of Sacagawea, a female Native American guide who helped explorers Lewis and Clark on their expedition in the American West from 1804 to 1806.

Roosevelt also radically changed the policy of American neutrality in foreign affairs, pledging the country to the *Good Neighbor Policy,* which called for mutual action against aggressors. Although he tried to remain neutral, he did send aid to the Allied powers in World War II, and when the Japanese attacked the U.S. at Pearl Harbor, the country was ready for war.

By the end of the war, Roosevelt's health had worsened, and he died of a cerebral hemorrhage on April 12, 1945.

Fighting for Women's Rights: Susan B. Anthony

One of American history's most influential women, Susan B. Anthony was born February 15, 1820, in Adams, Massachusetts. Anthony's Quaker background put her in the perfect position to champion the cause for women's rights. One of the first groups to practice equality between men and women, the Quakers based their religion on the belief that priests and churches are not necessary for a person to experience God.

After completing her education, Anthony worked as a schoolteacher in New York, one of the few "respectable" jobs a woman of the time could hold. Unfortunately, she was paid about one-fifth of what her male counterparts earned. When she protested this inequality, she was fired from her job. She found a better position and taught for about ten more years, although she eventually became disheartened by the lack of career opportunities for women.

She turned her attention to social and political causes. As a Quaker, Anthony didn't believe in the use of alcohol and she founded the Daughters of Temperance, the first women's temperance organization, after being denied the chance to speak at a Sons of Temperance meeting because she was a woman.

Anthony had a fateful meeting with women's rights leader Elizabeth Cady Stanton at a temperance meeting. From that point on, she worked tirelessly for the woman's *suffrage* (right-to-vote) movement, organizing state and national conventions on the issue. She helped to found the American Equal Rights Association in 1866.

Anthony and other women's rights activists also worked toward the *emancipation* (freeing) of slaves during the Civil War. They hoped to link women's rights to those of freed slaves. Unfortunately, the plan didn't work, and when the Fifteenth Amendment to the Constitution passed in 1870, it extended the right to vote only to black males.

Anthony challenged the Constitution on the basis of the Fourteenth Amendment, which stated that *all* people born in the United States were citizens and that no legal privileges could be denied them. As such, she argued on that basis that women could not be denied the right to vote. She and 15 other women voted in the presidential election of 1872 in Rochester, New York. Days later, the women were all arrested, although only Anthony was actually brought to trial. The judge, who opposed women's right to vote, found her guilty and fined her $100,000. She refused to pay and no further action was taken.

Undaunted, Anthony continued her campaign for women's rights, and her efforts resulted in new career opportunities for women. At the time of her death in 1906, only four states — Colorado, Idaho, Utah, and Wyoming — had granted women the right to vote. But the cause she fought so hard for continued even after she was gone. In 1920, Congress finally passed the Nineteenth Amendment, giving women the right to vote.

Marching for Civil Rights: Martin Luther King, Jr.

Our nation's most important civil-rights leader was born on January 15, 1929, at his family's home in Atlanta, Georgia. King entered Morehouse College at the age of 15 and graduated in 1948 with a BA degree in Sociology. During his academic career, he won numerous honors and earned several degrees, including a PhD in Theology.

At the age of 19, King was ordained a minister at the Ebenezer Baptist Church in Atlanta. Although he left this post for periods of time throughout his life, he returned from 1960 until his death in 1968, serving as copastor with his father.

Arrested 30 times for his participation in civil-rights activities, King was instrumental in effecting change through peaceful, nonviolent means, such as boycotts, protests, and *civil disobedience,* a form of protest in which demonstrators intentionally break the law and risk arrest in order to make their point.

In 1964, at age the age of 35, King's efforts in the fight for civil rights earned him the prestigious Nobel Peace Prize. He was the youngest man ever, the second American, and the third black man to be awarded this honor.

In 1968, Dr. King traveled to Memphis, Tennessee, to help lead sanitation workers there in a protest against low wages and unsavory working conditions. While in Memphis, he was shot down by an assassin's bullet. The President of the United States, Lyndon Johnson, proclaimed a national day of mourning, and flags throughout the country were flown at half-staff.

Today, the King Center, established in Atlanta, Georgia, by Dr. King's widow, Coretta Scott King, continues Martin Luther King, Jr.'s work of equality, civil rights, and nonviolent social change. Over 600,000 visitors make the trip to Atlanta annually to honor the work of this great civil-rights leader and pay their respects at his final resting place.

Chapter 16

Emblems of America

In This Chapter

- Honoring the flag
- Singing America's praises: the national anthem
- Recognizing symbols of the United States

Americans take their patriotic symbols seriously. From the flag to the national anthem, the Great Seal to the national bird, symbols of the United States surround us. This chapter gives you a crash course in symbolic ways to celebrate patriotism. It also prepares you for the questions a BCIS officer may ask during your naturalization interview.

Symbolizing the United States: Old Glory

More than any other symbol, the American Flag — also known as Old Glory — best represents the country and her people. With over 225 years of history behind it, the flag, like the country it represents, has gone through many important changes through the years.

Understanding the symbolism and significance of the flag

For almost a year after the U.S. first gained its independence from England, the American flag still bore the British Union Jack along with its red and white stripes. On June 14, 1777, the Marine Committee of the Second Continental Congress at Philadelphia changed the look of the American flag by authorizing the first official flag of the United States of America:

> Resolved, that the flag of the United States be thirteen stripes, alternate red and white; that the union be thirteen stars, white in a blue field representing a new constellation.

And so it came to be that the American flag was composed of stars and stripes. However, the resolution gave no specific instructions as to how many points the stars should have, or where they should be arranged on the blue union. If you look at historic flags in books or museums, you'll find all kinds of creative variations. Some flags have their stars staggered in rows, others made circles of the 13 stars, while still others opted for completely random placement. On some flags the stars had six points, while others sported eight. The proportion ratio of the blue field to stripes also varied from flag to flag. The matter was never completely resolved until the signing of the Executive Order of June 24, 1912, which outlined specific instructions on how the flag should look.

Celebrating Flag Day

June 14 is the flag's official birthday, commemorated each year in Flag Day ceremonies throughout the country. The Stars and Stripes first flew in Flag Day festivities in 1861 in Hartford, Connecticut, and the first national observance of Flag Day took place on the 100-year anniversary of the flag — June 14, 1877. Although not celebrated as a federal holiday, Americans everywhere continue to honor the flag and the ideals she represents to them through school programs and civic observances on June 14.

The 13 stripes represent the 13 original British colonies that formed the United States of America after they gained independence from England after the Revolutionary War. The stars, now 50 in all, represent each of the country's 50 states. The flag's colors also have special significance:

- Red represents hardiness and valor.
- White depicts purity and innocence.
- Blue represents vigilance, perseverance, and justice.

With the addition of Vermont and Kentucky to the union, the original flag of the United States grew to 15 stripes (8 red and 7 white), with 15 white stars in the union of blue. Even though more states were added over the years, the flag remained with 15 stars and 15 stripes until 1818. Congress had a problem. If they continued to add new stripes for each new state, the flag would simply grow too big. They eventually came up with the two-part solution:

- Return to a flag of 13 stripes, representing the original 13 colonies.
- Add a new white star for each new state that joined the union.

Displaying the flag

Many patriotic Americans are enthusiastic about displaying the flag. Unfortunately, a lot of people don't know the proper rules and etiquette of when and how to display the United States flag. Follow these guidelines, excerpted from the National Flag Code, and you'll always display your flag with dignity and pride, no matter what the occasion:

- It is the universal custom to display the flag only from sunrise to sunset on buildings and on stationary flagstaffs in the open. However, the flag may be displayed 24 hours a day if properly illuminated during the hours of darkness.
- The flag should not be displayed on days when the weather is inclement, except when an all-weather flag is displayed.
- The flag should be hoisted briskly and lowered ceremoniously.
- To display the flag on a building, hang it on a staff or rope with the stars away from the building.
- When marching, carry the flag on the right in a procession or parade. If there are many other flags, carry the American flag in the front center position.
- No other flag or pennant should be placed above or, if on the same level, to the right of the flag of the United States of America.

- When flags of states, cities, or societies are flown on the same halyard with the Stars and Stripes, the American flag should always be at the peak.
- When the flags of two or more nations are displayed, they are to be flown from separate staffs of the same height. The flags should be of approximately equal size. International usage forbids the display of the flag of one nation above that of another nation in times of peace.
- The U.S. flag should always be on its own right in relation to other flags on adjacent staffs — to the left of the observer.
- On a car, attach the flag to the antenna or clamp the flagstaff to the right fender of a vehicle, but never lay the flag over the vehicle.
- When displayed horizontally or vertically against a wall or in a window, the stars should be uppermost and to the observer's left.
- When carrying the flag, hold it at a slight angle from your body. It is also proper to carry the flag with one hand and rest it on your right shoulder.
- At a funeral, drape the flag over the casket with the stars at the head and over the left shoulder of the body. Do not lower the flag into the grave or allow it to touch the ground.

Half-staff rules

Flags are flown at half-staff to show respect for the dead. Even so, the practice comes with specific rules for flag etiquette and protocol:

- By order of the president, the flag shall be flown at half-staff upon the death of principal figures of the United States Government or the governor of a state, territory, or possession, as a mark of respect to their memory. In the event of the death of other officials or foreign dignitaries, the flag is to be displayed at half-staff according to presidential instructions or orders, or in accordance with recognized customs or practices not inconsistent with law.
- When flown at half-staff, the flag should be first hoisted to the peak for an instant and then lowered to the half-staff position. The flag should be again raised to the peak before it is lowered for the day.
- On Memorial Day, the flag should be displayed at half-staff until noon only, then raised to the top of the staff.

Saluting the flag

It may seem strange, but the clothing you wear affects how to properly salute the flag. Civilians should place their right hands over their hearts, except when wearing athletic clothing, in which case they should remove their hats and stand at attention; no hand salute is necessary. Civilian men wearing hats should remove the hat and hold it at their left shoulder, with hand over heart. Aliens should simply stand at attention. Those in uniform should render the military salute.

When the flag is moving, as in a parade, it is proper to salute when it is six paces in front of you and hold the salute until it passes six paces beyond. During the playing of the national anthem, the salute to the flag begins with the first note and continues until the song has ended. Even when a flag is not on display during the playing of the anthem, it is still proper to face the music and salute as if it were actually there.

Caring for the flag: Important etiquette

According to the United States Flag Code, when the flag is lowered, no part of it should touch the ground or any other object — it should be received by waiting hands and arms. The flag should also be cleaned and mended whenever necessary.

When a flag is so worn it is no longer fit to serve as a symbol of our country, it should be destroyed by burning in a dignified manner. Check with your local American Legion Post before Flag Day; most posts conduct flag-burning ceremonies on June 14.

The United States Flag Code provides many rules for how, when, and why the flag may be displayed, but it also warns of some important flag don'ts to avoid:

- The flag should not be displayed on a float in a parade, except from a staff, and should not be draped over the hood, top, sides, or back of any vehicle, railroad train, or boat.
- Although it's permissible for the flag to form a distinctive feature of the unveiling ceremony of a statue or monument, it should never be used as the actual covering piece.
- When it's permissible to use the flag to cover a casket, it should never be lowered into the grave or allowed to touch the ground.
- When being carried, the flag should not be dipped to any person or thing. Regimental colors, state flags, and organizational or institutional flags are to be dipped to the American flag as a mark of honor.
- The flag should never be displayed with the union down, except as a signal of dire distress in instances of extreme danger to life or property.
- The flag should never touch anything beneath it, such as the ground, water, or merchandise.
- The flag should never be carried flat or horizontally, but always aloft and free.
- The flag should never be used as wearing apparel, bedding, or drapery. It should never be festooned, drawn back, nor up, in folds, but always allowed to fall free. Bunting of blue, white, and red, always arranged with the blue above, the white in the middle, and the red below, should be used for covering a speaker's desk, draping the front of the platform, and for general decoration.
- The flag should never be fastened, displayed, used, or stored in such a manner as to permit it to be easily torn, soiled, or damaged in any way.
- The flag should never be used as a covering for a ceiling.
- The flag should never have placed upon it, nor on any part of it, nor attached to it, any mark, insignia, letter, word, figure, design, picture, or drawing of any nature.
- The flag should never be used as a receptacle for receiving, holding, carrying, or delivering anything.
- The flag should never be used for advertising purposes in any manner whatsoever. It should not be embroidered on such articles as cushions or handkerchiefs and the like, printed or otherwise impressed on paper napkins or boxes or anything that is designed for temporary use and discarded. Advertising signs should not be fastened to a staff or halyard from which the flag is flown.
- No part of the flag should ever be used as a costume or athletic uniform. However, a flag patch may be affixed to the uniform of military personnel, firemen, policemen, and members of patriotic organizations. The flag represents a living country and is itself considered a living thing. Therefore, the lapel flag pin being a replica, should be worn on the left lapel near the heart.

Folding the flag

A properly folded flag ends up in the shape of a tricornered hat, symbolic of the hats worn by colonial soldiers during the War for Independence. Here's how to fold the flag:

1. Start by holding the flag waist high with another person so that its surface is parallel to the ground.
2. Fold the flag in half, lengthwise, bringing the lower striped section up to meet the upper field of blue.
3. Fold lengthwise again, keeping the blue field on the outside.
4. Make a triangular fold by bringing the striped corner of the folded edge to meet the top (open) edge of the flag.
5. Fold the outermost point on the right inward, parallel to the top open edge, which forms a second triangle.
6. Continue the triangular folding until the entire length of the flag is folded in this manner. When complete, only a triangular blue field of stars should be visible.

Pledging Allegiance

> I pledge allegiance to the flag of the United States of America, and to the Republic for which it stands, one Nation, under God, indivisible, with liberty and justice for all.

Originally penned for a public-school program celebrating the 400th anniversary of Columbus's discovery of America, the pledge didn't receive formal recognition from Congress until it was officially adopted into the U.S. Flag Code on Flag Day of 1942. Even so, the official name "The Pledge of Allegiance" wasn't adopted until 1945.

The Pledge of Allegiance is now said with the right hand placed over the heart, but it wasn't always so. Prior to 1941, the pledge was said in the so-called *Bellamy Salute* (named for Francis Bellamy, the man credited with writing the pledge) — hand resting outward from the chest, the arm extending out from the body. After Adolf Hitler came to power in Europe, many Americans became concerned that the Bellamy salute too closely resembled the Nazi military salute, so in 1942, Congress established the current practice of reciting the pledge with the right hand over the heart.

Singing Out Freedom: The National Anthem

Francis Scott Key wrote the National Anthem of the United States of America on September 14, 1814. The site of an enormous 30-x-42-foot flag that flew over Fort McHenry during the War of 1812, a historic flag that now hangs at the Smithsonian's National Museum of American History in Washington, D.C., inspired Key to pen his poem.

Technically, our national anthem has four verses, although you'll almost never hear anything but the first.

Attending a public event and joining in the singing of this proud song can be an uplifting patriotic experience. So you're ready next time you attend a ballgame or other public event, here are the words, so you too can sing proudly along:

Oh, say can you see by the dawn's early light
What so proudly we hailed at the twilight's last gleaming?
Whose broad stripes and bright stars thru the perilous fight,
O'er the ramparts we watched were so gallantly streaming?
And the rocket's red glare, the bombs bursting in air,
Gave proof through the night that our flag was still there.
Oh, say does that star-spangled banner yet wave
O'er the land of the free and the home of the brave?

Investigating American Icons

Although the flag is undoubtedly our most important symbol, there are still more American icons you'll frequently encounter, and their history and symbolism are no less fascinating.

The Great Seal

Our Founding Fathers believed an emblem and national coat of arms would help solidify the identity of the United States as an independent nation of free people. Benjamin Franklin, John Adams, and Thomas Jefferson undertook the task of creating the seal for the United States of America in 1776. Six years later on June 20, 1782, the Great Seal was finalized and approved.

The Secretary of State serves as the official custodian of the Great Seal, and it can only be affixed to certain documents, such as foreign treaties and presidential proclamations. An officer from the Department's Presidential Appointments Staff does the actual embossing of documents after the Secretary of State has countersigned the president's signature.

Rich with patriotic symbolism, next time you gaze at the Great Seal of the United States, keep these points in mind:

- Central to the seal is a bald eagle, our national bird, holding in its beak a scroll inscribed *E pluribus unum* (Latin for "out of many, one," symbolizing how our 13 original colonies came together to form one nation).
- The eagle's right claw clutches an olive branch while the left talon holds 13 arrows, denoting "the power of peace and war."
- A shield with 13 red and white stripes covers the eagle's breast. Supported solely by the eagle, the shield reminds Americans to rely on their own virtue.
- The blue field on the shield represents the President and Congress, being supported by the states, denoted by the red and white stripes.
- As with our flag, red signifies hardiness and valor, white purity and innocence, and blue vigilance, perseverance, and justice.
- Floating above the eagle's head in a field of blue is a constellation formed of 13 stars. The constellation symbolized that America, a new state, was taking its place among other nations.

On the seal's reverse side you'll find a familiar image — it's also used on the back of U.S. dollar bills:

- An unfinished 13-step pyramid symbolizes strength and duration, and once again, the 13 original colonies.
- Atop the pyramid, the Eye of Providence. The words *Annuit Coeptis* appear above the pyramid, meaning, "God has favored our undertakings."
- A scroll beneath the pyramid, proclaiming 1776 as the beginning of the American new era with the Latin words *Novus Ordo Seclorum*, meaning "New Order of the Ages."

The national bird

The bald eagle, our national bird, is the only eagle unique to North America. When America adopted the bird as its national symbol in 1782, as many as 100,000 nesting bald eagles lived in the continental United States, and the bald eagle populated every state in the union except Hawaii. By 1963, only 417 nesting pairs were counted in the lower 48, although eagle populations in Alaska and Canada have always been healthy. Today, due to efforts by the Interior Department's U.S. Fish and Wildlife Service — in partnership with other federal agencies, tribes, state and local governments, conservation organizations, universities, corporations, and thousands of individual Americans — the number of nesting pairs has risen to an estimated 5,748, and the eagle is close to being removed from the endangered species list.

Benjamin Franklin, one of our most respected Founding Fathers, disapproved of the choice of the bald eagle as the national bird. He believed the eagle was a bird of bad moral character because it steals food from weaker animals. Franklin thought the best bird for the job was none other than the humble turkey, which Franklin described as "a bird of courage that would not hesitate to attack a grenadier of the British guards, who should presume to invade his farmyard with a red coat on."

The national motto

Increased religious sentiment during the Civil War spurred Congress to include the national motto "In God We Trust" on United States currency. Despite being barraged with appeals urging then Secretary of the Treasury Salmon P. Chase to recognize God on United States coins, his hands were tied because an 1837 Act of Congress specifically prescribed exactly which mottoes and devices could be placed on U.S. currency. Another Act of Congress changed that in 1864 and the words *In God We Trust* were first seen that year on the newly minted two-cent coins. More congressional acts throughout the years have authorized the motto to appear on various other currency denominations. But it wasn't until July 30, 1956, that the words officially became the national motto of the United States.

The national motto comes with a certain degree of controversy, because the constitutionality of the words has been challenged on many occasions. Nevertheless, the courts, which tend to favor looking at the motto in a historical rather than religious context, have consistently upheld the legality of the motto's use on the basis that it is not a specific endorsement of religion.

Many people think the Latin words *E pluribus unum* ("out of many, one") form the national motto. You'll hear national figures who should know better make this mistake on television and radio all the time. In fact, you can even find the words labeled as such in some government publications. Although the Latin phrase is used in many patriotic emblems — including the Great Seal of the United States — In God We Trust remains the officially recognized national motto.

Part V
Practicing for the Citizenship Test

"Over two dozen questions about being an American, and not one about baseball, mom, or apple pie."

In this part . . .

It's often been said that practice makes perfect, and preparing for your citizenship test is no different. The good news is that opportunities to practice your English and civics skills are everywhere, if you know where to look. In fact, with a little creativity, practicing for your citizenship test can actually be a lot of fun. The secret is this: Don't take things too seriously and don't be afraid to make mistakes. After all, you're learning, and with every mistake you make, you improve.

In this part, we give you ideas for ways to improve your English — reading, writing, and speaking. Although English can be one of the world's most difficult languages to master — there are as many exceptions to rules of English grammar as there are rules themselves — if you're living in the U.S., you'll find help in learning English everywhere. The more you communicate in your new language, the stronger your skills will get — and before you know it, you'll be conversing fluently. In this part, we also suggest ways to help you brush up on your American history and civics, both on your own and through the fun quizzes and games included in this book.

So relax, look at learning as fun, and you'll be well on your way to passing your citizenship exam.

Chapter 17

Preparing for the English Test

In This Chapter

- Brushing up on your English skills
- Figuring out where to practice your English

Part of your citizenship test involves demonstrating that you can read, write, and speak the English language. Many people worry needlessly about the English portion of the test. Relax. The examiner is not expecting you to speak flawless English with perfect pronunciation and precise grammar. Instead, he or she merely wants to know that you have a good basic understanding of the language — that you can converse in and read and write *basic* English. Although this may seem challenging, you can easily practice your skills every day. Before you know it, you'll be holding fluent English conversations with friends, family, co-workers, and your citizenship examiner.

This chapter gives you study hints and tips that should help you easily pass this part of your test.

Building Your Vocabulary

Living in the U.S., you'll find opportunities to practice English everywhere — you'll encounter native English speakers in your job or daily activities, and wherever you look you'll see signs in English.

TIP

What to look for when you buy a dictionary

When you go shopping for a dictionary, make sure it has these features:

- **A pronunciation key:** This is important to help you *pronounce* (or say) the words correctly.
- **The parts of speech:** Knowing whether a word is a noun, a verb, an adjective, an adverb, or another part of speech will help you to use the word correctly in sentences.
- **Other forms of the word such as prefixes, suffixes and irregular forms:** This information will help you to recognize words in conversation that may be close in meaning to the word you looked up.
- **Size:** Dictionaries come in all price ranges and sizes. Try to buy one that's large enough to cover the words you'll need, but small enough to be easily carried in a pocket or purse.

Getting a high-school diploma

Even though you may not have completed school, you can still get the equivalent of a U.S. high-school diploma by taking the General Educational Development (GED) test. Because preparing for the GED test involves general knowledge, as well as an essay question that demonstrates your ability to effectively write and communicate, you'll improve your English skills and civics knowledge while working toward credentials that can help you get a better job or continue your education. Passing the GED test documents that you have at least high-school-level academic skills. About 96 percent of employers accept GED credentials as equal to a traditional high-school diploma and 95 percent of U.S. colleges and universities accept GED graduates who meet their other qualifications for admission.

A good way to prepare for the GED test is by enrolling in a community GED-preparedness class — check listings in your local phonebook for classes near you. You can also prepare on your own without taking classes. Your local bookstore will have a selection of books to help you prepare, including *GED For Dummies* by Murray Shukyn and Dale Shuttleworth, PhD (published by Wiley).

Every chance you get to speak or read English is an opportunity to improve your skills and add to your *vocabulary* (the group of words you know well enough to use in everyday conversations). Speak and read English whenever possible and you can't help but improve your speaking, reading, and writing abilities. Use some or all the following hints to speed up the process:

- **Take an English as a Second Language (ESL) course.** Check local adult-education centers and community colleges. Some ESL courses are even geared toward people taking the naturalization test.
- **Read and watch materials geared toward children.** Books, magazines, and even television shows produced for kids are great ways for nonnative English speakers to pick up new words. The same programming that teaches kids how to read, write, and pronounce words can also help you. You may even find it handy to get a children's dictionary when you start out; dictionaries geared toward children explain definitions in terms that are easy to understand. As your language skills improve, start reading books or newspapers or watching TV shows that are aimed at older kids, until you're fully up to speed.
- **Buy a good dictionary.** A good dictionary is essential. Try to find one that's small enough to carry with you wherever you go, so you'll always be able to look up unfamiliar words. A good dictionary can help you master English, and you'll probably find yourself reaching for yours constantly. In addition to having on hand a good English dictionary, you'll probably also want one that gives words in your native language. Although stopping and looking up every unfamiliar word you encounter may seem time consuming, the more you do it now, the less you'll need to do it in the future, because more and more words will become familiar to you. You can use the frequency of your need to consult your dictionary as a good barometer of your progress — the less you need your dictionary, the more fluent you are in English.
- **Buy a good thesaurus.** A thesaurus gives you *synonyms* (words with similar meanings), and can help expand your vocabulary. When you become confident with a new vocabulary word, look it up in the thesaurus to find new ways to communicate your precise meaning.
- **Read BCIS forms.** Reading BCIS forms may be a tough assignment, but if you read and understand every important immigration document, you'll not only understand English very well, you'll be a step ahead in preparing for immigration and/or naturalization, because you'll know a lot about the requirements and restrictions. Of course, immigration is a complex process, so regardless of how much you read, you should still consult qualified people to help with your unique circumstances.

- **Enlist help from friends and co-workers.** Tell friends, co-workers, and anyone else who will listen that you're trying to improve your English. Tell them you would appreciate their honest critiques and help. In other words, ask them to tell you about your mistakes so you can benefit from them.
- **Each and every day, pick an unfamiliar word (any word you don't understand in a newspaper, book, or magazine will do), look up the word in the dictionary, and find out its meaning.** Play a game with yourself and see how many times that day you can use the word in conversation. If you can handle it, make a conscious effort to practice two, three, or even more words this way every day.
- **Use flashcards.** A good way to master new words and reinforce their meanings over time is to make your own flashcards. Small index cards work well. Print the vocabulary word on one side, and on the reverse side print the word's meaning, as well as clues to help you pronounce and use the word properly in conversation. You may even want to go so far as to list a few synonyms from your thesaurus. Try making flashcards for your words of the day. Studying with your flashcards is easy — keep them with you and run through a few flashcards every time you have an extra minute or two.
- **Find a friend to practice with.** Find a friend who is also trying to improve his or her English so you can study and practice together. Share new words and flashcards with your friend, and you'll double the speed of building your vocabulary.
- **Take classes.** Improve your language skills and discover something new by taking a class. Don't limit yourself to English classes — anything you study will require reading and writing (and possibly even speaking English).
- **Pick up a copy of *Vocabulary For Dummies* by Laurie E. Rozakis (published by Wiley).** This book can help native and nonnative speakers increase the number of words they know and improve communication skills by showing ways to figure out the meanings of words on the spot using their root languages, common prefixes and suffixes, and even conversational context. It really is an invaluable reference that also manages to make increasing your vocabulary fun.

Talking the Talk: Practicing Your Speaking Skills

If you're like most people, you probably understand more words by reading them than by speaking or hearing them. English pronunciation can be tricky — some words that sound alike have completely different meanings. Refer to Figure 17-1 for a pronunciation key that can help you when you look up words in the dictionary.

The quickest and easiest way to improve your English-speaking skills is to simply keep talking and keep listening. Speak English as much as possible to anyone who is willing to talk with you. The more you speak, the easier it will get, and the more you'll want to continue speaking English. Not only will you be able to converse, you'll also be able to enjoy English television and movies, newspapers, magazines, and books.

In addition to simply talking as much as possible, consider these tips for improving your speaking ability:

- **Listen.** In addition to talking, listen — listen to the radio, to the television, to the people you're talking to. You can even discreetly listen in on conversations going on around you — just to help you practice English, of course.
- **Insist to friends and relatives that you really do *want* them to correct your word pronunciation and English grammar.** Some people, in their efforts to be encouraging, may not want to constantly point out your mistakes to you. Assure them that you want to improve and this is the only way you can do so. And be sure to keep a good attitude about their feedback — you don't want to ask for their help and then act annoyed when you get it.
- **Ask questions.** If you don't know how to pronounce a word, ask a native English speaker to help you.
- **Use children's phonics programs.** Books, videos, and television shows that coach children in phonics will also help you sound out written words. English is filled with exceptions to rules, so not all words are pronounced the way they're written, but studying phonics will help you make the best guess.

PRONUNCIATION KEY

Vowel Sounds		Consonant Sounds	
Symbol	*Key Words*	*Symbol*	*Key Words*
a	at, cap, parrot	b	bed, table, rob
ā	ape, play, sail	d	dog, middle, sad
ä	cot, father, heart	f	for, phone, cough
e	ten, wealth, merry	g	get, wiggle, dog
ē	even, feet, money	h	hat, hope, ahead
i	is, stick, mirror	hw	which, white
ī	ice, high, sky	j	joy, badge, agent
ō	go, open, tone	k	kill, cat, quiet
ô	all, law, horn	l	let, yellow, ball
o͝o	could, look, pull	m	meet, number, time
yo͝o	cure, furious	n	net, candle, ton
ōō	boot, crew, tune	p	put, sample, escape
yōō	cute, few, use	r	red, wrong, born
oi	boy, oil, royal	s	sit, castle, office
ou	cow, out, sour	t	top, letter, cat
u	mud, ton, blood, trouble	v	voice, every, love
ʉ	her, sir, word	w	wet, always, quart
ə	ago, agent, collect, focus	y	yes, canyon, onion
'l	cattle, paddle	z	zoo, misery, rise
'n	sudden, sweeten	ch	chew, nature, punch
		sh	shell, machine, bush
		th	thin, nothing, truth
		th	then, other, bathe
		zh	beige, measure, seizure
		ŋ	ring, anger, drink

Figure 17-1: A pronunciation key.

Courtesy of Webster's New World Collegiate Dictionary, Fourth Edition

Joining Toastmasters

Joining a Toastmasters club is a wonderful way to improve your speaking ability and communication skills. Members of this not-for-profit organization sharpen their skills by speaking to groups and working with others in a supportive environment.

A typical club is made up of 20 to 30 people who meet once a week for a couple of hours. Everyone gets a chance to practice speaking at each meeting, by presenting short impromptu speeches or by giving prepared speeches. Members offer each other constructive evaluations and suggestions for ways to improve. Most Toastmasters clubs include at least a few folks who speak English as a second language.

The help and support of the club can really help you not only improve English, but also develop important leadership and team-building skills that can be used in business. In fact, many large companies who want to help their employees gain valuable communication skills sponsor Toastmasters clubs at their place of business (check to see if the company you work for has a Toastmasters club). If you don't find a club through your job, don't worry, there are clubs open to the public throughout the United States and the world. The cost of joining is low. For more information on meetings in your area, check your local phonebook or visit www.toastmasters.org.

Brushing Up on Your Reading and Writing

Practice by doing — read and write English at every opportunity possible — and you'll see rapid improvement in your comprehension of the English language. Reading on your own allows you the luxury of taking your time — as much time as you need — to really understand the words before you. Keep your dictionary handy to look up any unfamiliar words. You may want to make flashcards to help you remember the new words later.

Here are some additional tips to help you improve at reading and writing English:

- **Try to read a newspaper every day.** You'll not only stay up to date with civics and current events, you'll also improve your reading and English-comprehension skills.
- **In addition to reading books, magazines, and newspapers, read everything else you can during your daily activities.** Road signs, advertisements, menus, and other pieces of material will all help you get used to reading English.
- **Play word games such as Scrabble or Boggle.** These fun games will help you in your efforts to write and read in English. Children's versions of these games also exist, so don't be afraid to start there and progress to the adult versions as your skills grow.
- **Do word puzzles such as crossword puzzles and word searches.** Word puzzles come in all skill levels. Start with easy puzzles and progress.
- **Rent subtitled movies.** Watching foreign movies with English subtitles will help you to read and comprehend English. Watching these films at home, as opposed to in a movie theatre, will allow you to pause the tape when you need to look up unfamiliar words.
- **Help your kids with their homework and you can all improve your skills at the same time (in addition to spending some quality family time together).**

Chapter 18

Preparing for the Civics Test

In This Chapter

- Staying up to date with current events
- Understanding local and state governments
- Testing yourself: Review quizzes and questions

How well do you know U.S. history and government? The fun review quizzes in this chapter will help you find out. Here you'll also find 100 sample questions, similar to those asked on the citizenship history and civics test, so you should know what to expect on test day.

Be prepared to answer the question, "Why do you want to be a United States citizen?" The examiner wants to be sure you understand the duties and benefits that come with citizenship. See Chapter 1 for a review, then think about what these duties and benefits mean to you personally. Put it into words, and there's your answer!

Keeping Current

Your citizenship examiner may ask you about important events — events of national importance — currently happening and being covered in the news. The examiner may also ask you about the current representatives in your local or state government or your state's representatives in the U.S. Congress. Don't worry, keeping up with the events and people who shape our world is easy.

Current events

To stay up to date with current events, try to read at least one English newspaper every day. You'll improve your English comprehension and reading skills while keeping current with news and events of local, state, and national importance.

You can also stay informed by listening to radio news or watching the news on TV. Be sure to watch or listen to shows in English in order to improve your language skills at the same time.

History books make great review tools, too. Books like *The Civil War For Dummies* and *World War II For Dummies,* both by Keith D. Dickson (published by Wiley), give you the kind of information you can use to prepare for your citizenship test. They make for fascinating reading and will help you find out about some of history's most important events in easy-to-understand terms.

National, state, and local governments

Your citizenship examiner may ask you about the current representatives in your local or state government or in the U.S. government — know your senator and representative in Congress, your state's governor, and your city's mayor. If you read a local newspaper every day, you should become familiar with the names of your state and local government officials.

You can call or visit your state capitol to find out about your governor and state government representatives or your city hall to find out about your mayor and other local government officials. Or you can locate your state's official Web site, which will list at least your state's governor and members of your state's legislature, and your city's Web site, which will list the mayor and other elected city officials. Go to a search engine like Yahoo! (`www.yahoo.com`), and search for "State of [INSERT YOUR STATE NAME HERE]" or search for your city and state (for example, type in "Chicago, Illinois"), and you'll find the official Web site for your city and your state.

On the national level, you can find out about your state representatives to the United States Congress by calling the U.S. House switchboard operator at 202-225-3121. You can find out about your state's U.S. senators by phoning the United States Capitol switchboard at 202-224-3121. Online you can surf to `www.congress.org` for a central location to identify your state's elected officials in Congress, e-mail elected officials, and stay abreast of current legislation and issues on the national level.

Quizzing Yourself on Civics

Get ready to have some fun and test your knowledge about U.S. government and civics at the same time. Try your hand at these quizzes, based on questions that may be asked on your citizenship test.

The government quiz

In the following questions, identify which branch of government — executive, legislative, or judicial — has the power or responsibility listed. For extra credit, on questions dealing with the legislative branch of government, tell whether the duty belongs to the House of Representatives, the Senate, or both. (You'll find the answers at the end of this section.)

1. The power to impeach the president and federal court judges or justices
2. The power to declare laws unconstitutional
3. The power to veto bills before they become law
4. The power to conduct foreign policy
5. The power to borrow money on behalf of the government
6. The responsibility to serve as the Commander in Chief of the U.S. military
7. The power, "when appropriate," to pardon people found guilty of breaking a federal law
8. The power to levy and collect taxes
9. The responsibility to oversee the Department of Agriculture, the Department of Labor, and the Department of Energy
10. The responsibility to maintain the defense of the U.S., including the Army, Navy, and Air Force, and the power to declare war

11. The power to pass laws governing the District of Columbia
12. The power to determine guilt or innocence in impeachment cases
13. The power to confirm presidential appointments
14. The power to settle disagreements between U.S. states and foreign governments and/or their citizens
15. The power to ratify treaties between the U.S. and foreign governments
16. The power to introduce tax or budget bills
17. The power to settle legal disagreements between citizens of different U.S. states
18. The responsibility to administer the Federal Election Commission, the Small Business Administration, the United States Postal Service, and the Veterans Administration
19. The power to settle disputes between two or more U.S. states

Answers: (1) Legislative — the House of Representatives retains the power to impeach if they deem it necessary; (2) Judicial — the Supreme Court can declare laws unconstitutional or against the supreme law of the land; (3) Executive — the president has the power to veto bills; (4) Executive — the president is responsible for conducting foreign policy (of course, he has help from his advisors); (5) Legislative — both the Senate and the House of Representatives share responsibilities for borrowing money on the country's behalf; (6) Executive — the president serves as our military's Commander in Chief; (7) Executive — the president has the authority to pardon people charged with federal crimes; (8) Legislative — levying and collecting taxes are the shared duties of the House and Senate; (9) Executive — these departments and others like them come under the authority of the executive branch of government; (10) Legislative — although the president serves as Commander in Chief, it is both houses of Congress that must declare war and maintain our military forces; (11) Legislative — because our nation's capital is not within the borders of any state, the House of Representatives and the Senate pass the laws that govern the District of Columbia; (12) Legislative — the power to determine guilt or innocence in impeachment cases is held by the Senate; (13) Legislative — the power to confirm presidential appointments is held by the Senate; (14) Judicial — the federal courts decide on legal matters between the states and between the U.S. and foreign governments and their citizens; (15) Legislative — the power to ratify treaties between the U.S. and foreign governments is held by the Senate; (16) Legislative — House of Representatives (although both the House and the Senate can introduce most bills, *only* the House of Representatives may introduce tax or budget bills); (17) Judicial — when citizens of different states bring legal action against one another, the federal courts have the authority to decide the outcome; (18) Executive — these independent agencies, which can change according to the country's current needs and circumstances, fall under the authority of the executive branch; (19) Judicial — when states have legal disputes, they look to the federal courts to settle them.

The Constitution versus Declaration of Independence quiz

Here's a fun quiz that will help you become more familiar with the U.S.'s two most important documents — the Declaration of Independence and the Constitution. Many of the ideas and values from the Declaration carried over to the Constitution. Some of the people responsible for the first document were also instrumental in the second. Other ideas or people are directly involved with one or the other. Which of the following ideas, statements, and people are more closely associated with the Declaration of Independence, the Constitution, or both? (You'll find the answers at the end of this section.)

1. King George III
2. Taxation without representation
3. Thomas Jefferson
4. We the people
5. The supreme law of the land
6. Quartering
7. June 21, 1788
8. Federalists
9. Self-evident rights
10. Separation of powers or checks and balances
11. July 4, 1776
12. The Bill of Rights
13. James Madison

Answers: (1) The Declaration of Independence. George III was the ruler of England at the time the colonists declared independence. His unfair treatment of the colonies spurred the colonists to revolt and fight for independence. (2) The Declaration of Independence. Of all George III's policies, being taxed without the ability to send representatives to the British parliament most angered the colonists. (3) Both. Although Jefferson wrote much of the Declaration of Independence, many of his ideas were also incorporated into the Constitution, so he had a big influence on both important American documents. (4) The Constitution. These are the first three words to the United States Constitution. (5) The Constitution. No other laws may contradict any of the principles set forth in the Constitution, and no person or entity is exempt from following its laws. (6) The Declaration of Independence. Colonists were required by British law not only to house British soldiers in their own homes, but also to provide them with meals and basic supplies. (7) The Constitution. The Constitution was ratified on this day. (8) The Constitution. This political party supported the ratifying of the Constitution. (9) Both. Thomas Jefferson talked about the rights to life, liberty, and the pursuit of happiness in the Declaration of Independence, and the Constitution exists to guarantee those rights to all people living in the United States. (10) The Constitution. Our government structure, including the ability of the three branches to check and balance each other's powers, is outlined in the Constitution. (11) The Declaration of Independence. This is the day when the American colonies officially declared independence from England. (12) The Constitution. The first ten amendments or changes to the Constitution are known as the Bill of Rights. (13) The Constitution. Madison is also known as the "Father of the Constitution" because of his impact in getting the document ratified.

The important Americans quiz

Draw a line between the important American in the left column to his or her description in the right column. (You'll find the answers at the end of this section.)

Important American	*Description*
Alexander Hamilton	Freed the slaves with his Emancipation Proclamation
Martin Luther King, Jr.	Important Founding Father, statesman, and inventor

Abraham Lincoln	The 32nd president of the United States, responsible for giving the U.S. a "New Deal" during the Great Depression
Susan B. Anthony	The first Secretary of the Treasury
Benjamin Franklin	Also known as the father of our country, he was our first president
George Washington	An important civil-rights leader
Thomas Jefferson	An important Founding Father, the principal writer of the Declaration of Independence, and our third president
Franklin Delano Roosevelt	A fighter for women's right to vote

Answers: Alexander Hamilton: The first Secretary of the Treasury; Martin Luther King, Jr.: An important civil rights leader; Abraham Lincoln: Freed the slaves with his Emancipation Proclamation; Susan B. Anthony: A fighter for women's right to vote; Benjamin Franklin: Important Founding Father, statesman, and inventor; George Washington: Also known as the father of our country, he was our first president; Thomas Jefferson: An important Founding Father, the principal writer of the Declaration of Independence, and our third President; Franklin Delano Roosevelt: The 32nd President of the United States, responsible for giving the US a "New Deal" during the Great Depression.

The citizen responsibilities quiz

The following are important responsibilities or duties of *all* adult United States citizens, born or naturalized — true or false? (You'll find the answers at the end of this section.)

1. Serving in the military
2. Voting
3. Serving on a jury
4. Obeying laws
5. Paying taxes
6. Contributing to political campaigns
7. Allowing their homes to be searched at any time by law enforcement officials
8. Attending the church of their choice

Answers: (1) False. All citizens are not automatically required to serve in the military. Men between the ages of 18 and 26 years old are required, by law, to register with the Selective Service System, an independent agency within the executive branch of the government that works to provide manpower to the armed forces in times of emergency. They may or may not be required to serve (as of this writing there hasn't been a draft since 1973, when the U.S. converted to an all-volunteer military). (2) True. Although there is no law that compels all citizens to exercise their right to vote, voting nonetheless remains an important citizen responsibility, because those who don't exercise this right lose their voice in government. (3) True. Jurors perform an essential role in sustaining the U.S. system of justice. The right to a trial by a jury of one's peers is guaranteed in the Constitution, and a jury's honest and impartial decisions help protect our fundamental rights to fair and efficient justice for all. Although not all citizens will actually serve on a jury, the government has the right to require every citizen to serve periodically. (4) True. Everyone living in the United States, whether or not a citizen, is expected to obey the laws of the land. (5) True. Everyone who resides in the U.S., whether or not a citizen, is required to honestly pay taxes, and the money is used to provide government services that we all benefit from. (6) False. U.S. citizens are not compelled to contribute to any political campaigns. (7) False. The Constitution guarantees the right of the people against unreasonable searches and seizures of their persons, houses, papers, and effects. The officers must produce a search warrant from the court in order to search your home. (8) False. The Constitution guarantees freedom of religion, which also gives citizens the right not to attend church at all, should they choose.

Preparing for Your BCIS Interview: 100 Sample Questions

Want to know exactly what kinds of questions will be asked during your naturalization test? The BCIS gives the 100 sample questions below. Does this mean you'll be asked all these questions? No, not by a long shot. These are merely examples of the types of questions the examiner may ask. Can the examiner ask you questions that aren't on this list? Yes. Again, these are *not* actual test questions, but they do illustrate the subject, scope, and difficulty level of questions normally asked during a BCIS naturalization test.

1. **What are the colors of our flag?**

   Red, white, and blue.

2. **How many stars are on our flag?**

   50.

3. **What color are the stars on our flag?**

   White.

4. **What do the stars on the flag mean?**

   There is one star for each state in the union.

5. **How many stripes are on our flag?**

   13.

6. **What color are the stripes?**

   Red and white.

7. **What do the stripes on the flag mean?**

   They represent the 13 original states.

8. **How many states are there in the union?**

   50.

9. **What is the Fourth of July?**

   Independence Day.

10. **What is the date of Independence Day?**

    July 4.

11. **From whom did the US gain independence?**

    England.

12. What country did we fight during the Revolutionary War?

England.

13. Who was the first President of the United States?

George Washington.

14. Who is the President of the United States today?

George W. Bush (as of this writing).

15. Who is the Vice President of the United States?

Dick Cheney (as of this writing).

16. Who elects the President of the United States?

The Electoral College.

17. Who becomes President of the United States if the President dies?

The Vice President.

18. For how long do we elect the president?

Four years.

19. What is the Constitution?

The supreme law of the land.

20. Can the Constitution be changed?

Yes.

21. What do we call a change to the Constitution?

An amendment.

22. How many changes or amendments to the Constitution are there?

27 (as of this writing).

23. How many branches are there in our government?

Three.

24. What are the branches of our government?

Executive, legislative, and judicial.

25. What is the legislative branch of our government?

Congress.

26. Who makes the laws in the United States?

Congress.

27. What is Congress?

The Senate and the House of Representatives.

28. What are the duties of Congress?

To make laws.

29. Who elects Congress?

The people.

30. How many senators are there in Congress?

100.

31. **Can you name the U.S. Senators from your state?**

    To find your state's U.S. Senators, go to `www.senate.gov`.

32. **For how long do we elect each senator?**

    Six years.

33. **How many representatives are there in Congress?**

    435 (as of this writing). The number of representatives may change with changes in a given state's population.

34. **For how long do we elect representatives?**

    Two years.

35. **What is the executive branch of our government?**

    The President, the cabinet, and the departments under the cabinet members.

36. **What is the judicial branch of our government?**

    The Supreme Court.

37. **What are the duties of the Supreme Court?**

    To interpret laws.

38. **What is the supreme law of the United States?**

    The Constitution.

39. **What is the Bill of Rights?**

    The first ten amendments to the Constitution.

40. **What is the capital of your state?**

    To find your state's capital, go to `www.50states.com`.

41. **Who is the current governor of your state?**

    To find your state's governor, go to `www.50states.com`.

42. **Who becomes President of the United States if the President and the Vice President should die?**

    The Speaker of the House of Representatives.

43. **Who is the Chief Justice of the Supreme Court?**

    William Rehnquist (as of this writing).

44. **Can you name the 13 original states?**

    Connecticut, Delaware, Georgia, Maryland, Massachusetts, New Hampshire, New Jersey, New York, North Carolina, Pennsylvania, Rhode Island, South Carolina, and Virginia.

45. **Who said, "Give me liberty or give me death?"**

    Patrick Henry.

46. **Which countries were our enemies during World War II?**

    Germany, Italy, and Japan.

47. **What were the 49th and 50th states admitted to the union?**

    Alaska and Hawaii.

48. How many terms can a president serve?

Two.

49. Who was Martin Luther King, Jr.?

A civil rights leader.

50. Who is the head of your local government?

The answer depends on where you live. We provide ways for you to discover who your representatives are earlier in this chapter in the "National, state, and local governments" section.

51. According to the Constitution, a person must meet certain requirements in order to become President. Name one of the requirements.

He or she must be a natural-born citizen, must be at least 35 years old by the time he or she will serve, and must have lived in the United States for at least 14 years.

52. Why are there 100 senators in the senate?

There are two from each state.

53. Who selects the Supreme Court justices?

The President appoints them.

54. How many Supreme Court justices are there?

Nine.

55. Why did the pilgrims come to America?

For religious freedom.

56. What is the head executive of a state government called?

The governor.

57. What is the head executive of a city government called?

The mayor.

58. What holiday was celebrated for the first time by the American colonists?

Thanksgiving.

59. Who was the main writer of the Declaration of Independence?

Thomas Jefferson.

60. When was the Declaration of Independence adopted?

July 4, 1776.

61. What is the basic belief of the Declaration of Independence?

That all men are created equal.

62. What is the national anthem of the United States?

"The Star-Spangled Banner."

63. Who wrote "The Star-Spangled Banner"?

Francis Scott Key.

64. Where does freedom of speech come from?

The Bill of Rights.

65. What is the minimum voting age in the United States?

18.

66. Who signs bills into laws?

The President.

67. What is the highest court in the United States?

The Supreme Court.

68. Who was the president during the Civil War?

Abraham Lincoln.

69. What did the Emancipation Proclamation do?

Freed many slaves.

70. What special group advises the President?

The Cabinet.

71. Which president is called "the father of our country"?

George Washington.

72. What Bureau of Citizenship and Immigration Services (BCIS) form is used to apply to become a naturalized citizen?

Form N-400, "Application to File Petition for Naturalization."

73. Who helped the pilgrims in America?

The Native Americans or American Indians.

74. What is the name of the ship that brought the pilgrims to America?

The *Mayflower.*

75. What were the 13 original states of the United States called?

Colonies.

76. Name three rights or freedoms guaranteed by the Bill of Rights.

A. A person has the right to freedom of speech, press, religion, peaceable assembly, and the right to request a change of government or government policies.

B. A person has the right to bear arms (the right to have weapons or own a gun, though this right is subject to certain regulations).

C. The government may not quarter or house soldiers in the people's homes during peacetime without the people's consent.

D. The government may not search or take a person's property without a warrant.

E. A person may not be tried twice for the same crime and does not have to testify against himself or herself.

F. A person charged with a crime still has some rights, such as the right to a trial and to have a lawyer.

G. A person has the right to a trial by jury in most cases.

H. People are protected from excessive or unreasonable fines or cruel and unusual punishment.

I. The people have rights other than those mentioned in the Constitution. Any power not given to the federal government by the Constitution is a power of either the state or the people.

77. Who has the power to declare war?

Congress.

78. What kind of government does the United States have?

Republican. (In this case, the word "Republican" has nothing to do with the political party; it refers to Republican government structure, meaning the government is not headed by a monarch, and elected representatives act on behalf of the citizens they represent.)

79. Which President freed the slaves?

Abraham Lincoln.

80. In what year was the Constitution written?

1787.

81. What are the first ten amendments to the Constitution called?

The Bill of Rights.

82. Name one purpose of the United Nations.

For countries to discuss and try to resolve problems; to provide economic aid to many countries.

83. Where does Congress meet?

In the Capitol in Washington, D.C.

84. Whose rights are guaranteed by the Constitution and the Bill of Rights?

Everyone, citizen and noncitizen alike, living in the United States.

85. What is the introduction to the Constitution called?

The Preamble.

86. Name one benefit of being a citizen of the United States.

You can obtain federal government jobs, travel with a U.S. passport, and petition for close relatives to come to the U.S. to live.

87. What is the most important right guaranteed to U.S. citizens?

The right to vote.

88. What is the United States Capitol?

The place where Congress meets.

89. What is the White House?

The President's official home.

90. Where is the White House located?

In the capital of Washington, D.C. (1600 Pennsylvania Avenue NW).

91. What is the name of the President's official home?

The White House.

92. Name one right guaranteed by the First Amendment.

Freedom of speech, press, religion, peaceable assembly, and requesting change of the government.

93. Who is the Commander in Chief of the military?

The President.

94. Which President was the first Commander in Chief of the military?

George Washington.

95. In what month do we vote for President?

November.

96. In what month is the new President inaugurated?

January.

97. How many times may a senator be reelected?

There is no limit.

98. How many times may a congressman be reelected?

There is no limit.

99. What are the two major political parties in the United States today?

The Democratic and Republican parties.

100. How many states are there in the United States?

50.

Remembering facts

You can memorize facts easier by using mnemonics or other memory techniques. A *mnemonic* is a word, rhyme, abbreviation, or similar verbal shorthand that you create to help trigger your memory. You can trick yourself into remembering facts in many different ways. For example, if you're trying to remember the names of the 13 original colonies of the U.S. (Connecticut, Delaware, Georgia, Maryland, Massachusetts, New Hampshire, New Jersey, New York, North Carolina, Pennsylvania, Rhode Island, South Carolina, and Virginia), you can just remember the first letters of their names — C, D, G, two Ms, four Ns, P, R, S, and V. If you set those letters to a familiar tune, it'll be even easier to remember.

The trick is to do whatever works for you. Try out several different techniques and see which one works best for you.

Part VI
The Part of Tens

"We're still learning the language and Martin tends to act out things he doesn't know the word for. He tried buying a toilet seat the other day and they almost threw him out of the store."

In this part . . .

Every *For Dummies* book contains The Part of Tens — a collection of chapters, each consisting of ten key pieces of information. In this part, you'll find information examining the accomplishments of our last ten presidents. The remaining two chapters in this section are good checklists to look over from time to time during the immigration process, because they'll help keep you on track. Chapter 20 shares ten ways to improve your immigration chances — put these into practice at every stage of the game. Equally (if not more) important, refer frequently to Chapter 21 to make sure you're not doing anything that can hurt your immigration goals.

Chapter 19

The Historical Impact of Our Last Ten Presidents

In This Chapter

- Meeting our modern leaders
- Understanding the roots of current events
- Keeping up with recent history

Finding out about American history involves far more than just looking back at the country's origins. Some of the most profound events and important challenges in American history are happening right now. Most have roots in our recent history.

One of the quickest ways to get an overview of the United States today is to examine the administrations of our latest presidents. By examining the major events that took place during their times in office and the legacies they left, we can better understand how the United States came to its current place in world history.

Dwight David Eisenhower

34th President (Served 1953–1961)
Party affiliation: Republican
Born: October 14, 1890, in Denison, Texas
Married to: Mamie Geneva Doud Eisenhower
Died: March 28, 1969, in Washington, D.C.
Buried in: The Place of Meditation at the Eisenhower Center in Abilene, Kansas, the town where he grew up

Dwight David Eisenhower enjoyed a prestigious military career long before he ever sought the office of Commander in Chief, serving in the army under Generals John J. Pershing, Douglas MacArthur, and Walter Krueger. After the Japanese attack on Pearl Harbor on December 17, 1941, Eisenhower was called to Washington for a war-plans assignment.

General Eisenhower never actually commanded troops in combat, but rather directed strategy and coordinated Allied forces. He commanded the Allied forces landing in North Africa in November 1942 and served as the Supreme Commander of the troops invading France on D-Day, June 6, 1944. By November 1945, Eisenhower was promoted to Chief of Staff, U.S. Army.

After the war, Dwight Eisenhower became President of Columbia University. He took a leave from this position in 1951 to assume supreme command over the new North Atlantic Treaty Organization (NATO) forces. The following year, high-ranking members of the Republican Party traveled to his Paris office to convince him to run for president. Eisenhower defeated Illinois Governor Adlai Stevenson in the presidential election of 1952 to become the first Republican president in 20 years.

During his two terms in office, Eisenhower continually worked to ease Cold War tensions. He proposed worldwide development of atomic energy in his Atoms for Peace speech to the United Nations in 1953, while the same year a truce brought an armed peace along the border of North and South Korea, and Russia consented to a peace treaty neutralizing Austria.

As president, he navigated the country through foreign affairs crises in Lebanon, Suez, Germany, and Hungary. With the signing of the Eisenhower Doctrine in 1957, he proposed and obtained a joint resolution from Congress authorizing the use of U.S. military forces to aid any country that appeared likely to fall to communism.

Considered a political moderate, Eisenhower stressed *fiscal* (financial) responsibility in domestic affairs. Concerned with civil-rights issues, he sent troops to Little Rock, Arkansas, to enforce court-ordered school integration. With the signing of the Federal Highway Bill, he authorized construction of the interstate highway system.

Historical highlights that happened during Eisenhower's time in office include the following:

- The U.S. and North Korea signed a peace agreement to end the Korean War in 1952.
- Soviet leader Joseph Stalin died in 1953.
- The Supreme Court ruled segregated schools were illegal in the case of *Brown* v. *the Board of Education of Topeka, Kansas* (1954).
- A CIA-sponsored coup overthrew the elected government in Guatemala in 1954.
- The first civil-rights legislation in 82 years, the Civil Rights Act of 1957 was passed, largely due to the efforts of Eisenhower and Lyndon Johnson (then a senator from Texas).
- Eisenhower signed a bill establishing the National Aeronautics and Space Administration (NASA) in 1958.
- Alaska and Hawaii became states in 1959.
- Eisenhower broke off diplomatic relations with Cuba in 1961.

John Fitzgerald Kennedy

35th President (Served 1961–1963)
Party affiliation: Democrat
Born: May 29, 1917, in Brookline, Massachusetts
Married to: Jacqueline Lee Bouvier Kennedy
Died: November 22, 1963, in Dallas, Texas
Buried in: Arlington National Cemetery in Arlington, Virginia

After graduating from Harvard in 1940, John Fitzgerald Kennedy joined the navy as a lieutenant assigned to command a patrol torpedo boat in the South Pacific. Kennedy became a national hero when a Japanese destroyer rammed and sunk *PT109.* Despite extreme pain and serious injuries, Kennedy led survivors to safety through the treacherous waters. His courage earned him the Navy and Marine Corps Medal.

After the war, Kennedy became a Democratic congressman from the Boston area. He advanced to the Senate in 1953. Still plagued by the pain caused by his war injuries, he wrote the Pulitzer Prize–winning history book *Profiles in Courage* while recovering from back surgery in 1955.

John Kennedy won the presidency by a narrow margin against Republican candidate Richard M. Nixon. In 1960, he became America's first Roman Catholic president and the youngest man to ever hold the office of President of the United States.

In the early days of his presidency, Kennedy dealt with many historic events, decisions, and political maneuverings. From the previous presidential administration, he inherited a secret plan to overthrow the communist Cuban regime of Fidel Castro. The unsuccessful attempt by American-trained and American-supported Cuban exiles to overthrow the communist government — which became known as the Bay of Pigs Invasion (1961) — proved a dismal failure that seriously embarrassed the new President and his administration.

One year later, when the U.S. discovered that the Russians planned to install nuclear missiles in Cuba, the Kennedy administration announced a quarantine on all offensive weapons bound for Cuba. The Cuban Missile Crisis is the closest the world has come to nuclear war up to this point in history. The Soviet Union, convinced of the futility of nuclear blackmail, ultimately backed down, agreeing to dismantle the launch sites. The crisis was over, with both sides realizing they had a vital interest in stopping the spread of nuclear weapons and slowing the arms race.

A positive side effect of the Cold War, in terms of scientific advancement and study, was the space race. A huge proponent of space exploration, Kennedy vowed that the United States would put a man on the moon before the Soviets. Space programs started during the Kennedy administration opened the door to worldwide progress in the exploration of space.

During his time in office, Kennedy fought hard for equal rights, calling for new civil-rights legislation. He brought American idealism to the world by forming the Peace Corps, which sent trained American volunteers to help people of developing countries in meeting their need for trained and educated workers.

On November 22, 1963, while riding in an open car in a parade in Dallas, Texas, John F. Kennedy was shot and killed by an assassin named Lee Harvey Oswald. The stunned nation mourned our youngest president — also the youngest president to die.

Other historical highlights that took place during Kennedy's time in office include the following:

- In 1961, newly elected President Kennedy sent the first military advisors and soldiers to South Vietnam, to help keep stability in the region and fight corruption and a growing Communist force.
- Cesar Chavez established the National Farm Workers Union in 1962.
- The Test Ban Treaty of 1963 banned nuclear tests in the atmosphere, underwater, and in space. The USSR and the United States agreed to establish a hot line between Moscow and Washington, D.C., to facilitate communication in times of crisis.
- Kennedy sent 3,000 federal troops to control riots when the Supreme Court ordered the University of Mississippi to accept African American student James Meredith.
- The March on Washington of 1963 brought attention to civil rights and held the record for the largest gathering of people to that date.

Lyndon Baines Johnson

36th President (Served 1963–1969)
Party affiliation: Democrat
Born: August 27, 1908, near Stonewall, Texas
Married to: Claudia Taylor "Lady Bird" Johnson
Died: January 22, 1973, in Johnson City, Texas
Buried in: The Johnson Family Cemetery at the Johnson Ranch in Stonewall, Texas

Born in the area of central Texas that his family first helped settle, Lyndon Johnson came into the world a man of modest means. He worked his way through Southwest Texas State Teachers College, dropping out of school for a year to serve as the principal of and teacher for fifth, sixth, and seventh grades at Welhausen School, a Mexican American school in south Texas.

During World War II, Johnson served briefly as a lieutenant commander in the Navy, winning a Silver Star in the South Pacific for gallantry in action during an aerial combat mission over New Guinea.

In 1937, he campaigned successfully for the House of Representatives. After six terms in the House, Johnson was elected to the Senate in 1948, becoming the youngest Minority Leader in Senate history, and when the Democrats won control the following year, he became the youngest Majority Leader.

In 1960, Johnson campaigned as John F. Kennedy's vice-presidential running mate. Lyndon Johnson assumed the presidency on November 22, 1963, the day of John Kennedy's assassination.

Continuing the slain president's work, he obtained enactment of the measures Kennedy had been fighting for at the time of his death, including a new civil-rights bill and a tax cut. When it came time for reelection in 1964, Johnson had the widest popular vote margin in American history — 61 percent.

Johnson's Great Society program became the focus of his agenda for Congress. This ambitious and wide-reaching social plan included aid to education, Medicare, urban renewal, beautification, and conservation; attack on disease; development of depressed regions; a wide-scale fight against poverty; control and prevention of crime and delinquency; and removal of obstacles to the right to vote. Space exploration also continued to flourish under the Johnson administration.

Despite the beginning of new antipoverty and antidiscrimination programs, also known as the War on Poverty, Johnson's era was troubled by riots and unrest in the inner cities of America, largely in response to the assassination of civil-rights leader Martin Luther King, Jr. The president steadfastly exerted his influence against segregation, but there were often no easy solutions.

Communist aggression in Vietnam, a problem that had been brewing for some time, continued to escalate. By the end of 1968, the U.S. found itself divided over the war. Johnson surprised the world by withdrawing as a candidate for reelection. He felt he could work more effectively toward peace without having to play politics.

Peace talks were underway when he left office. Unfortunately, he didn't live to see them completed. Lyndon Johnson died suddenly of a heart attack at his Texas ranch on January 22, 1973.

Historical highlights that took place during the Johnson administration include the following:

- The 1964 Civil Rights Act included provisions to protect the right to vote, guarantee access to public accommodations, and withhold federal funds from programs administered in a discriminatory fashion.
- Congress passed the Southeast Asia Resolution (often called the Gulf of Tonkin Resolution) on August 7, 1964, backing Johnson in taking "all necessary measures to repel any armed attack against the forces of the United States and to prevent further aggression." Johnson signed the resolution on August 10, formally committing America's involvement in Vietnam.
- Millions of elderly people received medical help through the 1965 Medicare amendment to the Social Security Act.
- Three astronauts successfully orbited the moon in December 1968.

Richard Milhous Nixon

37th President (Served 1969–1974)
Party affiliation: Republican
Born: January 9, 1913, in Yorba Linda, California
Married to: Patricia Ryan Nixon
Died: April 22, 1994, in New York, New York
Buried in: The grounds of the Nixon Library in Yorba Linda, California

Richard Nixon should have been nicknamed the Comeback Kid. He enjoyed early career success as a lawyer and politician, then was defeated at a run for president in 1960 and a bid for Governor of California in 1962. He astonished his political allies and enemies alike when he went on to become the 37th President of the United States, easily winning reelection in 1972 with 60.6 percent of the electoral vote, a historic margin for reelection.

During World War II, Nixon served as a Navy lieutenant commander in the Pacific. After the war, he was elected to represent the people of California in Congress, advancing to the Senate in 1950. Nixon was only 39 years old when General Dwight Eisenhower chose him as his running mate. He served in the office of Vice President for eight years.

Nixon lost his first bid for the presidency by a narrow margin to John F. Kennedy, but in the 1968 election, he defeated then Vice President Hubert H. Humphrey and third-party candidate, Alabama Governor George C. Wallace.

When Richard Nixon took office, the country was deeply divided over the issue of the Vietnam War, with protests and civil unrest at home and abroad dominating the news. With peace a priority of his administration, the war came to an end during Nixon's time in office.

Despite all his accomplishments, Richard Nixon is perhaps most remembered for his involvement in the Watergate scandal. Five men were arrested for breaking into the Democratic National Committee's executive quarters in the Watergate Hotel in Washington, D.C., on June 17, 1972. Traced to officials of the Committee to Re-Elect the President, suspicions surfaced that Richard Nixon himself took part in planning the break-in. The Supreme Court ordered Nixon to turn over tape recordings of the plans for the coverup of the scandal. Senate hearings began in 1973, and Nixon finally admitted his involvement. When his impeachment trial began — a trial that could remove him from office if he was found guilty — he opted to resign from office instead.

In his final years, Nixon gained praise as an elder statesman. He became a prolific writer after his retirement from political life, penning ten books about foreign policy and his experiences in public life — all bestsellers.

Historical highlights of the Nixon era include the following:

- American astronauts made the first moon landing in 1969.
- Nixon instigated a broad environmental program including creating the Environmental Protection Agency in 1970.
- In 1972, Nixon became the first president ever to visit the People's Republic of China, a nation that had remained isolated from the West since the communist revolution in 1949. The President's visit preceded a warming trend in U.S.-China diplomatic relations.
- Instead of continuing the arms race, Nixon proposed that the U.S. and the Soviet Union develop a *strategic parity* in nuclear weapons. Essentially, that meant that if both sides had enough weapons to guarantee the destruction of the other, neither would dare to start war. In theory, peace would prevail.
- Vice President Spiro T. Agnew resigned in 1973 over scandals unrelated to Watergate. Gerald R. Ford took over as Vice President.
- The draft ended in 1973. (Nonetheless, to this day, young men in the U.S. still must register with the Selective Service Administration, in case the need for another draft arises.)
- The Supreme Court legalized abortion in 1973.
- An accord with North Vietnam ended American involvement in Vietnam in 1973.

Gerald Rudolph Ford

38th President (Served 1974–1977)
Party affiliation: Republican
Born: July 14, 1913, in Omaha, Nebraska
Married to: Elizabeth "Betty" Bloomer Ford

Gerald Ford holds the distinction of being the only American President to never win a presidential election. When Richard Nixon's Vice President, Spiro Agnew, resigned over a political scandal, Nixon appointed Gerald Ford to fill the position, according to terms set in the Twenty-fifth Amendment (the first and only time the law has ever been put to use). Congress approved the choice. When Nixon became the first president to ever resign, Ford stepped up to the highest office in the land.

Before he found himself in the position of Commander in Chief, Gerald Ford spent 25 years in Congress, serving as House Minority Leader from 1965 to 1973. Nonetheless, he faced enormous challenges upon assuming the presidency, including a depressed economy, ballooning economic inflation, and ongoing energy shortages.

In foreign affairs, Ford acted vigorously to maintain U.S. power and prestige after the collapse of Cambodia and South Vietnam. Preventing a new war in the Middle East remained another major foreign policy goal of the Ford administration. By providing aid to both Egypt and Israel, the two countries were convinced to form an interim peace agreement. Tensions with the USSR continued to lessen during the Ford years and the world's two superpowers set further limits on nuclear weapons.

Despite opposition from a largely Democratic Congress, Ford fought to limit inflation by reversing the trend from government intervention in solving societal problems — although when the country entered a recession, he initiated measures aimed at boosting the economy, like reducing taxes and lessening regulatory-agency controls over business and industry.

Although Gerald Ford won the Republican nomination for President in 1976, the problems he inherited with the office proved too difficult to overcome — the aftereffects of a divisive war in Southeast Asia, rising inflation, and fears of energy shortages. He lost the election to Democrat Jimmy Carter, the former Governor of Georgia.

After resuming private life, President and Mrs. Ford moved to Rancho Mirage, California, where the President wrote his memoirs, *A Time to Heal: The Autobiography of Gerald R. Ford.* He has lectured at over 179 colleges and universities since leaving office.

Historical highlights of the Ford years include the following:

- One month after taking office, Ford exercised his presidential power to give former President Richard Nixon a full and complete pardon (turn to Chapter 10 for more information on this process).
- President Ford survived two unsuccessful assassination attempts in the month of September 1975.
- The United States celebrated its *bicentennial* (200th) birthday in 1976.

James Earl Carter, Jr.

39th President (Served 1977–1981)
Party affiliation: Democrat
Born: October 1, 1924, in Plains, Georgia
Married to: Rosalynn Smith Carter

President Jimmy Carter, who rarely used his full name, graduated in 1946 from the Naval Academy in Annapolis, Maryland. Carter served seven years as a naval officer before returning to his home in Plains, Georgia.

He began his career in state politics in 1962, and was elected Governor of Georgia in 1970, on a political platform that emphasized ecology and equality. After first announcing his candidacy for president in 1974, he worked tirelessly on a two-year campaign with Minnesota senator Walter "Fritz" Mondale as his running mate. Carter won the election by 297 electoral votes to Gerald Ford's 241.

Ever an idealist, Carter sought to make a "competent and compassionate" government, an impossible feat in an era of rampant inflation, unemployment, and rising energy costs. Despite the fact that the economy saw a turn for the better — Carter decreased the budget deficit (measured as a percentage of the gross national product) — he never received the credit he deserved. Record high interest and inflation rates sent the country into a short recession, which damaged his popularity.

Carter shone in foreign affairs, although many of his achievements had a solid base in the work of some of his presidential predecessors, such as Richard Nixon and Gerald Ford. The Camp David Agreement of 1978 brought peace between Egypt and Israel. He established full diplomatic relations with the People's Republic of China and completed negotiations with the Soviet Union on the SALT II Nuclear Limitation Treaty, although the Soviet invasion of Afghanistan caused a suspension of ratification plans.

In addition to economic woes, Carter's popularity took another blow when Iranian militants stormed the United States embassy in Tehran and took about 70 Americans captive. The terrorist act triggered a media storm that dominated the public's consciousness for the remainder of Carter's time in office. In April 1980, an ill-fated military rescue operation ended with the deaths of eight U.S. servicemen. At the end of the disastrous mission, the hostages remained captive and would remain so for another 270 days. In a press conference about the failed rescue mission, President Carter took full responsibility for the tragedy.

Carter lost the 1980 election to republican Ronald Reagan. Despite the electoral defeat, he never stopped his endless negotiations to free the hostages. Right up until their final hours in office, Carter and his senior staff worked intensely to finalize a deal with the Iranians. Ironically, the hostages were released on January 20, 1981, on the same day Carter officially left office.

Jimmy Carter has stayed busy since leaving politics. In 1982, he became University Distinguished Professor at Emory University in Atlanta, Georgia. He has authored 16 books. Well known and respected for his charity work, he and Mrs. Carter volunteer one week a year for Habitat for Humanity, an organization that helps needy people in the United States and in other countries to renovate and build homes for themselves. He also founded the Carter Center, a nonpartisan and nonprofit center that addresses national and international issues of public policy in an effort to resolve conflict, promote democracy, protect human rights, and prevent disease and other afflictions around the globe. He also teaches Sunday school and is a deacon in the Maranatha Baptist Church in Plains, Georgia.

On December 10, 2002, Jimmy Carter received the Nobel Peace Prize "for his decades of untiring effort to find peaceful solutions to international conflicts, to advance democracy and human rights, and to promote economic and social development."

Important historical events that took place during the Carter administration include the following:

- Carter pardoned draft evaders of the Vietnam War period upon taking office.
- In 1977, there was deregulation of the trucking and airline industries and the ratification of the Panama Canal treaties.
- Following 12 days of secret negotiations between Israel and Egypt, the 1978 Camp David Accord outlined the framework for peace in the Middle East.
- The Department of Education was established in 1978.
- The National Parks Service expanded in 1980 to include the 19-million-acre Arctic National Wildlife Refuge in Alaska — the same land currently under hot debate for its rich oil resources.
- More than 50 nations, including the United States, boycotted the 1980 Olympic Games in Moscow in protest of the Soviet invasion of Afghanistan.

Ronald Wilson Reagan

40th President (Served 1981–1989)
Party affiliation: Republican
Born: February 6, 1911, in Tampico, Illinois
Married to: Nancy Davis Reagan

Ronald Reagan worked his way through Illinois's Eureka College, studying economics and sociology, excelling on the football team, acting in school plays, and serving as student-body president. After graduating, he got a job as a radio sports announcer, but more than just a great voice, Reagan's good looks helped land him a Hollywood movie contract. Over the next 20 years, Ronald Reagan appeared in 53 films.

Before he ever became President of the United States, Reagan served as president of the Screen Actors Guild — an actor's union — where he became involved in the issue of communism in the film industry. Around this time, his political philosophy changed from liberal to conservative.

He was elected Governor of California in 1966 and won reelection in 1970. When he ran as the Republican candidate for President in 1980, he chose former Texas Congressman George Bush as his running mate.

The public had been weathering the effects of double-digit inflation and high interest rates under the Ford and Carter administrations, as well as stress over the Iran hostage crisis.

Reagan won the election in an electoral vote landslide: 489 electoral votes to President Jimmy Carter's 49. At 73 years old, Ronald Reagan became the oldest man ever elected president. In his inaugural address, Reagan announced that the 52 American hostages held in Iran for 444 days were at that moment being released and would soon return to freedom.

His first-term economic policies — which came to be known in popular language as *Reaganomics* — so boosted America's confidence that he easily won his second presidential election against Democratic challengers Walter Mondale and Geraldine Ferraro (the first woman vice-presidential candidate on a national party ticket).

Reagan's overhaul of the federal income-tax code eliminated many deductions. His other economic policies included cutting taxes and government spending, while obtaining legislation to stimulate economic growth and strengthen national defense. This last point ultimately led to a large deficit. Nonetheless, by the end of the Reagan administration, the nation was enjoying its longest period of peacetime prosperity without recession or depression. Over the course of his administration, Ronald Reagan facilitated the passage of $39 billion in budget cuts into law.

The economic gains, however, came at a cost of a growing national debt and a record annual deficit, made worse by a trade deficit — Americans were buying more foreign-made goods than they were selling. Nonetheless, Reagan maintained his free-trade political platform.

Reagan believed that the United States should negotiate with the Soviet Union from a position of strength. During his two terms in office, he managed to increase defense spending while simultaneously negotiating arms treaties with the Soviets. He gave support to anti-communist organizations in Asia, Africa, and Central America. He sent a naval escort task force to insure the free flow of oil in the Persian Gulf during the Iraq-Iran War, a plan that resulted in tragedy when an Iraqi warplane missile killed 37 sailors aboard the U.S.S. *Stark*.

In spite of his significant accomplishments, Reagan's years in office could not escape controversy. In a scandal that became known as the *Iran Contra Affair,* a special congressional hearings review board reported that Reagan authorized the sale of arms to Iran in exchange for help in freeing U.S. hostages in Lebanon. Even worse, the money from the arms sales was funneled to aid the contras — opponents of Nicaragua's Sandinista government. In the course of the proceedings, National Security Advisors Robert McFarlane and John Poindexter, as well as National Security Council aide Colonel Oliver North, were indicted by a federal grand jury and convicted of lying to Congress.

After retiring from politics Ronald and Nancy Reagan returned to their Southern California home. The former president celebrated his 92nd birthday in 2003, making him not only the oldest man ever elected president, but also the oldest living president in American history.

Historical highlights of the Reagan era include the following:

- After only 69 days in office, a would-be assassin shot President Reagan and Press Secretary James Brady. The president quickly recovered and returned to duty. Despite a serious gunshot wound to the head, Brady remained Press Secretary until the end of the Reagan administration.
- Reagan gave striking air-traffic controllers 48 hours to return to work, and in 1981, fired those who refused.
- The U.S. retaliated against Libya for terrorist acts against Americans with air attacks in 1981 and again in 1986 after the terrorist-related deaths of Americans in a Berlin discotheque.
- A suicide truck bomber crashed into marine barracks and killed 241 members of the U.S. peacekeeping force in Beirut, Lebanon, in 1983.
- Reagan's Secretary of State, Charles Shultz, designated Iran as a sponsor of international terrorism in 1984.
- Reagan signed legislation in 1986 to make slain civil-rights leader Reverend Martin Luther King, Jr.'s birthday a national holiday, celebrated each year on the third Monday of January.
- The U.S. space shuttle *Challenger* exploded seconds after takeoff in 1986, killing the six astronauts on board as well as teacher Christa McAuliffe, the first civilian to go into space.
- In the beginning of 1988, the Soviets agreed to begin pulling troops out of Afghanistan, pledging to be completely out by February 15, 1989.

George Herbert Walker Bush

41st President (Served 1989–1993)
Party affiliation: Republican
Born: June 12, 1924, in Milton, Massachusetts
Married to: Barbara Pierce Bush

The Bush family has a long legacy of public service that continues to grow to this day. George Herbert Walker Bush's father, Prescott Bush, served as a United States senator from Connecticut from 1952 to 1962.

On his eighteenth birthday George Bush enlisted in the armed forces where he became a navy pilot, flying 58 combat missions during World War II and receiving the Distinguished Flying Cross for bravery in action. He was still a mere 18 years old in June of 1943 when he received his wings and commission, making him the youngest pilot in the Navy at that time.

After the war, Bush attended Yale University where he excelled in both sports and academics. After graduating, he moved his family to West Texas to start a career in the oil industry. While there, he followed his father's footsteps into politics.

He served two terms as a representative to Congress from Texas, although he was defeated twice at runs for the senate. After leaving Congress he held a series of high-level positions including Ambassador to the United Nations, Chairman of the Republican National Committee, Chief of the U.S. Liaison Office in the People's Republic of China, and Director of the Central Intelligence Agency (CIA).

Although he lost the 1980 Republican Party nomination for President, Ronald Reagan chose him as his running mate. He finally won the presidential nomination in 1988, with Senator Dan Quayle of Indiana as his vice president, defeating the Massachusetts Governor, Democrat Michael Dukakis.

The world was in transition when George Herbert Walker Bush took office. The communist empire that was the USSR broke up and the Berlin Wall, which separated Communist East Berlin from Democratic West Berlin, came tumbling down.

In Panama, the regime of dictator/president General Manuel Noriega threatened the security of the Panama Canal. Bush sent troops to overthrow the corrupt government, and brought Noriega to the United States to face drug-trafficking charges.

The Bush Administration faced its biggest challenge when Iraqi President Saddam Hussein invaded Kuwait on August 2, 1990, threatening to move on to Saudi Arabia. After rallying the United Nations for support, Congress authorized sending 425,000 American troops to the Middle East. The American forces were helped by 118,000 allied troops, launching Operation Desert Storm, a massive air war that destroyed Iraq's military foundation. The main coalition ground forces invaded Kuwait and Iraq on February 24 and defeated the Iraqis in only four days, freeing Kuwait. Despite victory, both sides sustained enormous losses.

Although Bush experienced a high public approval rating on the issue of the Gulf War, the faltering domestic economy took its toll on his administration's popularity. George Herbert Walker Bush lost his 1992 bid for reelection to Bill Clinton — but this would not be the last the White House would see of the Bush family.

After retiring from political life, the President and Mrs. Bush moved to Houston, Texas, where they serve on the Board of Visitors of M.D. Anderson Hospital and are members of St. Martin's Episcopal Church. The senior George Bush also serves on the board of the Episcopal Church Foundation.

Historical highlights of the Bush years include the following:

- The Berlin Wall, separating East and West Berlin, fell in 1989.
- An accident aboard the Exxon *Valdez* in 1989 created one of the worst oil spills and environmental disasters in history.
- The Cold War ended, the Communist empire broke up, and the Soviet Union ceased to exist after 1991.
- Anita Hill accused then Supreme Court Justice nominee Clarence Thomas of sexual harassment in 1991. Thomas was found not guilty and went on to serve on the Supreme Court.
- The signing of the historic arms reduction treaties, START I and START II, in 1991 created the first-ever agreements to dismantle and destroy strategic weapons since the start of the nuclear age.
- The signing of the North American Free Trade Agreement (NAFTA) in 1992 removed most barriers to trade and investment between the United States, Canada, and Mexico.

William Jefferson Clinton

42nd President (Served 1993–2001)
Party affiliation: Democrat
Born: August 19, 1946, in Hope, Arkansas
Married to: Hillary Rodham Clinton

Three months after William Jefferson Blythe IV was born on August 19, 1946, his father died in a traffic accident. A few years later, his mother remarried. During his high-school years, he adopted his stepfather's family name, Clinton. During that same period, as a delegate to Boys Nation, he had the opportunity to meet President John F. Kennedy in the White House Rose Garden. The encounter inspired young Bill Clinton to enter a life of public service.

While attending Georgetown University, Clinton served as an intern for Senator J. William Fulbright of Arkansas before receiving his BS degree in 1968. He won a Rhodes Scholarship to Oxford University, then received a law degree from Yale University in 1973.

A year later he was defeated in his campaign for Congress in Arkansas's Third District. Clinton was elected Arkansas Attorney General in 1976, and won the governor's race in 1978, becoming the nation's youngest governor. He lost his bid for a second term but regained control of the governor's office four years later.

In the 1992 presidential election, Clinton and his running mate, Tennessee Senator Albert Gore, Jr., defeated President George Bush and third-party candidate Ross Perot. For the first time in well over a decade, the same party controlled both the White House and Congress. By 1994, however, the Republicans won majorities in both houses of Congress putting an end to the Democratic edge (the U.S. system of checks and balances at work). Nonetheless, Clinton won the 1996 presidential election against Republican Bob Dole by a comfortable margin, making William Jefferson Clinton the first Democratic president in over 60 years to be elected to the office twice.

The U.S. enjoyed the lowest unemployment rate and lowest inflation in 30 years during Clinton's first year in office. He proposed the first balanced budget in decades, and the U.S. actually had a budget surplus.

His second year in office was plagued by the overwhelming failure of his health-care reform plan. Public concerns over the proposal's complexity dampened congressional enthusiasm for the policy initiative, which had been the cornerstone of the Clinton campaign.

Scandal regarding a sexual-harassment lawsuit and issues of personal indiscretions with a White House intern followed in 1998. As a result of the Monica Lewinsky scandal, Clinton became the second U.S. president to be impeached by the House of Representatives (Andrew Johnson was the first). As outlined in the impeachment procedure set forth in the Constitution, Clinton was tried in the Senate. Found not guilty of the charges brought against him, he nonetheless apologized to the nation for his actions. The public accepted the apology and Clinton enjoyed record popular approval ratings.

In foreign affairs, he became a worldwide advocate for an expanded North Atlantic Treaty Organization (NATO), including more open international trade. The Clinton administration successfully initiated peacekeeping forces in war-torn Bosnia and maintained a worldwide battle against drug trafficking.

When Iraq's Saddam Hussein stopped United Nations inspections for evidence of nuclear, chemical, and biological weapons and appeared to be threatening neighbor Kuwait, Clinton deployed troops. He later ordered air strikes against Iraq for violating the terms of peace agreed to at the end of the Persian Gulf War.

In the spring of 1999, Clinton and his British counterpart, Prime Minister Tony Blair, led the push for NATO intervention in response to reports of continued ethnic cleansing in the Serbian province of Kosovo. A 78-day bombing campaign against Serbia began in March. On June 19, 1999, Serbian President Slobodan Milosevic finally signed a peace treaty.

During his final year in office, Clinton lent his support to Vice President Al Gore's unsuccessful run for the presidency as well as his wife Hillary Clinton's successful bid for U.S. Senator from New York.

Historical highlights of the Clinton years include the following:

- During his first term Clinton succeeded in appointing two members to the U.S. Supreme Court — Ruth Bader Ginsburg and Stephen G. Breyer — the first appointments to the high court made by a Democratic president in 25 years.

- Clinton's 1994 crime bill included a ban on assault weapons and added 100,000 new community police officers to the streets. The bill also represented the federal government's first attempt to address issues of domestic violence with the Violence Against Women Act.
- The 1995 Bosnian Peace Agreement ended the largest campaign of force in NATO history. U.S. troops were deployed to Bosnia to enforce the agreement.
- At around 9 a.m. on April 19, 1995, a bomb inside a rental truck parked outside the federal building in Oklahoma City, Oklahoma, exploded, killing 168 people. Until the bombings of September 11, 2001, the Oklahoma City bombing was the worst terrorist attack on U.S. soil. Ironically, the man responsible, Timothy McVeigh was an American. McVeigh has since been executed for the crime.
- The Telecommunications Reform Bill of 1996 improved competition in the industry and allowed parents to monitor television programs with violent content.
- The 1993 bombing of the World Trade Center became a motivating factor in enacting the 1996 Anti-Terrorism and Effective Death Penalty Act (AEDPA) and the Illegal Immigration Reform and Immigrant Responsibility Act (IIRAIRA) of 1996. Both impacted the rights of many immigrants. Included in the acts were provisions allowing the Immigration and Naturalization Service (now the Bureau for Citizenship and Immigration Services) to immediately deport, without a hearing, immigrants for minor crimes, including misdemeanors. The IIRAIRA further expanded the number of crimes that constitute aggravated felonies.
- The 1996 Personal Responsibility and Work Opportunity Reconciliation Act eliminated many immigrants from eligibility for public benefits.

George Walker Bush

43rd President (Served 2001–)
Party affiliation: Republican
Born: July 6, 1946, in New Haven, Connecticut
Married to: Laura Welch Bush

George W. Bush received a bachelor's degree from Yale University in 1968 before going on to serve as an F-102 fighter pilot in the Texas Air National Guard. He received a Master of Business Administration from Harvard Business School in 1975, then followed in his father's footsteps, moving back to Texas to work in the oil business. He took a leave of absence to work on his father's presidential campaign. After the election, he assembled the group of partners that purchased the Texas Rangers baseball franchise in 1989. He served as the managing general partner of the Texas Rangers until winning the Texas governor's election of November 8, 1994. He served for six years as the 46th Governor of the State of Texas, becoming the first Texas governor to be elected to two consecutive four-year terms.

In a close and hotly contested election, Bush and running mate Dick Cheney won the 2000 presidential race against Democrat Al Gore and his running mate, Connecticut Senator Joseph Lieberman.

Since taking office, Bush has signed into law initiatives to improve public schools and initiated tax relief that provided lower tax rates and rebate checks for everyone who pays income taxes in the United States, as well as increased pay for military personnel.

The terrorist attacks of September 11, 2001, in New York City and Washington, D.C., forever changed life in the United States. President Bush immediately made the war against terror a priority of his administration. To date, the United States military, with help from a coalition of nations, has defeated Afghanistan's brutal Taliban regime, sending members of the terrorist organization Al Qaeda running to find safe operation headquarters. Terrorist operations throughout the world have been disbanded or disrupted.

As we write this book, issues of nuclear arms and weapons inspections that began in the Reagan era and plagued George Herbert Walker Bush and Bill Clinton, still dominate U.S. foreign policy. The current Bush administration claims that Iraq has refused to cooperate with UN weapons inspectors and nuclear disarmament requirements and as a result, the U.S. and its allies find themselves at war with Iraq, without regard to the United Nations processes for addressing such situations. Exactly how long it will take to rebuild a free and democratic Iraq, and what the final effects the war will have on international politics and domestic security is anyone's guess.

Historical events of George W. Bush's administration, as of this writing, include the following:

- In a disputed election, George W. Bush won the electoral college to become the 43rd President of the United States, despite losing the popular vote.
- Terrorists attacked the World Trade Center in New York City and the Pentagon in Washington, D.C., on September 11, 2001.
- On January 24, 2003, the President signed the law that created the new Department of Homeland Security, representing the most significant and extensive transformation of the U.S. government in over 50 years. The new department incorporated 22 previously different domestic agencies under the authority of one department.
- As part of the new Department of Homeland Security, the Immigration and Naturalization Service (INS) ceased to exist as of March 1, 2003. Two separate government agencies — the Bureau for Citizenship and Immigration Services (BCIS) and the Directorate of Border and Transportation Security (BTS) — took over the roles formerly performed by the INS.

Chapter 20

Ten Tips to Help You Pass Your Immigration Interview

In This Chapter

- Making sure you put your best foot forward
- Knowing what to expect ahead of time
- Being honest with your interviewer

Use this chapter as a checklist of items to put into practice before going to your naturalization interview. Each of the ideas in the following pages can actually improve your chances of successfully passing the interview and becoming a naturalized citizen of the United States.

Be On Time

Get to the interview on time. That means on BCIS time, which means that if you have an 8 a.m. interview, you should arrive at the building by at least at 7 a.m., to allow time to get into the building.

Security procedures at government buildings may significantly increase the amount of time it takes to even enter the building. Allow plenty of extra time so you don't risk being late.

Before the day of your interview, take a trip to the building where your interview will be held, leaving at the same time of day as you'll need to leave for the real thing. This way, you can time how long it takes you to get to the building, allowing for traffic or other delays. Then allow even more time than that on the day of your interview, in case something unexpected comes up.

Present Yourself Favorably

You only get one chance to make a first impression. Dress like you're going to a job interview, and be polite to everyone you meet. Even if you have to wait three hours before being called in, don't take it out on the immigration officer.

Listen Carefully

Listen carefully to the questions the examiner asks you. If, for any reason, you don't understand a question, politely ask to have it repeated or explained until you do. You're better off getting clarification on the question than answering it incorrectly.

Answer the Right Questions

When you're sure you understand the question, take care to answer the question the officer asks you. For example, if the examiner asks, "What do the stripes on the flag mean?" don't say, "Red." Answer that the stripes on the flag represent our 13 original colonies. And limit your response to the question asked (there are no extra points for showing off, and it will only lengthen the interview).

Know Your Application

Be familiar with your naturalization application. Knowing there is a mistake on your application and asking the officer to correct it is much easier than having the officer ask you to explain a discrepancy or inconsistency (for instance, you correctly recall your dates of travel out of the U.S. as being less than six months, corroborated by your passport, but the dates are wrong on the application, stating a much longer trip).

Be Prepared

If something in your application requires an explanation, such as an extended trip abroad, past membership in the Communist Party, or a criminal record, don't let your interview be the first time you try to explain it to someone. If you have issues like this, you should have already included an explanatory affidavit with your naturalization application and, ideally, you would have consulted with a knowledgeable immigration lawyer or accredited representative before filing.

Know Your Stuff

If you're required to take the English and history/civics tests, which you most likely will be, remember, they are called *tests* for a reason. Study, practice, and be prepared. Yes, you can get another chance if you fail this portion of the interview, but why delay things and have to come back? Study hard the first time.

Bring What You Need

Bring all your original documents — green card, passport, affidavits, criminal records, and so on. If you've taken our advice, you have neat compact files that include copies of all your immigration-related documents and correspondence. Take your file along, and you'll be sure to have any paperwork you need.

Be Honest and Honorable

This may seem obvious, but don't lie, cheat, steal, or attempt to bribe your examining officer. Any of these can and probably will get you immediately disqualified from naturalization.

Treat Immigration Officers with Respect

BCIS adjudicators deal with huge caseloads. You aren't the only applicant your adjudicator will see that day. To ensure fair and prompt treatment of your application, try to make his job easier. Limit your discussions in the interview to the topics covered by the BCIS officer.

Note that this tip should not make you feel compelled to tolerate inappropriate behavior by a BCIS officer. If you think the officer is acting inappropriately or asking inappropriate questions, you should ask to speak with a supervisor immediately to report the incident. Be prepared to have your interview rescheduled with another officer. Inappropriate questions or behavior can include derogatory or discriminatory statements, sexual advances, or suggestions of favorable treatment in exchange for money or other favors.

Chapter 21

Ten Things That Can Hurt Your Immigration Chances

In This Chapter

- Knowing what *not* to do if you want to be a U.S. citizen
- Making sure you keep your nose clean

Just as there are things you can do to help your immigration chances, there are also some definite immigration don'ts. If any of the items on this list apply to you, we strongly urge you to seek the help of a qualified immigration attorney — long before you ever get to the stage of interviewing with the BCIS.

Some of the items here can prevent you from ever becoming a U.S. citizen; others present temporary problems. Again, a qualified attorney can best advise you on how to deal with the situation.

Committing a Crime

Murder, along with aggravated felonies committed on or after November 29, 1990, constitutes a *permanent bar to naturalization.* Other crimes present *temporary bars,* meaning you must wait a designated period of time before applying for citizenship. Furthermore, the BCIS can and will take your criminal record into consideration when determining whether you have good moral character. The bottom line: Obey the law, and you'll have a lot less to worry about.

Doing Drugs

Violating any controlled-substance law of the United States, any state, or any foreign country can get your application bounced on grounds of a lack of good moral character. Translation: In order to protect your immigration chances, don't use, sell, traffic, or otherwise be involved with drugs or other controlled substances of any kind, anywhere.

Abandoning Your Application

You must follow up on your application, make and meet appointments, and deliver necessary forms and documents to the appropriate immigration authorities in a timely manner.

The BCIS takes deadlines seriously, and missing them can result in your application being denied and your having to start the entire process all over again (complete with all the fees involved).

Also, make sure you notify the BCIS each and every time you change your address, so they'll always know where to send you information or get in touch when needed. If mail sent to you is returned to the BCIS, they will assume you've abandoned your application. Failure to keep the BCIS informed of changes of address is a crime and can be grounds for removal.

Participating in Subversive Activities

You can't expect to be welcomed as a citizen if you devote yourself to opposing the ideals upon which that citizenship is based. Anarchists, recent willful communists, supporters of totalitarian governments, and those who advocate for the overthrow of the U.S. government by force are barred from naturalization. And besides, if you're so opposed to the ideals of the U.S., why become a citizen anyway?

Behaving Poorly (Even If You're Not Breaking a Law)

Criminal convictions are not the only criteria upon which a negative determination of good moral character can be made. Other transgressions can include failing to pay child support; committing adultery that destroys a viable marriage, affects minor children, or is otherwise scandalous; having practiced polygamy; having been or being a habitual drunkard; or committing other unlawful acts that undermine moral character.

Supporting Terror

Of course, the U.S. government does not allow known terrorists to legally enter the country, much less to naturalize. Also excluded are those who support terrorism, financially or otherwise.

Perpetrating Fraud

Fraud encompasses lying on your naturalization application, as well as seeking immigration benefits that you know you aren't entitled to by putting forth a fraudulent claim (for instance, staging a marriage just to gain immigration benefits).

Unlawfully Staying in the U.S.

Being caught illegally in the United States can seriously impact your immigration and naturalization goals in a negative way. Make sure your immigration status is legal and up to date, and never stay in the U.S. beyond the date stamped on your I-94. If you have recently been ordered to leave the country, you aren't eligible for citizenship. If you're currently in removal proceedings, you may not apply for citizenship until the proceedings are complete and you've been allowed to remain in the country as a lawful permanent resident.

Failing to Register with the Selective Service (If You're a Male)

All male legal permanent residents between the ages of 18 and 26 must register with the Selective Service. Failure to register can be found to undermine good moral character. Desertion from the armed forces during a time of war may subject an applicant to a permanent bar to naturalization.

Failing to Meet Deadlines

Immigration proceedings come with strict time deadlines. From knowing when you're eligible to apply to knowing how long you have to file an appeal, you need to monitor the calendar to make sure you don't miss out.

Remember the following:

- You can file your N-400 three months before your naturalization eligibility date (five years; three years for spouses of U.S. citizens).
- You must have lived within the BCIS district in which you file at least three months before the filing date.
- You must have been physically present in the U.S. for at least half the required residence time (30 months out of 5 years; 18 months out of 3 years).

Don't forget to keep track of your absences from the U.S. — absences of more than six months require an explanation, and those over a year break the continuity of residence. After you've filed your application, be sure to read all government correspondence carefully.

Make sure you follow all instructions carefully and that you provide the BCIS with any paperwork and documentation they need within the time period that they specify. Failing to meet deadlines will cause the BCIS to think you've abandoned your application; your application will be thrown out and you'll have to start the process all over again.

Part VII
Appendixes

The 5th Wave
By Rich Tennant
THE JUSTICES RULE ON PAPER VS SCISSORS VS STONE
©RICHTENNANT

In this part . . .

In this part, you'll find extra information that you may want to refer to throughout your immigration and naturalization process. If you're interested in reading the actual text of the most important documents in the United States, we've reproduced the Declaration of Independence and the Constitution of the United States of America here. We've also supplied you with a handy document checklist that can really help when preparing your naturalization applications. The government designed this checklist so that applicants could see, at a glance, the documents, forms and paperwork they need to send when applying for naturalization.

Appendix A

The Declaration of Independence

WHEN in the Course of human Events, it becomes necessary for one People to dissolve the Political Bands which have connected them with another, and to assume among the Powers of the Earth, the separate and equal Station to which the Laws of Nature and of Nature's God entitle them, a decent Respect to the Opinions of Mankind requires that they should declare the causes which impel them to the Separation.

WE hold these Truths to be self-evident, that all Men are created equal, that they are endowed by their Creator with certain unalienable Rights, that among these are Life, Liberty, and the Pursuit of Happiness-That to secure these Rights, Governments are instituted among Men, deriving their just Powers from the Consent of the Governed, that whenever any Form of Government becomes destructive of these Ends, it is the Right of the People to alter or to abolish it, and to institute new Government, laying its Foundation on such Principles, and organizing its Powers in such Form, as to them shall seem most likely to effect their Safety and Happiness. Prudence, indeed, will dictate that Governments long established should not be changed for light and transient Causes; and accordingly all Experience hath shewn, that Mankind are more disposed to suffer, while Evils are sufferable, than to right themselves by abolishing the Forms to which they are accustomed. But when a long Train of Abuses and Usurpations, pursuing invariably the same Object, evinces a Design to reduce them under absolute Despotism, it is their Right, it is their Duty, to throw off such Government, and to provide new Guards for their future Security. Such has been the patient Sufferance of these Colonies; and such is now the Necessity which constrains them to alter their former Systems of Government. The History of the present King of Great-Britain is a History of repeated Injuries and Usurpations, all having in direct Object the Establishment of an absolute Tyranny over these States. To prove this, let Facts be submitted to a candid World.

HE has refused his Assent to Laws, the most wholesome and necessary for the public Good.

HE has forbidden his Governors to pass Laws of immediate and pressing Importance, unless suspended in their Operation till his Assent should be obtained; and when so suspended, he has utterly neglected to attend to them.

HE has refused to pass other Laws for the Accommodation of large Districts of People, unless those People would relinquish the Right of Representation in the Legislature, a Right inestimable to them, and formidable to Tyrants only.

HE has called together Legislative Bodies at Places unusual, uncomfortable, and distant from the Depository of their public Records, for the sole Purpose of fatiguing them into Compliance with his Measures.

HE has dissolved Representative Houses repeatedly, for opposing with manly Firmness his Invasions on the Rights of the People.

HE has refused for a long Time, after such Dissolutions, to cause others to be elected; whereby the Legislative Powers, incapable of Annihilation, have returned to the People at large for their exercise; the State remaining in the mean time exposed to all the Dangers of Invasion from without, and Convulsions within.

HE has endeavoured to prevent the Population of these States; for that Purpose obstructing the Laws for Naturalization of Foreigners; refusing to pass others to encourage their Migrations hither, and raising the Conditions of new Appropriations of Lands.

HE has obstructed the Administration of Justice, by refusing his Assent to Laws for establishing Judiciary Powers.

HE has made judges dependent on his Will alone, for the Tenure of their Offices, and the Amount and Payment of their Salaries.

HE has erected a Multitude of new Offices, and sent hither Swarms of Officers to harrass our People, and eat out their Substance.

HE has kept among us, in Times of Peace, Standing Armies, without the consent of our Legislatures.

HE has affected to render the Military independent of and superior to the Civil Power.

HE has combined with others to subject us to a Jurisdiction foreign to our Constitution, and unacknowledged by our Laws; giving his Assent to their Acts of pretended Legislation:

FOR quartering large Bodies of Armed Troops among us:

FOR protecting them, by a mock Trial, from Punishment for any Murders which they should commit on the Inhabitants of these States:

FOR cutting off our Trade with all Parts of the World:

FOR imposing Taxes on us without our Consent:

FOR depriving us, in many Cases, of the Benefits of Trial by Jury:

FOR transporting us beyond Seas to be tried for pretended Offences:

FOR abolishing the free System of English Laws in a neighbouring Province, establishing therein an arbitrary Government, and enlarging its Boundaries, so as to render it at once an Example and fit Instrument for introducing the same absolute Rule into these Colonies:

FOR taking away our Charters, abolishing our most valuable Laws, and altering fundamentally the Forms of our Governments:

FOR suspending our own Legislatures, and declaring themselves invested with Power to legislate for us in all Cases whatsoever.

HE has abdicated Government here, by declaring us out of his Protection and waging War against us.

HE has plundered our Seas, ravaged our Coasts, burnt our Towns, and destroyed the Lives of our People.

HE is, at this Time, transporting large Armies of foreign Mercenaries to compleat the Works of Death, Desolation, and Tyranny, already begun with circumstances of Cruelty and Perfidy, scarcely paralleled in the most barbarous Ages, and totally unworthy the Head of a civilized Nation.

HE has constrained our fellow Citizens taken Captive on the high Seas to bear Arms against their Country, to become the Executioners of their Friends and Brethren, or to fall themselves by their Hands.

HE has excited domestic Insurrections amongst us, and has endeavoured to bring on the Inhabitants of our Frontiers, the merciless Indian Savages, whose known Rule of Warfare, is an undistinguished Destruction, of all Ages, Sexes and Conditions.

IN every stage of these Oppressions we have Petitioned for Redress in the most humble Terms: Our repeated Petitions have been answered only by repeated Injury. A Prince, whose Character is thus marked by every act which may define a Tyrant, is unfit to be the Ruler of a free People.

NOR have we been wanting in Attentions to our British Brethren. We have warned them from Time to Time of Attempts by their Legislature to extend an unwarrantable jurisdiction over us. We have reminded them of the Circumstances of our Emigration and Settlement here. We have appealed to their native justice and Magnanimity, and we have conjured them by the Ties of our common Kindred to disavow these Usurpations, which, would inevitably interrupt our Connections and Correspondence. They too have been deaf to the Voice of Justice and of Consanguinity. We must, therefore, acquiesce in the Necessity, which denounces our Separation, and hold them, as we hold the rest of Mankind, Enemies in War, in Peace, Friends.

WE, therefore, the Representatives of the UNITED STATES OF AMERICA, in GENERAL CONGRESS, Assembled, appealing to the Supreme Judge of the World for the Rectitude of our Intentions, do, in the Name, and by Authority of the good People of these Colonies, solemnly Publish and Declare, That these United Colonies are, and of Right ought to be, FREE AND INDEPENDENT STATES; that they are absolved from all Allegiance to the British Crown, and that all political Connection between them and the State of Great-Britain, is and ought to be totally dissolved; and that as FREE AND INDEPENDENT STATES, they have full Power to levy War, conclude Peace, contract Alliances, establish Commerce, and to do all other Acts and Things which INDEPENDENT STATES may of right do. And for the support of this Declaration, with a firm Reliance on the Protection of divine Providence, we mutually pledge to each other our Lives, our Fortunes, and our sacred Honor.

[illegible]

[illegible]

[illegible]

[illegible]

[illegible]

[illegible]

[illegible]

Appendix B

The United States Constitution

We the People of the United States, in Order to form a more perfect Union, establish Justice, insure domestic Tranquility, provide for the common defence, promote the general Welfare, and secure the Blessings of Liberty to ourselves and our Posterity, do ordain and establish this Constitution for the United States of America.

Article. 1.

Section. 1.

All legislative Powers herein granted shall be vested in a Congress of the United States, which shall consist of a Senate and House of Representatives.

Section. 2.

Clause 1: The House of Representatives shall be composed of Members chosen every second Year by the People of the several States, and the Electors in each State shall have the Qualifications requisite for Electors of the most numerous Branch of the State Legislature.

Clause 2: No Person shall be a Representative who shall not have attained to the Age of twenty five Years, and been seven Years a Citizen of the United States, and who shall not, when elected, be an Inhabitant of that State in which he shall be chosen.

Clause 3: Representatives and direct Taxes shall be apportioned among the several States which may be included within this Union, according to their respective Numbers, which shall be determined by adding to the whole Number of free Persons, including those bound to Service for a Term of Years, and excluding Indians not taxed, three fifths of all other Persons. The actual Enumeration shall be made within three Years after the first Meeting of the Congress of the United States, and within every subsequent Term of ten Years, in such Manner as they shall by Law direct. The Number of Representatives shall not exceed one for every thirty Thousand, but each State shall have at Least one Representative; and until such enumeration shall be made, the State of New Hampshire shall be entitled to chuse three, Massachusetts eight, Rhode-Island and Providence Plantations one, Connecticut five, New-York six, New Jersey four, Pennsylvania eight, Delaware one, Maryland six, Virginia ten, North Carolina five, South Carolina five, and Georgia three.

Clause 4: When vacancies happen in the Representation from any State, the Executive Authority thereof shall issue Writs of Election to fill such Vacancies.

Clause 5: The House of Representatives shall chuse their Speaker and other Officers; and shall have the sole Power of Impeachment.

Section. 3.

Clause 1: The Senate of the United States shall be composed of two Senators from each State, chosen by the Legislature thereof, for six Years; and each Senator shall have one Vote.

Clause 2: Immediately after they shall be assembled in Consequence of the first Election, they shall be divided as equally as may be into three Classes. The Seats of the Senators of the first Class shall be vacated at the Expiration of the second Year, of the second Class at the Expiration of the fourth Year, and of the third Class at the Expiration of the sixth Year, so that one third may be chosen every second Year; and if Vacancies happen by Resignation, or otherwise, during the Recess of the Legislature of any State, the Executive thereof may make temporary Appointments until the next Meeting of the Legislature, which shall then fill such Vacancies.

Clause 3: No Person shall be a Senator who shall not have attained to the Age of thirty Years, and been nine Years a Citizen of the United States, and who shall not, when elected, be an Inhabitant of that State for which he shall be chosen.

Clause 4: The Vice President of the United States shall be President of the Senate, but shall have no Vote, unless they be equally divided.

Clause 5: The Senate shall chuse their other Officers, and also a President pro tempore, in the Absence of the Vice President, or when he shall exercise the Office of President of the United States.

Clause 6: The Senate shall have the sole Power to try all Impeachments. When sitting for that Purpose, they shall be on Oath or Affirmation. When the President of the United States is tried, the Chief Justice shall preside: And no Person shall be convicted without the Concurrence of two thirds of the Members present.

Clause 7: Judgment in Cases of Impeachment shall not extend further than to removal from Office, and disqualification to hold and enjoy any Office of honor, Trust or Profit under the United States: but the Party convicted shall nevertheless be liable and subject to Indictment, Trial, Judgment and Punishment, according to Law.

Section. 4.

Clause 1: The Times, Places and Manner of holding Elections for Senators and Representatives, shall be prescribed in each State by the Legislature thereof; but the Congress may at any time by Law make or alter such Regulations, except as to the Places of chusing Senators.

Clause 2: The Congress shall assemble at least once in every Year, and such Meeting shall be on the first Monday in December, unless they shall by Law appoint a different Day.

Section. 5.

Clause 1: Each House shall be the Judge of the Elections, Returns and Qualifications of its own Members, and a Majority of each shall constitute a Quorum to do Business; but a smaller Number may adjourn from day to day, and may be authorized to compel the Attendance of absent Members, in such Manner, and under such Penalties as each House may provide.

Clause 2: Each House may determine the Rules of its Proceedings, punish its Members for disorderly Behaviour, and, with the Concurrence of two thirds, expel a Member.

Clause 3: Each House shall keep a Journal of its Proceedings, and from time to time publish the same, excepting such Parts as may in their Judgment require Secrecy; and the Yeas and Nays of the Members of either House on any question shall, at the Desire of one fifth of those Present, be entered on the Journal.

Clause 4: Neither House, during the Session of Congress, shall, without the Consent of the other, adjourn for more than three days, nor to any other Place than that in which the two Houses shall be sitting.

Section. 6.

Clause 1: The Senators and Representatives shall receive a Compensation for their Services, to be ascertained by Law, and paid out of the Treasury of the United States. They shall in all Cases, except Treason, Felony and Breach of the Peace, be privileged from Arrest during their Attendance at the Session of their respective Houses, and in going to and returning from the same; and for any Speech or Debate in either House, they shall not be questioned in any other Place.

Clause 2: No Senator or Representative shall, during the Time for which he was elected, be appointed to any civil Office under the Authority of the United States, which shall have been created, or the Emoluments whereof shall have been encreased during such time; and no Person holding any Office under the United States, shall be a Member of either House during his Continuance in Office.

Section. 7.

Clause 1: All Bills for raising Revenue shall originate in the House of Representatives; but the Senate may propose or concur with Amendments as on other Bills.

Clause 2: Every Bill which shall have passed the House of Representatives and the Senate, shall, before it become a Law, be presented to the President of the United States; If he approve he shall sign it, but if not he shall return it, with his Objections to that House in which it shall have originated, who shall enter the Objections at large on their Journal, and proceed to reconsider it. If after such Reconsideration two thirds of that House shall agree to pass the Bill, it shall be sent, together with the Objections, to the other House, by which it shall likewise be reconsidered, and if approved by two thirds of that House, it shall become a Law. But in all such Cases the Votes of both Houses shall be determined by yeas and Nays, and the Names of the Persons voting for and against the Bill shall be entered on the Journal of each House respectively. If any Bill shall not be returned by the President within ten Days (Sundays excepted) after it shall have been presented to him, the Same shall be a Law, in like Manner as if he had signed it, unless the Congress by their Adjournment prevent its Return, in which Case it shall not be a Law.

Clause 3: Every Order, Resolution, or Vote to which the Concurrence of the Senate and House of Representatives may be necessary (except on a question of Adjournment) shall be presented to the President of the United States; and before the Same shall take Effect, shall be approved by him, or being disapproved by him, shall be repassed by two thirds of the Senate and House of Representatives, according to the Rules and Limitations prescribed in the Case of a Bill.

Section. 8.

Clause 1: The Congress shall have Power To lay and collect Taxes, Duties, Imposts and Excises, to pay the Debts and provide for the common Defence and general Welfare of the United States; but all Duties, Imposts and Excises shall be uniform throughout the United States;

Clause 2: To borrow Money on the credit of the United States;

Clause 3: To regulate Commerce with foreign Nations, and among the several States, and with the Indian Tribes;

Clause 4: To establish an uniform Rule of Naturalization, and uniform Laws on the subject of Bankruptcies throughout the United States;

Clause 5: To coin Money, regulate the Value thereof, and of foreign Coin, and fix the Standard of Weights and Measures;

Clause 6: To provide for the Punishment of counterfeiting the Securities and current Coin of the United States;

Clause 7: To establish Post Offices and post Roads;

Clause 8: To promote the Progress of Science and useful Arts, by securing for limited Times to Authors and Inventors the exclusive Right to their respective Writings and Discoveries;

Clause 9: To constitute Tribunals inferior to the supreme Court;

Clause 10: To define and punish Piracies and Felonies committed on the high Seas, and Offences against the Law of Nations;

Clause 11: To declare War, grant Letters of Marque and Reprisal, and make Rules concerning Captures on Land and Water;

Clause 12: To raise and support Armies, but no Appropriation of Money to that Use shall be for a longer Term than two Years;

Clause 13: To provide and maintain a Navy;

Clause 14: To make Rules for the Government and Regulation of the land and naval Forces;

Clause 15: To provide for calling forth the Militia to execute the Laws of the Union, suppress Insurrections and repel Invasions;

Clause 16: To provide for organizing, arming, and disciplining, the Militia, and for governing such Part of them as may be employed in the Service of the United States, reserving to the States respectively, the Appointment of the Officers, and the Authority of training the Militia according to the discipline prescribed by Congress;

Clause 17: To exercise exclusive Legislation in all Cases whatsoever, over such District (not exceeding ten Miles square) as may, by Cession of particular States, and the Acceptance of Congress, become the Seat of the Government of the United States, and to exercise like Authority over all Places purchased by the Consent of the Legislature of the State in which the Same shall be, for the Erection of Forts, Magazines, Arsenals, dock-Yards, and other needful Buildings; — And

Clause 18: To make all Laws which shall be necessary and proper for carrying into Execution the foregoing Powers, and all other Powers vested by this Constitution in the Government of the United States, or in any Department or Officer thereof.

Section. 9.

Clause 1: The Migration or Importation of such Persons as any of the States now existing shall think proper to admit, shall not be prohibited by the Congress prior to the Year one thousand eight hundred and eight, but a Tax or duty may be imposed on such Importation, not exceeding ten dollars for each Person.

Clause 2: The Privilege of the Writ of Habeas Corpus shall not be suspended, unless when in Cases of Rebellion or Invasion the public Safety may require it.

Clause 3: No Bill of Attainder or ex post facto Law shall be passed.

Clause 4: No Capitation, or other direct, Tax shall be laid, unless in Proportion to the Census or Enumeration herein before directed to be taken.

Clause 5: No Tax or Duty shall be laid on Articles exported from any State.

Clause 6: No Preference shall be given by any Regulation of Commerce or Revenue to the Ports of one State over those of another: nor shall Vessels bound to, or from, one State, be obliged to enter, clear, or pay Duties in another.

Clause 7: No Money shall be drawn from the Treasury, but in Consequence of Appropriations made by Law; and a regular Statement and Account of the Receipts and Expenditures of all public Money shall be published from time to time.

Clause 8: No Title of Nobility shall be granted by the United States: And no Person holding any Office of Profit or Trust under them, shall, without the Consent of the Congress, accept of any present, Emolument, Office, or Title, of any kind whatever, from any King, Prince, or foreign State.

Section. 10.

Clause 1: No State shall enter into any Treaty, Alliance, or Confederation; grant Letters of Marque and Reprisal; coin Money; emit Bills of Credit; make any Thing but gold and silver Coin a Tender in Payment of Debts; pass any Bill of Attainder, ex post facto Law, or Law impairing the Obligation of Contracts, or grant any Title of Nobility.

Clause 2: No State shall, without the Consent of the Congress, lay any Imposts or Duties on Imports or Exports, except what may be absolutely necessary for executing it's inspection Laws: and the net Produce of all Duties and Imposts, laid by any State on Imports or Exports, shall be for the Use of the Treasury of the United States; and all such Laws shall be subject to the Revision and Controul of the Congress.

Clause 3: No State shall, without the Consent of Congress, lay any Duty of Tonnage, keep Troops, or Ships of War in time of Peace, enter into any Agreement or Compact with another State, or with a foreign Power, or engage in War, unless actually invaded, or in such imminent Danger as will not admit of delay.

Article. II.

Section. 1.

Clause 1: The executive Power shall be vested in a President of the United States of America. He shall hold his Office during the Term of four Years, and, together with the Vice President, chosen for the same Term, be elected, as follows

Clause 2: Each State shall appoint, in such Manner as the Legislature thereof may direct, a Number of Electors, equal to the whole Number of Senators and Representatives to which the State may be entitled in the Congress: but no Senator or Representative, or Person holding an Office of Trust or Profit under the United States, shall be appointed an Elector.

Clause 3: The Electors shall meet in their respective States, and vote by Ballot for two Persons, of whom one at least shall not be an Inhabitant of the same State with themselves. And they shall make a List of all the Persons voted for, and of the Number of Votes for each; which List they shall sign and certify, and transmit sealed to the Seat of the Government of the United States, directed to the President of the Senate. The President of the Senate shall, in the Presence of the Senate and House of Representatives, open all the Certificates, and the Votes shall then be counted. The Person having the greatest Number of Votes shall be the President, if such Number be a Majority of the whole Number of Electors appointed; and if there be more than one who have such Majority, and have an equal Number of Votes, then the House of Representatives shall immediately chuse by Ballot one of them for President; and if no Person have a Majority, then from the five highest on the List the said House shall in like Manner chuse the President. But in chusing the President, the Votes shall be taken by States, the Representation from each State having one Vote; A quorum for this Purpose shall consist of a Member or Members from two thirds of the States, and a Majority of all the States shall be necessary to a Choice. In every Case, after the Choice of the President, the Person having the greatest Number of Votes of the Electors shall be the Vice President. But if there should remain two or more who have equal Votes, the Senate shall chuse from them by Ballot the Vice President.

Clause 4: The Congress may determine the Time of chusing the Electors, and the Day on which they shall give their Votes; which Day shall be the same throughout the United States.

Clause 5: No Person except a natural born Citizen, or a Citizen of the United States, at the time of the Adoption of this Constitution, shall be eligible to the Office of President; neither shall any Person be eligible to that Office who shall not have attained to the Age of thirty five Years, and been fourteen Years a Resident within the United States.

Clause 6: In Case of the Removal of the President from Office, or of his Death, Resignation, or Inability to discharge the Powers and Duties of the said Office, the Same shall devolve on the Vice President, and the Congress may by Law provide for the Case of Removal, Death, Resignation or Inability, both of the President and Vice President, declaring what Officer shall then act as President, and such Officer shall act accordingly, until the Disability be removed, or a President shall be elected.

Clause 7: The President shall, at stated Times, receive for his Services, a Compensation, which shall neither be encreased nor diminished during the Period for which he shall have been elected, and he shall not receive within that Period any other Emolument from the United States, or any of them.

Clause 8: Before he enter on the Execution of his Office, he shall take the following Oath or Affirmation: — "I do solemnly swear (or affirm) that I will faithfully execute the Office of President of the United States, and will to the best of my Ability, preserve, protect and defend the Constitution of the United States."

Section. 2.

Clause 1: The President shall be Commander in Chief of the Army and Navy of the United States, and of the Militia of the several States, when called into the actual Service of the United States; he may require the Opinion, in writing, of the principal Officer in each of the executive Departments, upon any Subject relating to the Duties of their respective Offices, and he shall have Power to grant Reprieves and Pardons for Offences against the United States, except in Cases of Impeachment.

Clause 2: He shall have Power, by and with the Advice and Consent of the Senate, to make Treaties, provided two thirds of the Senators present concur; and he shall nominate, and by and with the Advice and Consent of the Senate, shall appoint Ambassadors, other public Ministers and Consuls, Judges of the supreme Court, and all other Officers of the United States, whose Appointments are not herein otherwise provided for, and which shall be established by Law: but the Congress may by Law vest the Appointment of such inferior Officers, as they think proper, in the President alone, in the Courts of Law, or in the Heads of Departments.

Clause 3: The President shall have Power to fill up all Vacancies that may happen during the Recess of the Senate, by granting Commissions which shall expire at the End of their next Session.

Section. 3.

He shall from time to time give to the Congress Information of the State of the Union, and recommend to their Consideration such Measures as he shall judge necessary and expedient; he may, on extraordinary Occasions, convene both Houses, or either of them, and in Case of Disagreement between them, with Respect to the Time of Adjournment, he may adjourn them to such Time as he shall think proper; he shall receive Ambassadors and other public Ministers; he shall take Care that the Laws be faithfully executed, and shall Commission all the Officers of the United States.

Section. 4.

The President, Vice President and all civil Officers of the United States, shall be removed from Office on Impeachment for, and Conviction of, Treason, Bribery, or other high Crimes and Misdemeanors.

Article. III.

Section. 1.

The judicial Power of the United States, shall be vested in one supreme Court, and in such inferior Courts as the Congress may from time to time ordain and establish. The Judges, both of the supreme and inferior Courts, shall hold their Offices during good Behaviour, and shall, at stated Times, receive for their Services, a Compensation, which shall not be diminished during their Continuance in Office.

Section. 2.

Clause 1: The judicial Power shall extend to all Cases, in Law and Equity, arising under this Constitution, the Laws of the United States, and Treaties made, or which shall be made, under their Authority; — to all Cases affecting Ambassadors, other public Ministers and Consuls; — to all Cases of admiralty and maritime Jurisdiction; — to Controversies to which the United States shall be a Party; — to Controversies between two or more States; — between a State and Citizens of another State; — between Citizens of different States, — between Citizens of the same State claiming Lands under Grants of different States, and between a State, or the Citizens thereof, and foreign States, Citizens or Subjects.

Clause 2: In all Cases affecting Ambassadors, other public Ministers and Consuls, and those in which a State shall be Party, the supreme Court shall have original Jurisdiction. In all the other Cases before mentioned, the supreme Court shall have appellate Jurisdiction, both as to Law and Fact, with such Exceptions, and under such Regulations as the Congress shall make.

Clause 3: The Trial of all Crimes, except in Cases of Impeachment, shall be by Jury; and such Trial shall be held in the State where the said Crimes shall have been committed; but when not committed within any State, the Trial shall be at such Place or Places as the Congress may by Law have directed.

Section. 3.

Clause 1: Treason against the United States, shall consist only in levying War against them, or in adhering to their Enemies, giving them Aid and Comfort. No Person shall be convicted of Treason unless on the Testimony of two Witnesses to the same overt Act, or on Confession in open Court.

Clause 2: The Congress shall have Power to declare the Punishment of Treason, but no Attainder of Treason shall work Corruption of Blood, or Forfeiture except during the Life of the Person attainted.

Article. IV.

Section. 1.

Full Faith and Credit shall be given in each State to the public Acts, Records, and judicial Proceedings of every other State. And the Congress may by general Laws prescribe the Manner in which such Acts, Records and Proceedings shall be proved, and the Effect thereof.

Section. 2.

Clause 1: The Citizens of each State shall be entitled to all Privileges and Immunities of Citizens in the several States.

Clause 2: A Person charged in any State with Treason, Felony, or other Crime, who shall flee from Justice, and be found in another State, shall on Demand of the executive Authority of the State from which he fled, be delivered up, to be removed to the State having Jurisdiction of the Crime.

Clause 3: No Person held to Service or Labour in one State, under the Laws thereof, escaping into another, shall, in Consequence of any Law or Regulation therein, be discharged from such Service or Labour, but shall be delivered up on Claim of the Party to whom such Service or Labour may be due.

Section. 3.

Clause 1: New States may be admitted by the Congress into this Union; but no new State shall be formed or erected within the Jurisdiction of any other State; nor any State be formed by the Junction of two or more States, or Parts of States, without the Consent of the Legislatures of the States concerned as well as of the Congress.

Clause 2: The Congress shall have Power to dispose of and make all needful Rules and Regulations respecting the Territory or other Property belonging to the United States; and nothing in this Constitution shall be so construed as to Prejudice any Claims of the United States, or of any particular State.

Section. 4.

The United States shall guarantee to every State in this Union a Republican Form of Government, and shall protect each of them against Invasion; and on Application of the Legislature, or of the Executive (when the Legislature cannot be convened) against domestic Violence.

Article. V.

The Congress, whenever two thirds of both Houses shall deem it necessary, shall propose Amendments to this Constitution, or, on the Application of the Legislatures of two thirds of the several States, shall call a Convention for proposing Amendments, which, in either Case, shall be valid to all Intents and Purposes, as Part of this Constitution, when ratified by the Legislatures of three fourths of the several States, or by Conventions in three fourths thereof, as the one or the other Mode of Ratification may be proposed by the Congress; Provided that no Amendment which may be made prior to the Year One thousand eight hundred and eight shall in any Manner affect the first and fourth Clauses in the Ninth Section of the first Article; and that no State, without its Consent, shall be deprived of its equal Suffrage in the Senate.

Article. VI.

Clause 1: All Debts contracted and Engagements entered into, before the Adoption of this Constitution, shall be as valid against the United States under this Constitution, as under the Confederation.

Clause 2: This Constitution, and the Laws of the United States which shall be made in Pursuance thereof; and all Treaties made, or which shall be made, under the Authority of the United States, shall be the supreme Law of the Land; and the Judges in every State shall be bound thereby, any Thing in the Constitution or Laws of any State to the Contrary notwithstanding.

Clause 3: The Senators and Representatives before mentioned, and the Members of the several State Legislatures, and all executive and judicial Officers, both of the United States and of the several States, shall be bound by Oath or Affirmation, to support this Constitution; but no religious Test shall ever be required as a Qualification to any Office or public Trust under the United States.

Article. VII.

The Ratification of the Conventions of nine States, shall be sufficient for the Establishment of this Constitution between the States so ratifying the Same.

Attest William Jackson Secretary

Done in Convention by the Unanimous Consent of the States present the Seventeenth Day of September in the Year of our Lord one thousand seven hundred and Eighty seven and of the Independence of the United States of America the Twelfth In witness whereof We have hereunto subscribed our Names,

G[o]. Washington
Presidt and deputy from Virginia

Delaware

Geo: Read
Gunning Bedford jun
John Dickinson
Richard Bassett
Jaco: Broom

Maryland

James McHenry
Dan of St Thos. Jenifer
Danl. Carroll.

Virginia

John Blair
James Madison Jr.

North Carolina

Wm. Blount
Richd. Dobbs Spaight.
Hu Williamson

South Carolina

J. Rutledge
Charles Cotesworth Pinckney
Charles Pinckney
Pierce Butler

Georgia

William Few
Abr Baldwin

New Hampshire

John Langdon
Nicholas Gilman

Massachusetts

Nathaniel Gorham
Rufus King

Connecticut

Wm. Saml. Johnson
Roger Sherman

New York

Alexander Hamilton

New Jersey

Wil: Livingston
David Brearley.
Wm. Paterson
Jona: Dayton

Pennsylvania

B Franklin
Thomas Mifflin
Robt. Morris
Geo. Clymer
Thos. FitzSimons
Jared Ingersoll
James Wilson
Gouv Morris

Appendix C

Document Checklist

U.S. Department of Justice
Immigration and Naturalization Service

OMB No. 1115-0009

Document Checklist

All applicants must send the following 3 things with their N-400 application:

1. A photocopy of both sides of your Permanent Resident Card (formerly known as the Alien Registration Receipt Card or "Green Card"). If you have lost the card, submit a photocopy of the receipt of your Form I-90, Application to Replace Alien Registration Receipt Card;
2. Two (2) identical color photographs, with your name and "A" number written lightly in pencil on the back of each. For details about the photo requirements, see part 5 of *A Guide to Naturalization* and the Form M-378 instructions distributed with your application. Do not wear eyeglasses or earrings for the photo. Note that if your religion requires you to wear a head covering, your facial features and your right ear must still be exposed in the photo for purposes of identification; AND
3. A check or money order for the application fee and the fingerprinting fee, as stated in the M-479 Current Naturalization Fees enclosure in the *Guide*. (Applicants 75 years of age or older are exempted from fingerprinting and the fingerprinting fee). Write your "A" number on the back of the check or money order.

Send COPIES of the following documents, unless we ask for an original.

If an attorney or accredited representative is acting on your behalf, send:
❑ A completed original Form G-28, "Notice of Entry of Appearance as Attorney or Representative."

If your current legal name is different from the name on your Permanent Resident Card, send:
❑ The document(s) that legally changed your name (marriage certificate, divorce decree, or court document).

If you are applying for naturalization on the basis of marriage to a U.S. citizen, send the following 4 things:

1. Evidence that your spouse has been a U.S. citizen for the last 3 years:
   - birth certificate (if your spouse never lost citizenship since birth), OR
   - naturalization certificate, OR
   - certificate of citizenship, OR
   - the inside of the front cover and signature page of your spouse's current U.S. passport, OR
   - Form FS240, "Report of Birth Abroad of a Citizen of the United States of America"
2. Your current marriage certificate; AND
3. Proof of termination of ALL prior marriages of your spouse (divorce decree(s), annulment(s), or death certificate(s)); AND
4. Documents referring to you and your spouse:
   - tax returns, bank accounts, leases, mortgages, or birth certificates of children, OR
   - IRS-certified copies of the income tax forms that you both filed for the past 3 years, OR
   - an IRS tax return transcript for the last 3 years.

If you were married before, send:
❑ Proof that ALL earlier marriages ended (divorce decree(s), annulment(s), or death certificate(s)).

If you were previously in the U.S. military service, send:
❑ A completed original Form G-325B, "Biographic Information."

If you are currently in U.S. military service AND are seeking citizenship based on that service, send:
❑ A completed original Form N-426, "Request for Certification of Military or Naval Service;" AND

❑ A completed original Form G-325B, "Biographic Information."

If you have taken any trip outside of the United States that lasted for 6 months or more since becoming a Permanent Resident, send evidence that you (and your family) continued to live, work, and/or keep ties to the United States, such as:

- ❑ An IRS tax return "transcript" or an IRS-certified tax return listing tax information for the last 5 years (or for the last 3 years if you are applying on the basis of marriage to a U.S. citizen)
- ❑ Rent or mortgage payments and pay stubs.

If you have a dependent spouse or children who do not live with you, send:

- ❑ Any court or government order to provide financial support; AND
- ❑ Evidence of your financial support (including evidence that you have complied with any court or government order), such as:
  - cancelled checks
  - money order receipts
  - a court or agency printout of child support payments
  - evidence of wage garnishments
  - a letter from the parent or guardian who cares for your children

If you answer "Yes" to any of questions 1 through 15 in Part 7, send:

- ❑ A written explanation on a separate sheet of paper.

If you answer "No" to any of questions 1 through 5 in Part 8, send:

- ❑ A written explanation on a separate sheet of paper.

If you have ever been arrested or detained by any law enforcement officer for any reason, and no charges were filed, send:

- ❑ An original official statement by the arresting agency or applicable court confirming that no charges were filed.

If you have ever been arrested or detained by any law enforcement officer for any reason, and charges were filed, send:

- ❑ An original or court-certified copy of the complete arrest record and disposition for each incident (dismissal order, conviction record, OR acquittal order).

If you have ever been convicted or placed in an alternative sentencing program or rehabilitative program (such as a drug treatment or community service program), send:

- ❑ An original or court-certified copy of the sentencing record for each incident; AND
- ❑ Evidence that you completed your sentence:
  - An original or certified copy of your probation or parole record, OR
  - Evidence that you completed an alternative sentencing program or rehabilitative program

If you have ever had any arrest or conviction vacated, set aside, sealed, expunged, or otherwise removed from your record, send:

- ❑ An original or court-certified copy of the court order vacating, setting aside, sealing, expunging, or otherwise removing the arrest or conviction, OR an original statement from the court that no record exists of your arrest or conviction.

If you have ever failed to file an income tax return since you became a Permanent Resident, send:

- ❑ All correspondence with the Internal Revenue Service (IRS) regarding your failure to file.

If you have any federal, state, or local taxes that are overdue, send:

- ❑ A signed agreement from the IRS or state or local tax office showing that you have filed a tax return and arranged to pay the taxes you owe; AND
- ❑ Documentation from the IRS or state or local tax office showing the current status of your repayment program.

If you are applying for a disability exception to the testing requirement, send:

- ❑ An original Form N-648, "Medical Certification for Disability Exceptions," completed less than 6 months ago by a licensed medical or osteopathic doctor or licensed clinical psychologist.

If you did not register with the Selective Service and you 1) are male, 2) are 26 years old or older, and 3) lived in the United States in a status other than as a lawful nonimmigrant between the ages of 18 and 26, send:

- ❑ A "Status Information Letter" from the Selective Service (Call 1-847-688-6888 for more information).

Form M-477
(Rev. 12/00)N

Index

• A •

• B •

• C •

• D •

• E •

• F •

• G •

• H •

• I •

• J •

• K •

• L •

• M •

• N •

• O •

• P •

• Q •

• R •

• S •

• T •

U

V

W

• Y •

Notes

Notes

Notes

Notes

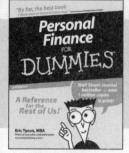

COMPUTER BASICS

0-7645-0838-5

0-7645-1663-9

0-7645-1548-9

Also available:

PCs All-in-One Desk Reference For Dummies (0-7645-0791-5)

Pocket PC For Dummies (0-7645-1640-X)

Treo and Visor For Dummies (0-7645-1673-6)

Troubleshooting Your PC For Dummies (0-7645-1669-8)

Upgrading & Fixing PCs For Dummies (0-7645-1665-5)

Windows XP For Dummies (0-7645-0893-8)

Windows XP For Dummies Quick Reference (0-7645-0897-0)

BUSINESS SOFTWARE

0-7645-0822-9

0-7645-0839-3

0-7645-0819-9

Also available:

Excel Data Analysis For Dummies (0-7645-1661-2)

Excel 2002 All-in-One Desk Reference For Dummies (0-7645-1794-5)

Excel 2002 For Dummies Quick Reference (0-7645-0829-6)

GoldMine "X" For Dummies (0-7645-0845-8)

Microsoft CRM For Dummies (0-7645-1698-1)

Microsoft Project 2002 For Dummies (0-7645-1628-0)

Office XP For Dummies (0-7645-0830-X)

Outlook 2002 For Dummies (0-7645-0828-8)

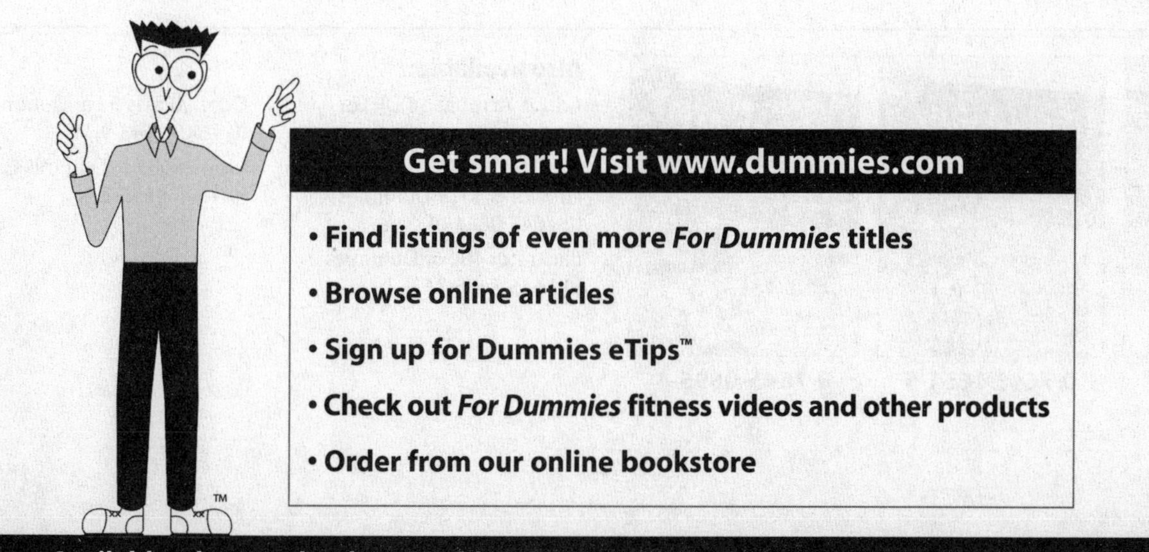

Available wherever books are sold. Go to www.dummies.com or call 1-877-762-2974 to order direct.

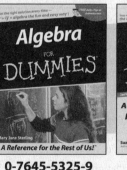